This volume is one of a series devoted to the art and technology of photography. The books present pictures by outstanding photographers of today and the past, relate the history of photography and provide practical instruction in the use of equipment and materials.

LIFE LIBRARY OF PHOTOGRAPHY

Special Problems

Revised Edition

BY THE EDITORS OF TIME-LIFE BOOKS

TIME-LIFE BOOKS, ALEXANDRIA, VIRGINIA

For information about any
Time-Life book, please write:
Reader Information, Time-Life Books,
541 North Fairbanks Court,
Chicago, Illinois 60611.

TIME-LIFE is a trademark of
Time Incorporated U.S.A.

Library of Congress Cataloguing in Publication Data
Main entry under title:
Special problems.
   (Life Library of photography)
   Bibliography: p.
   Includes index.
   1. Photography, Applied. I. Time-Life Books.
II. Series.
TR624.S63 1982   770'.28   81-18389
          AACR2
ISBN 0-8094-4402-X
ISBN 0-8094-4401-1 (lib. bdg.)
ISBN 0-8094-4400-3 (Retail ed.)

ON THE COVER: Two examples of
nature's extremes—the swirling dust and
blistering heat of a Hawaiian volcano,
and the peculiar light and piercing cold of
an Antarctic fog—suggest the range of
special problems that photographers may
face. Robert Goodman (in Hawaii) and
Emil Schulthess (in Antarctica) did more
than meet the challenges: They
demonstrated that distinguished images
can be wrested from the most daunting
photographic circumstances.

Contents

LIFE LIBRARY OF PHOTOGRAPHY
EDITORIAL STAFF FOR
THE ORIGINAL EDITION OF
SPECIAL PROBLEMS:
SERIES EDITOR: Richard L. Williams
Editor: Robert G. Mason
Picture Editor: Patricia Maye
Text Editor: Jay Brennan
Designer: Raymond Ripper
Assistant Designer: Herbert H. Quarmby
Staff Writers: Paula Pierce, Suzanne Seixas,
John von Hartz, Bryce S. Walker
Chief Researcher: Peggy Bushong
Researchers: Sondra Albert, Kathleen Brandes,
Malabar Brodeur, Monica O. Horne, Myra Mangan,
Shirley Miller, Kathryn Ritchell
Copy Coordinators: Ruth Kelton, Barbara Quarmby
Art Assistant: Patricia Byrne
Picture Coordinator: Catherine Ireys

EDITORIAL STAFF FOR
THE REVISED EDITION OF *SPECIAL PROBLEMS:*
SENIOR EDITOR: Edward Brash
Picture Editor: Neil Kagan
Designer: Sally Collins
Chief Researcher: Jo Thomson
Text Editor: John Manners
Researchers: Rhawn Anderson, Charlotte Marine,
Jean Strong
Assistant Designer: Kenneth E. Hancock
Copy Coordinator: Ricki Tarlow
Picture Coordinator: Eric Godwin
Editorial Assistant: Jane H. Cody

Special Contributors:
Don Earnest (text);
Mel Ingber (technical research)

EDITORIAL OPERATIONS
Production Director: Feliciano Madrid
Assistants: Peter A. Inchauteguiz,
Karen A. Meyerson
Copy Processing: Gordon E. Buck
Quality Control Director: Robert L. Young
Assistant: James J. Cox
Associates: Daniel J. McSweeney,
Michael G. Wight
Art Coordinator: Anne B. Landry
Copy Room Director: Susan B. Galloway
Assistant: Celia Beattie

CORRESPONDENTS
Elisabeth Kraemer (Bonn); Margot Hapgood, Dorothy
Bacon (London); Susan Jonas, Lucy T. Voulgaris (New
York); Maria Vincenza Aloisi, Josephine du Brusle
(Paris); Ann Natanson (Rome). Valuable assistance
was also provided by: Judy Aspinall (London); Miriam
Hsia, Christina Lieberman, Donna Lucey, Tina
Voulgaris (New York); Mimi Murphy (Rome).

*The editors are indebted to the following individuals
of Time Inc.: George Karas, Chief, Time-Life Photo
Lab, New York City; Herbert Orth, Deputy Chief,
Time-Life Photo Lab; Photo Equipment Supervisor,
Albert Schneider; Photo Equipment Technician, Mike
Miller; Time-Life Photo Lab Color Lab Supervisor,
Peter Christopoulos; Time-Life Photo Lab B/W
Supervisor, Carmine Ercolano.*

The special problems of photography—and there are many—seldom discourage the serious photographer. On the contrary, these very problems stimulate his interest, their goad prodding him to some of his finest pictures. They excite him to stretch the outer limits of his knowledge, and in the process acquire a better understanding of the full capacities of his equipment and ingenuity.

The shot considered merely a routine assignment by an experienced professional may be a hazardous adventure for the beginner. But there are certain problems that are a challenge to photographers of every rank. One is the daunting power of nature's extremes; under the lash of a freezing rain or the intense heat of a summer sun, simply preserving film, lenses and camera—let alone getting a good photograph—is a severe test. More exotic perils include the dust, fire and explosions of an erupting volcano or an insidious fungus that will spread over equipment in the damp tropics.

Even in the mildest climates, however, photographers face problems of setting—reflections, obstacles, distances that get in the way of clear and dramatic pictures; yet all these can be avoided with proper technique and equipment.

This revised edition discusses rugged, lightweight new gear that is designed to perform in extreme climates, as well as other items useful for solving problems that occur in the most ordinary situations. The edition includes new material on diagnosing problems in color processing *(pages 126-127)* and a wholly new picture essay showing how professionals coped with problems they encountered on assignment or in pursuing their own creative goals *(pages 86-100)*.

One classic problem that has intrigued photographers since the development of the camera can never finally be solved: how to convey a sense of action in the utterly motionless medium of still photography. But the attempts to deal with this difficulty have produced stunning pictures that communicate the idea of action to the viewer *(pages 138-160)*.

These problems, while not those of all photographers, are basic to the photographic experience. To understand their traps is to begin to realize ways to avoid them. Or to make use of them. For some of the most exciting pictures are those that are purposely shot the wrong way—and turn problems into advantages.

The Editors

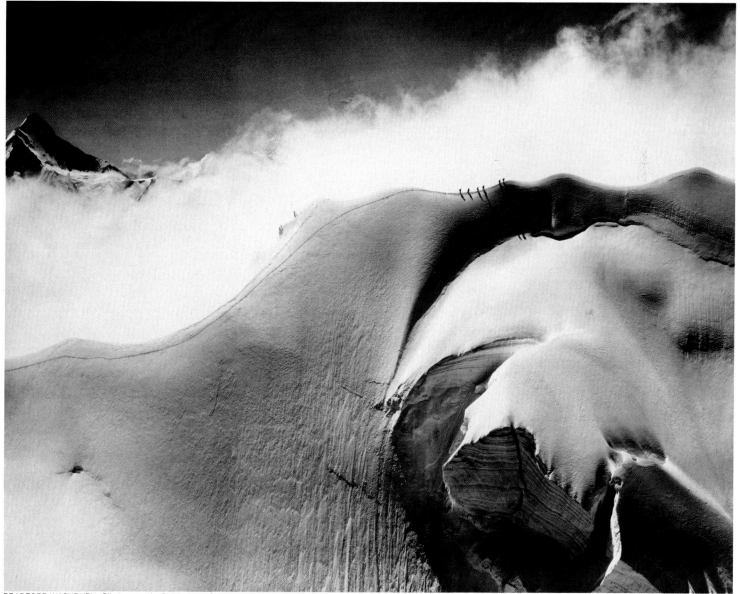

BRADFORD WASHBURN: *Climbers on the Doldenhorn, Switzerland,* 1960

Perils of Heat and Cold, Dust and Dampness

In many ancient cultures, weather was thought to depend on the moods of the gods — and rather irascible gods at that. Fei Lien, the Chinese deity of wind, had a dragon's body and a powerful set of lungs that could blow up a typhoon in an instant. The Norsemen placed the blame for thunder and rain on Thor, a muscular redhead who wore an iron glove and wielded a red-hot hammer. Such notions may seem outmoded, but photographers in particular might be forgiven for continuing to suspect the gods of weather of occasional malevolence. For nature itself is often the culprit when pictures fail to come out. It is not the only source of trouble, of course. Setting and lighting pose their own problems, action is difficult to convey in a still picture, equipment fails — and the photographer makes mistakes of his own. Yet photographic obstacles presented by the environment are in many ways the trickiest to surmount.

Heat, humidity, rain, snow and cold all jeopardize photographic materials and equipment. Dust, sand and salt spray also bring their share of troubles, and even the unusual lighting conditions of a summertime beach or a snow-clad mountain can play hob with exposure calculations. The harm caused by environmental extremes may be immediately obvious. If the camera shutter does not work, the film-advance mechanism jams or the film snaps, the trouble is announced at once. But more often it is impossible to learn that something went wrong until later, when developed film turns out to be ruined or the effects of camera corrosion begin to show up.

In an era when people travel widely and routinely chronicle their journeys with their cameras, an understanding of the depredations of nature has become essential. As might be expected, the types of problems vary with the climate. Troubles encountered in California's Mojave Desert differ greatly from those that bedevil the photographer in Florida's Everglades. And the difficulties of the Massachusetts seacoast scarcely resemble those of the Colorado ski slopes. Yet none of the problems are insurmountable, and often they can be solved in very simple ways.

Heat is one of the most prevalent sources of photographic miseries. At the beach, in the desert, and in practically any locale where the sun's rays are intense, the camera's lens can be harmed if it is not kept sufficiently cool. When the air is 90° F. — a level that is still reasonably comfortable if the humidity remains low — direct sunshine may cause the dark, heat-absorbing body of a camera to rise to 120° F. or more. A camera that is stored in the glove compartment or trunk of a car may be even worse off, for temperatures there sometimes go as high as 150° F.

Whenever the temperature of a camera exceeds 110° F., trouble is possible — and sometimes it is disastrous. The lubricants in the camera can thin so much they run and gum up the delicate leaves that set the size of the aperture in the lens diaphragm. The cement that holds the glass elements of a lens together can soften and permit the elements to separate. And above 120° F., bubbles could form in the optical cement, requiring expensive repairs.

To avoid such catastrophes on clear, hot days, keep equipment in the shade as much as possible. A durable carrying case will go a long way toward shielding the camera and lenses from the sun's heat (professional photographers often carry their equipment in sturdy aluminum cases that reflect sunlight). However, a good protective device is also one of the simplest: a foam plastic picnic cooler, the inexpensive kind sold in hardware stores and supermarkets to keep food and drink hot or cold. Such coolers *(page 25)* offer satisfactory insulation from the sun's rays because their rigid plastic material is filled with air bubbles. They are also fairly strong and very light in weight.

Even these insulators have their limits, and the interior will heat up if the cooler is out in the sun for a long time, particularly after it has been opened once or twice. One way to keep the temperature down under such conditions is to keep a moist towel on the hamper. Photographer Ralph Crane

Despite the climate, Ralph Crane chose an outdoor setting for his portrait of Sheik Shakbut bin Sultan, ruler of Abu Dhabi, an oil-rich sheikdom on the Persian Gulf, where temperatures routinely exceed 120° F. At the sheik's side is a $36,400, solid-gold model of an offshore oil derrick. It was presented by a grateful consortium of businessmen to whom Shakbut had granted an oil concession.

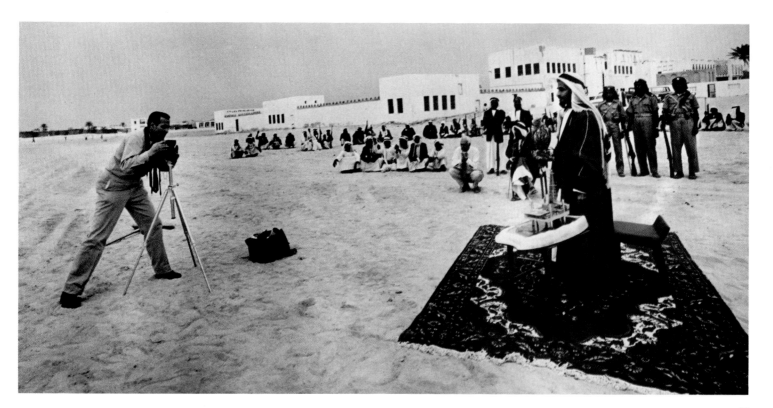

chose another trick when he did a story on the oil-rich—and blazingly hot—kingdom of Abu Dhabi for *Life* magazine *(preceding page):* Each morning he placed a jar of ice cubes in the foam plastic cooler that he used to store his film and equipment. A tidier, more compact alternative to the ice is a sealed container of refreezable gelatin, sold in supermarkets for such picnic coolers.

An air-conditioned car is, of course, a great asset in hot climates—although, in rare instances, trouble may arise when equipment, cool from air-conditioned storage, is taken out into the broiling sun. The sudden heat starts all parts of the camera expanding, but since glass and metal expand at different rates, a lens may jam and make focusing impossible. Another difficulty with air conditioning plagued photographer Henry Groskinsky several summers ago when he was shooting pictures of houses in Houston, Texas, using large-format 4 x 5 and 5 x 7 cameras. He loaded the sheets of cut film into their holders while he was inside an air-conditioned house, then went out to get some exterior shots. His mistake did not become evident until he developed the film and discovered all his pictures were blurred. The cool film, subjected to a sudden rise in temperature, expanded so rapidly it buckled in the holders, throwing much of the image out of focus. This mishap could have been avoided by giving the film and holders time to warm slowly to the temperature of the surrounding air. (Such extreme buckling is less likely with small-sized 35mm film.)

When high humidity is combined with heat, the problems worsen. In the swamps of Georgia or the bayous of Louisiana, the hostile alliance of these factors is at an extreme, yet a spell of muggy summer weather in Washington, D.C., may be troublesome too. The prime victim of hot, humid climates is film, especially after it has been unwrapped. Although modern film is very reliable and stable compared to that produced only a few decades ago, it still must be classed as a perishable product. This is hardly surprising, considering its make-up of organic gelatin (akin to gelatin foods used for desserts) and sensitive, microscopically small silver halide crystals that are easily triggered into changing their chemical form.

The combination of heat and humidity harms film in a number of ways. It can soften the gelatin so that developing solutions penetrate the emulsion at different rates when the film is processed. As a result, black-and-white pictures may seem unevenly exposed. Color pictures may appear washed out. And if color film's separate emulsion layers, which control the balance of color, are affected to different degrees, as is often the case in extremely humid tropical climates, pictures may have a reddish, bluish or greenish cast. In addition, extreme heat and humidity may act on the silver halide crystals just as light does, producing the unwanted overall exposure called fog. These types of damage can be inflicted either before or after the film has been exposed—although they do not show up until it is developed.

In hot, damp climates, film may also fall victim to fungus (sometimes called mildew or mold). Microscopic fungus spores are everywhere in the air, and given a suitably humid environment, they rapidly multiply on the film surface because its gelatin serves as food. In five or six weeks, they produce visible splotches or cobweb-like filaments on the emulsion. If the growth has not gone too far, the fungus can be removed from black-and-white film with special film-cleaning preparations, but color pictures may be hopelessly damaged, for the fungus releases substances that affect the color dyes. Fungus also attracts insects and bacteria that display a similarly voracious appetite for the gelatin. And over a period of three to six months, fungus can even grow on the lens, impairing light transmission and reducing the clarity of pictures.

Still another potential difficulty arises from the moisture-absorbing properties of film. In hot, damp weather the gelatin sops up humidity like a sponge, and when it becomes sufficiently swollen with moisture, the film may stick together in its cassette or on the take-up spool. If the photographer attempts to advance or rewind it, the emulsion side of the film may rip right off the film base, thoroughly ruining the pictures.

In any hot climate where the relative humidity remains above 60 per cent, film should be kept cool and (most important of all) dry, in order to avert loss of sensitivity, attacks by fungus and moisture absorption. One sound practice is to store the film in a refrigerator until it is to be used. However, this precaution will come to naught if the moistureproof wrapping is removed the moment that the film is taken out of the refrigerator, for water droplets may be condensed out of the humid air by the chilled emulsion, causing spotting on the film. To prevent such condensation, the film should be left in its plastic can or foil wrapping overnight so that it can warm up to the temperature of the surrounding air. In any case, it is best, in tropical climates, to load a camera during the daytime because the relative humidity is higher at night, making moisture condensation more likely then, even on film that is only slightly cooler than the air around it.

A second sound precaution is to keep film inside the camera for no more than a day or two so that it cannot swell up with moisture and stick together. This is particularly necessary on any extended field trip in a humid climate. For example, photographer Stan Wayman even went to the trouble of removing the film from his cameras every night when he was doing a story on fishing in Florida (overleaf); he qualified as an expert on the problems of damp environments, for he grew up on a small farm in the Everglades. But when an exposed roll of color film is removed from the camera outdoors, it should not be resealed in its original container until the photographer has reached some dry sanctuary, lest the humid outdoor air be locked up inside the can along with the film.

For travelers who will spend only a few days in a hot, damp climate, a conve-

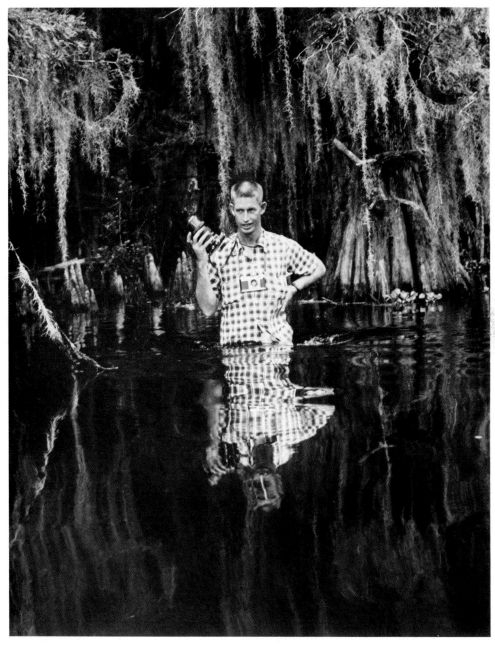

Hip-deep in a Florida waterway known as Fisheating Creek, Stan Wayman prepares to photograph an angler fly-casting for black bass. For 15 years, Wayman covered outdoor activities ranging from walrus hunts in the Bering Sea to scuba diving in Micronesia for Life magazine.

nient way to dry out exposed rolls of film—and keep them dry—is to place them in a suitcase containing freshly ironed clothes. Ironed linens absorb moisture well enough to hold humidity to a safe level. In the tropics, however, neither the suitcase nor the camera should be left in a hotel closet, for moth- and mildew-repellent compounds are often put there to protect clothes, and the vapor of these substances may react adversely with the dyes in color film. A slight amount of contaminated air may even remain in the camera long after it is taken from the hotel closet and even this trace of vapor is sufficient to continue to harm color film.

Much more reliable than ironed shirts as a defense against high humidity is a chemical drying agent, such as silica gel. Crystals of silica gel (white in their natural state but often treated with a bluish indicator dye) can keep the air in a small enclosed space as dry as Arizona. When the gel has collected all the moisture it can hold, the treated crystals turn reddish. But their humidity-countering powers can be revived by cooking them in an oven at 400° F. until they become bluish again. Silica gel is practically an ideal product: It is cheap; it can be reused indefinitely; and it is available at many photography supply stores, which sell it in small cans the size of shoe-polish tins.

On an extended trip in hot, wet climates, some photographers store equipment and exposed film with two or three perforated shoe-polish-can-sized containers of silica gel inside 10-gallon cans of the kind used for paint; their tight-sealing lids make them thoroughly moistureproof. A large, wide-mouthed glass or plastic jar with a vapor-tight cap will also serve as an excellent container for film and small items of equipment if silica gel is included. And even a foam plastic picnic cooler, despite its lack of a tightly fitted lid, will usually remain sufficiently dry if it contains a liberal amount of fresh silica gel.

When silica gel is not available, rice can substitute as a drying agent, although about eight times as much will be needed. Before putting it in the cooler, dry the rice over a low flame, then cool it in an airtight container so that it will not immediately absorb the moisture from surrounding air. For convenient packets to hold rice or bulk quantities of silica gel in a cooler or equipment case, try ordinary socks; moisture is easily absorbed through the fabric of the socks, and there is no problem of loose grains or crystals scattering about.

Far more troublesome than humidity, hot or cold, is water in any form—mist, rain, perspiration or ocean spray. When water gets inside a camera, it can rust metal parts, spot the film and cause other sorts of havoc such as shorting out the electrical circuit of the light meter. Perspiration is a worse offender than rain, for it contains salts and acids that quickly corrode metal. Prolonged exposure to salt spray is a foolproof recipe for rusting a camera.

In sweaty weather, many photographers wear towels around their necks so that perspiration does not drip into their cameras. Since hands will perspire, too, leaving salty moisture on camera surfaces, the camera should be wiped periodically with a lint-free cloth or chamois. Neck straps and camera cases made of leather are also prey to perspiration. Co Rentmeester once went through seven neck straps in 10 days when he was shooting a story for *Life* on orangutans in Borneo *(right)*. The solution to the neck-strap problem is simple: Use one made of metal, plastic or nylon.

In rainy weather some photographers wear a raincoat several sizes too large so that equipment can be carried underneath; but for all-around convenience, nothing beats an old-fashioned umbrella. However, it is no mean feat to hold an umbrella and shoot a picture at the same time, and occasionally the camera must be bared to raindrops. A lens hood will usually keep rain from getting on the lens and blurring the photograph. After the picture has been snapped, the camera should be dried as soon as possible to prevent corrosion. Wiping it with a lint-free cloth will get rid of some water. When the weather clears, the camera should be aired and then left in the sun briefly to exorcise the last of the moisture. A camera can also be dried in an oven for a few moments at very low heat, but this procedure must be performed with caution.

Plastic bags — the self-sealing transparent ones used for food storage — provide very effective shields against rain or salt spray, and they are ideal containers for camera, lenses and film in a driving rainstorm, out on a boat or near the surf. It is even possible to keep a plastic bag over the camera while shooting. Just cut a hole in the bottom of the bag, making it large enough for the lens to peek through, then place a rubber band around the hole to clamp the bag to the lens and look through the open end of the bag to use the viewfinder for framing and focusing. More permanent is a durable plastic cover made for cameras and available from large photography stores and some stores selling diving equipment.

If a camera actually falls into salt water, it stands little chance of survival. Drying it out will not help. The only hope is to rinse it thoroughly, then keep it immersed in a pail of fresh water and get it to a camera repair shop as fast as possible. The immersion may seem suicidal, but it actually prevents air from reacting with moist salt and oxidizing the metal.

The best protection against such a calamity when working near salt water is a waterproof housing — or a true underwater camera. The housing made of flexible soft plastic is also ideally suited for shooting in rain or near water sprays. Essentially a heavy-duty plastic sack with an opening that seals watertight, the flexible housing has two glass ports — one for the lens and the other for the viewfinder. A glove built into the sack gives the photographer access to the camera's controls. A soft housing is easier to use than the rigid plastic or metal models employed by professional underwater photographers, and it is also less expensive. Equally important, it is lightweight and can be quickly

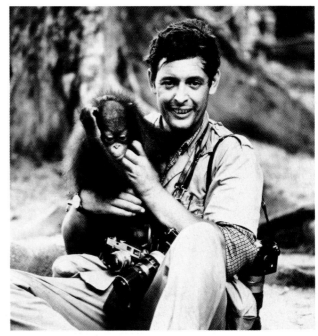

In the steamy atmosphere of a Borneo wildlife preserve, Co Rentmeester found an exceedingly friendly subject in one baby orangutan. Only a few of these primate relatives of man survive in the rain forests of Borneo and Sumatra.

folded and packed away. Its obvious drawback is the fragility of its soft plastic, which can be cut or punctured; reasonable precautions must be observed to avoid such damage. Cameras sealed in either metal or plastic cases may fog over because of condensation; packets of silica gel will solve the problem.

A soft housing can also protect a camera if submerged — deliberately or accidentally — but only up to a depth of 30 feet. Before using it for this purpose, however, it should be tested. Submerge the empty housing in a pail of water; a stream of bubbles will rise from even the tiniest hole.

Since wetness is so obviously harmful, logic suggests that photographic gear will be safe in very dry climates — but this is not the case, for dry weather usually means that dust or sand particles are floating or blowing about. Blowing dust and sand can etch the surface of a lens, gradually reducing its ability to give clear pictures. In addition, the fine, airborne particles penetrate the crevices of a camera. Once inside, they may jam the film-advance mechanism, slow down the shutter, or coat the inner surfaces of the lens so that light transmission is impaired. The dust may also get on the film, coating it with spots that block light and cause speckled pictures.

An indispensable safeguard for dusty regions is a clear or ultraviolet filter kept over the lens at all times. Since these filters do not significantly affect the transmission of light from the subject, there is no need to calculate new exposure settings — and the filter shields the expensive lens against the direct assaults of flying particles. (Such filters are also very useful in wet environments to guard the lens against dried salt.) Dust and sand can be quickly blown or wiped away with a cloth. The filter may not last long in a very dusty or sandy environment under such treatment, but a new one costs only a few dollars; placing a lens cap over the filter between shots will somewhat extend its life.

Not only the lens, but all other equipment needs protection from dust in dry regions. A coat or blanket can be thrown over photographic gear when it is not in use, but a case or plastic bag affords better protection. A plastic housing made to keep out water will also keep out particles of grit — although its optical glass ports will eventually become scratched and, in time, will have to be replaced. Despite the most meticulous precautions, however, some particles will probably find their way into a camera sooner or later, and the interior should always be checked before a new roll of film is loaded. Luckily, dust and sand are not especially hard to remove from a camera's innards. The simplest method is to blow them out by lung power — but there is always a danger that saliva will get into the camera. It is much safer to remove the offending particles with a sable or camel's-hair brush. A more effective device, sold at most photography stores, is a rubber bulb that emits a stream of air when squeezed; on the opposite end of the bulb is a soft brush to clear away any particles that remain.

In very cold climates, the photographer has to run yet another gantlet of difficulties, which are often just as arduous as those encountered in hot, humid, wet or dusty environments. Shutters slow down, lenses ice over, exposure calculations become mystifying, film snaps or is marred by electrostatic discharge, and the photographer himself runs the danger of frostbite from touching a freezing camera. However, several potential troubles can be eliminated by careful advance preparations.

Cameras with automatic electronic controls powered by batteries are the most trouble-prone in cold weather because batteries lose their ability to generate power as the temperature plunges. In many cameras, electronic circuits control not only the exposure meter but also such functions as the timing and release of the camera's shutter. For these cameras, a dead battery may mean much more than just a dead meter. Unless the camera has an emergency backup system that will permit its shutter to operate mechanically—most such systems work at just one shutter speed—a dead battery will make it impossible to open and close the camera shutter. And without a working shutter, a camera that is an electronic marvel at normal temperatures becomes little more than an expensive film canister.

Some types of batteries tend to withstand extreme cold better than others. In 1981 tests at –20° F., relatively inexpensive alkaline batteries outperformed both lithium and silver oxide batteries; but at +10° F., all three performed about equally, and silver and lithium batteries lasted much longer than alkaline.

The best way to prevent battery failure in cold weather is to use fresh cells and to keep them as warm as possible. Shield the camera from cold with a protective covering such as a felt-lined blimp bag *(page 25),* and carry spare batteries in a pocket warmed by body heat.

These precautions, however, offer only limited protection; a photographer planning extensive shooting in frigid climates should avoid relying on batteries at all if he can. A camera with a shutter that operates mechanically—either a nonautomatic camera, or an automatic with a full range of mechanical shutter speeds as a backup—is a wise choice. And he should supplement his camera's built-in light meter with a hand-held selenium-cell meter that does not require battery power to function.

Having a mechanical shutter does not solve all cold-weather shutter problems. Sometimes a chilled shutter does not operate as fast as the setting calls for, resulting in overexposure. In some cameras this lethargy is caused by the material used for their focal-plane shutters. It becomes so brittle at low temperatures that it resists movement; such cameras should be left home. More often, the problem is due to thickening of the oil that lubricates the shutter mechanism. This seldom happens nowadays because most new camera lubricants contain synthetic lubricants that do not become stiff until the temperature reaches –65° F. But it is wise to check the camera before a winter trip to ski resorts or to northern Alaska. A convenient way of gauging cold-weather performance is to put the camera in the freezer compartment of a refrigerator for several hours, then take pictures at various shutter speeds. If any pictures come out overexposed, the camera should be taken to a repair shop, where an expert will winterize it by removing most of the lubricants. (When the camera is brought back to a temperate climate, the lubricants must be replaced to avoid wear and tear on the mechanism.) It is also good policy to have an expert make sure that a camera is perfectly light-tight. In snowy regions, where bright light is reflected from all directions, even a minute light leak can fog negatives.

Other hazards await as the camera becomes cold in the chill outdoors. One common mistake is to take warm equipment out into blowing snow. Snowflakes strike the camera, melt on contact and then refreeze. The only way to get the ice coating off is to take the camera back into the warm indoors. Yet this problem can be easily avoided by giving the camera time to cool down before taking it out of its protective case. When the metal surface is cold, snow that gets on it will not stick and can be shaken or brushed off.

Even after the camera has chilled to a low air temperature, freezing problems remain; they are simply different. For one thing, the lens ices up if the warm vapor of breath gets on it—as often happens when f-stop adjustments are being made. The moisture will instantly freeze when it touches the cold glass, but it can sometimes be removed by breathing on the lens again and then immediately wiping the remelted droplets off with a cotton cloth. More serious is the possibility that human skin will freeze to very cold camera surfaces. If a photographer puts his eye to an uncushioned viewfinder or tries to adjust the camera controls with his bare hands, his flesh may actually stick to the metal. To counter this hazard, tape sponge rubber, chamois or felt to the camera wherever it is likely to be touched. Another wise safeguard is thin silk or cotton gloves worn under the usual heavy gloves or mittens. The inner gloves not only keep hands warmer when the outer ones are removed, the thin ones make much easier—and safer—the loading and adjustment of a camera in sub-zero weather.

Exposure troubles, when they occur in cold weather, come less from temperature than from the light often found in cold climates. Even with an accurate meter, there is a tendency to overexpose pictures in snow-covered terrain (as well as at the beach or in the desert), because reflectance of light is much higher than in an ordinary landscape. But if the picture includes a relatively dark subject—such as a person standing in the snow—underexposure rather than overexposure is likely. The strong light from the snow will distort the meter reading, and the person will come out dark and lacking in detail. To avoid underexposures, the meter should be held close to the person's face or clothes—or to the photographer's hand or any convenient object that has the same degree of reflectance as the subject. But the best course is extensive bracketing of all exposures.

An ultraviolet filter is a useful aid to correct exposure in wintertime. It is almost colorless, but cuts down on the invisible ultraviolet light scattered by air molecules in the atmosphere; the reduction in ultraviolet helps prevent overexposure, darkens the sky in an attractive way, and also keeps the snow from appearing artificially blue in color pictures—an effect due to the reflection by snow crystals of the sky's ultraviolet, which registers as blue in color film. On the ski slopes, an ultraviolet filter is indispensable because there is so much ultraviolet light at high altitudes that overexposure is very likely.

The film itself picks up peculiar ailments in extreme cold. Its sensitivity is not particularly affected, but it becomes very brittle. The edges of film hardened by the cold are so sharp that they can cut fingers during the loading operation. In the camera, the film must be advanced and rewound slowly or it will snap. When *Life* photographer Hank Walker was covering the Korean War in wintertime *(right),* his film often snapped because he advanced it too quickly during action-packed moments. He found that such mishaps could be greatly reduced by putting his cameras beneath his parka between shots; his body heat warmed the film and made it less brittle. Cautious movement of the film also avoids another cold-weather problem: electrostatic discharge. Moving film acts just like the rubbing surfaces in the electrostatic generators used for laboratory experiments; an electric voltage builds up on it, and a spark may actually leap from the film to the camera body, resulting in branchlike markings on pictures *(page 128).*

One final danger lurks at the end of the day's shooting in cold climates. If a chilled camera is taken back into the warm indoors, the moisture in the warmer air may condense on the lens, on the film and on the delicate inner mechanisms of the camera. The moisture may corrode the camera or spot the emulsion; and if the camera is taken back outside before the moisture has had time to evaporate, it will freeze solid and make picture taking impossible. The solution is to place the camera in an airtight plastic bag before going outdoors. Moisture will condense harmlessly on the outside of the bag while the equipment inside warms up.

Some tactics apply to the problems of all climates. Certainly the first and most important rule does: Keep the camera clean. Regularly use a cloth or camel's-hair brush to rid it of moisture, dirt or dust so that it does not fail at some crucial moment. It is bad enough to have picture quality slowly go downhill as camera performance deteriorates, but it is even worse to miss a great picture because the camera suddenly, without warning, refuses to work.

Some camera failures that occur in the field can be remedied on the spot. The old trick of making a portable darkroom out of a coat, for example, may

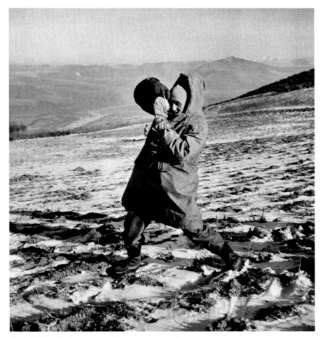

Hank Walker had to cope with temperatures that occasionally dipped to –30° F., while on assignment with an American patrol near the Yalu River (background) during the Korean War. In such extreme cold, film grows brittle. Film breakage was Walker's major problem.

save the day when film jams after half a roll has been shot. The technique is simple: Place the camera on the coat; button and fold the coat in such a manner that no light reaches the camera; reach backward through the sleeves to open up the camera back; then free the film from the sprockets of the take-up spool and wind it back into its light-tight cassette. With the film thus rescued, the photographer can remove the coat and go to work on the camera to eliminate the source of the trouble—perhaps a particle of sand or dirt that has gotten into the mechanism.

There are several other kinds of first-aid treatment for cameras. A small screwdriver comes in handy to tighten screws that have shaken loose on a trip across rough country. A roll of Gaffer's tape—very strong adhesive tape used by movie studio electricians—is particularly useful. Tape helps seal the crevices of a camera in very dusty regions. And if a camera has been accidentally dropped, bending the back of the camera so that light can penetrate it and fog the film, tape will provide a temporary seal until repairs are possible.

First aid will not always do the trick, of course, and the time may come when a photographer has to resign himself to the loss of a camera. To cover such an eventuality, professionals working with SLRs almost always carry a spare camera body (that is, a camera minus the lens). It provides an invaluable backstop and is not nearly so expensive as might be thought. The spare need not be an exact duplicate of the camera body ordinarily used. A less expensive model—perhaps a manually operated model or one lacking a very fast shutter—will be fine for backup purposes, as long as it takes the same lenses the regular camera does. A secondhand body is generally good enough and may cost only half as much as a new one. But before starting out on a trip, have it checked out at a camera shop and then shoot a roll or two of film with it to compare its performance with that of the regular equipment. A backup hand-held exposure meter is another essential piece of insurance in case the camera's built-in meter fails. It can be a batteryless selenium-cell type—ideal for frigid climates— or a more sensitive battery-powered model, which can be kept warm in a pocket if necessary. Either type will ensure that invaluable photographic opportunities are not lost for want of a functioning light meter.

The need for special gear and precautions to neutralize the hazards of nature may suggest that the camera should be left on the shelf at home except when the weatherman guarantees a perfect June day. Far from it. Most of the steps that safeguard equipment are simple. And some of the best pictures are obtained under the worst conditions. Photographers who surmount the problems of the environment find visual glories—the soft light and rich colors of rainy weather, the starkness of desert and plain, the translucent waters and dark tangle of the tropics, the fury of surf, the purity of snow. The difficulties are more than matched by the prize. □

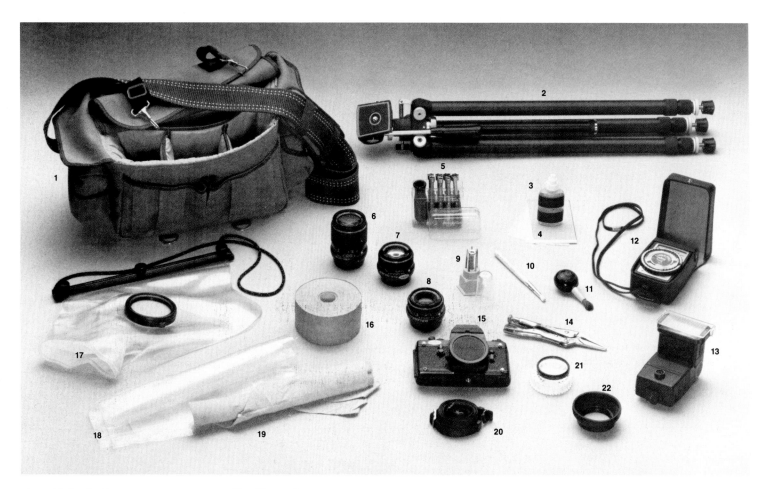

1 padded gadget bag	12 silicon-cell exposure meter
2 tripod	13 electronic flash
3 lens-cleaning solution	14 locking needle-nose pliers
4 lens-cleaning paper	15 35mm SLR camera
5 set of small socket wrenches	16 Gaffer's tape
6 135mm lens	17 waterproof flexible plastic housing
7 50mm lens	18 self-sealing plastic bags
8 28mm lens	19 chamois
9 set of jeweler's screwdrivers	20 moistureproof camera neck strap
10 stiff-bristled brush	21 ultraviolet filter
11 air-blower brush	22 collapsible rubber lens hood

Gearing Up for Heat and Cold

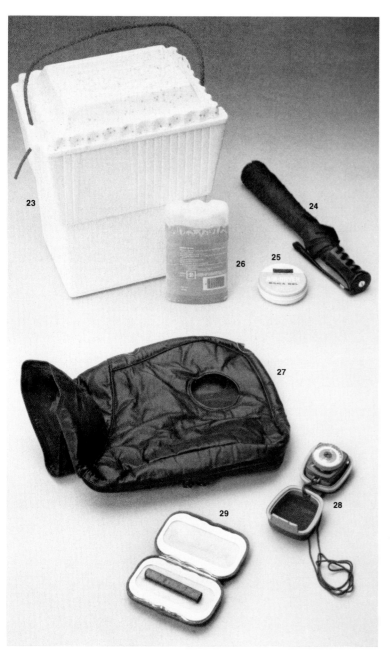

23 **foam plastic picnic cooler**

24 **folding umbrella**

25 **silica-gel drying agent**

26 **refreezable refrigerant**

27 **cold-weather camera cover**

28 **selenium-cell exposure meter**

29 **hand warmer**

The basic 35mm kit for rugged conditions *(opposite)* is centered on a single-lens-reflex camera (15) that can operate mechanically at more than one shutter speed in case batteries fail, and three lenses of fixed focal lengths: normal (7), wide-angle (8) and long (6).

A sturdy lightweight tripod (2), a relatively powerful flash unit (13) and a back-up hand-held exposure meter (12) serve their normal functions. Other accessories are dictated by harsh conditions. An ultraviolet filter (21) and a collapsible rubber hood (22) protect lenses from moisture and grit, while an airtight flexible plastic housing (17) will get the camera safely through rain, snow or sandstorms.

Essential cleaning supplies include a chamois (19), a stiff-bristled brush (10), an air-blower brush (11), special lens-cleaning fluid (3) and tissue (4).

Small socket wrenches (5) and tiny jeweler's screwdrivers (9) help fix loose screws and nuts while needle-nose locking pliers (14) can loosen jammed tripod joints. Strong Gaffer's tape (16) can cover a camera light leak, patch a rip or provide a grip for removing a stuck filter.

This equipment can be carried in a multipocketed bag (1). The model pictured keeps fragile equipment separated and cushioned with padded dividers. For storing film and accessories, carry self-sealing plastic bags (18).

For hot, damp regions *(left, top),* add a folding umbrella (24), a foam plastic picnic cooler (23), a tin of silica gel (25) to keep the cooler dry and reusable gelatin refrigerant (26) to keep it cool. For cold climates *(bottom),* take a solid-fuel hand warmer (29), a lined camera cover (27) and, most important, a selenium-cell exposure meter (28), which operates without batteries and is unaffected by cold. □

The Challenge of Nature at Its Worst

Professional photographers have been engaged in an endurance contest with nature since their craft began, willingly enduring punishment to their equipment and to themselves in an effort to get unusual pictures. More than a century ago, travel photographers ventured into broiling heat and biting sand in the Sahara, over snow on the Russian steppes, and up to chilling winds in the Swiss Alps, bringing back exotic views that delighted a huge audience of stay-at-homes.

Getting a good picture under such climatic conditions was a difficult business at best. The collodion emulsion of wet plates—a predecessor of modern film—sometimes boiled in hot regions or hardened and became insensitive where the air was very dry. Countless pictures were spoiled when the emulsion picked up flying dust or when a drop of perspiration fell on the plate.

The invention of dry, roll film and rugged cameras freed photographers from many of their former worries. But predictably enough, the professionals continue to strive for the outer limits of endurance. These days they tote their cameras to the South Pole where the temperature may sink to as low as –100° F.; they defy the fury of hurricanes; they press close to erupting volcanoes; and they will undoubtedly follow the astronauts to the airless mountains of the moon if they can wangle transportation.

Like battle-wise soldiers, they have devised dozens of small ways to protect their gear. Thus armed, the modern professional photographers have bested the worst that nature can present—and have brought back from their arduous campaigns such trophies of rare beauty as the ones that are shown on the following 16 pages.

Heeding Death Valley's reputation for furnace-like heat—so intense at midday that the color balance of film might be affected—Charles Moore photographed the California desert between 5:30 and 7 in the morning, before the temperature rose above 80° F. Even at that hour, the glare of the barren dunes required him to shoot at one or two f-stops smaller than the normal reading. An ultraviolet filter protected his lens from flying sand, but some tiny particles penetrated the crevices of his camera and he had to clean it later with a brush.

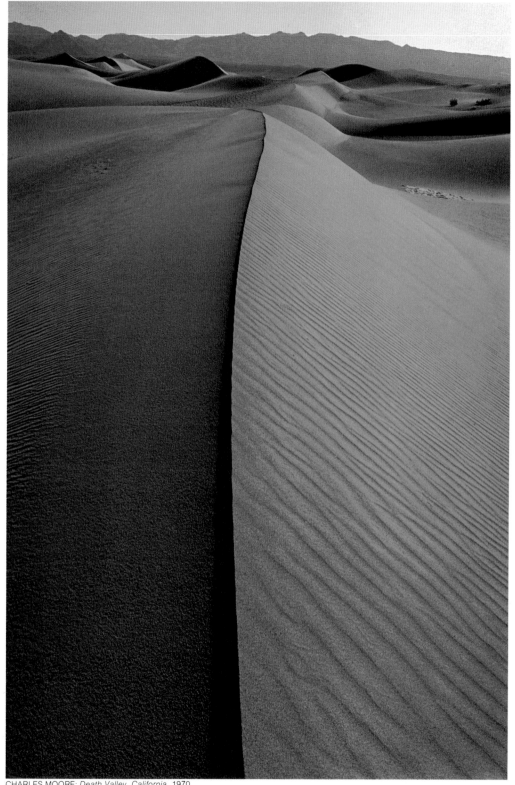

CHARLES MOORE: *Death Valley, California,* 1970

An Elusive Mirage

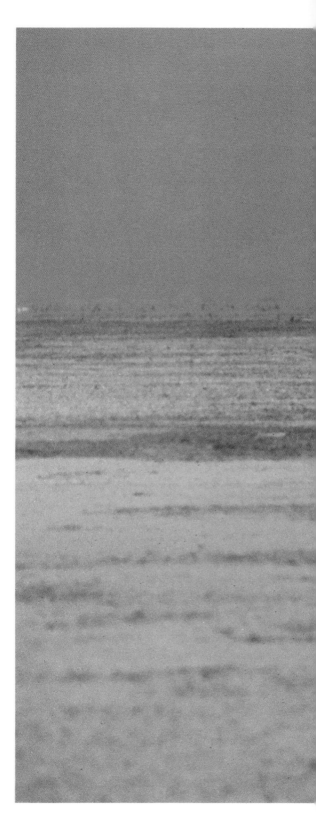

Defying noontime heat to record Indians crossing a desert in Colombia, the photographer unexpectedly encountered a desert mirage. The elusive phenomenon, which occurs when hot air just above the ground surface bends light waves, creates an inverted mirror image of objects on the surface. To guard against heat and grit, the camera was sealed in a plastic bag, film was stored in a foam plastic cooler and other equipment was carried in an aluminum case shaded from the sun.

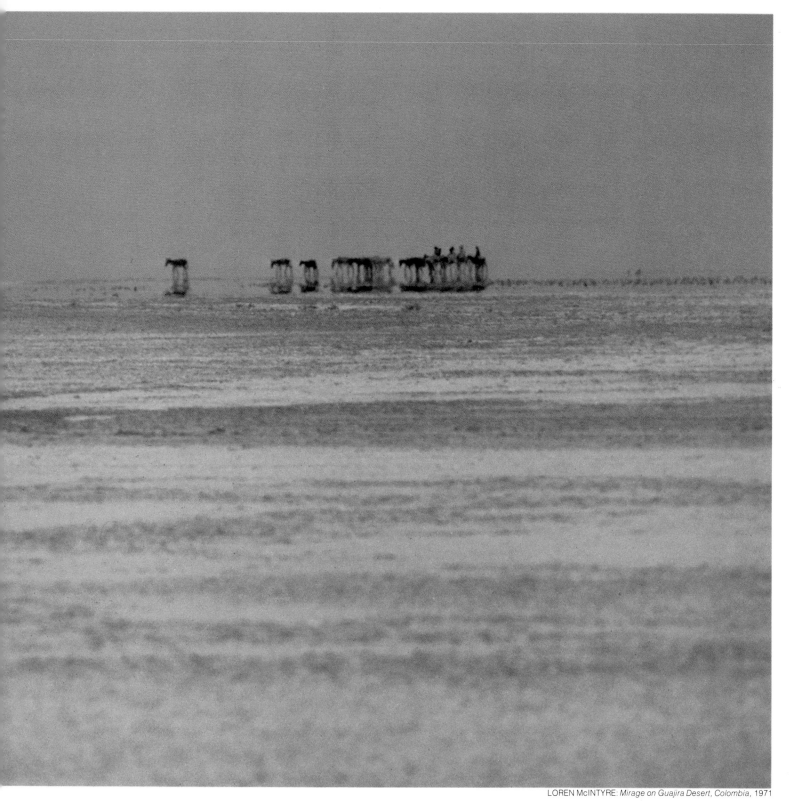

LOREN McINTYRE: *Mirage on Guajira Desert, Colombia,* 1971

A Volcano's Spectacular Hell-fire

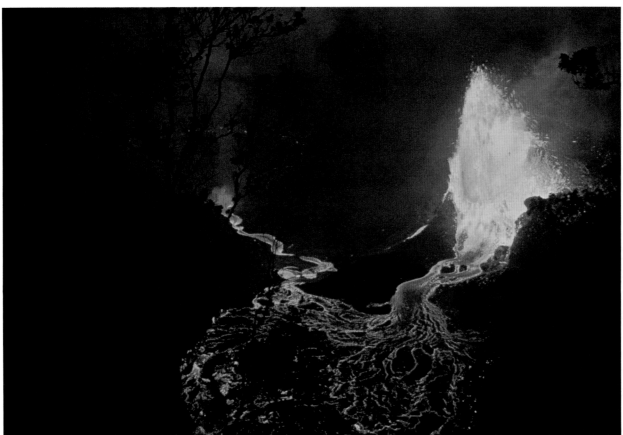

ROBERT B. GOODMAN: *Fountains of Lava, Hawaii,* 1959

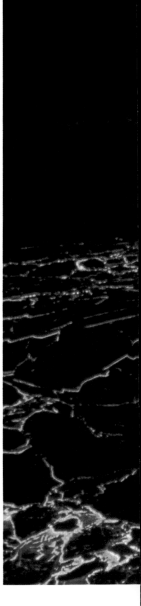

Despite its thrilling fireworks, the eruption of Kilauea Volcano in Hawaii seemed like a trial by torture to Robert B. Goodman, who photographed it for the National Geographic magazine. The shaking earth blurred many of his exposures, and he used up a pocketful of lens tissues wiping pumice and rain off the protective filters over his lenses. He needed several cameras because grit continually penetrated and jammed them, even though they were wrapped with protective tape. When Goodman came close to the seething lava (right), the heat was so fierce that he had to focus and shoot in a few brief seconds, and then turn his back to recover. Of this assignment he later said, "Photographing a volcano is just about the most miserable thing you can do, but also the most fascinating."

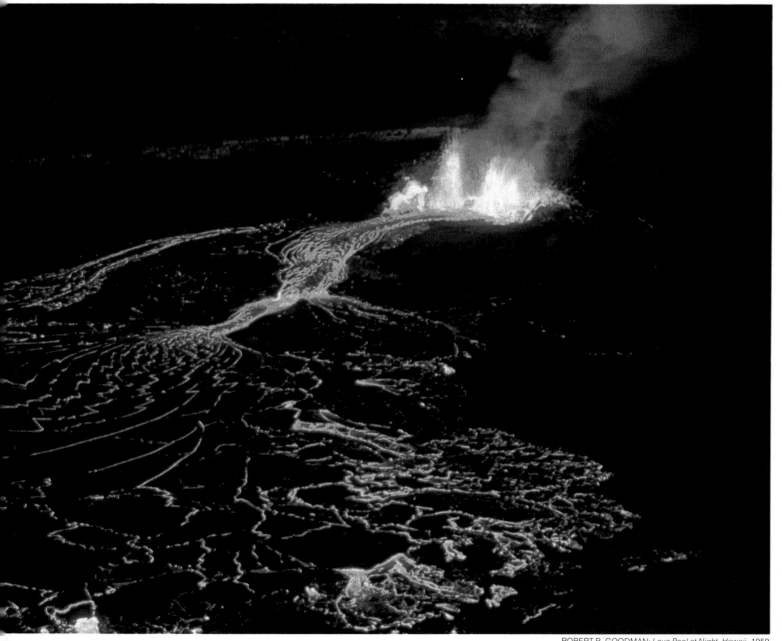

ROBERT B. GOODMAN: *Lava Pool at Night, Hawaii*, 1959

The Damp of Sea Air

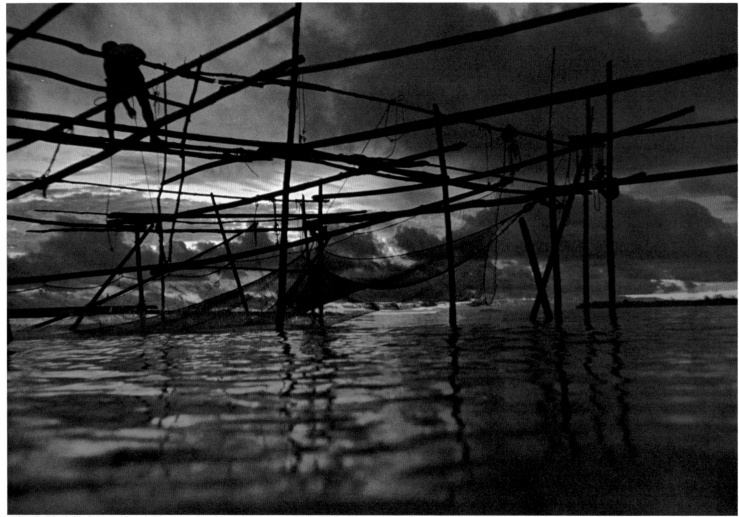

MICHAEL ROUGIER: *Fishing in Rajang River Delta, Borneo, 1964*

*A serene vision of a Borneo fisherman hauling
up his nets at sunset belies the difficulties that
Michael Rougier faced in this hot, humid
climate. To ward off fungus, he carried his film
in a picnic cooler lined with packets of the
chemical dehumidifier, silica gel. After a day of
shooting in the damp air, he used a portable
hair dryer to get all moisture out of his camera.*

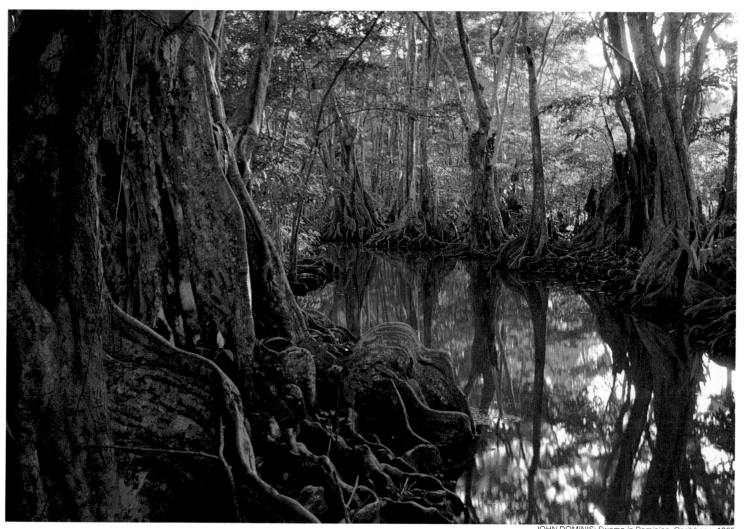

JOHN DOMINIS: *Swamp in Dominica, Caribbean, 1965*

On the Caribbean island of Dominica, giant pterocarpus trees hold within their gnarled embrace an invisible threat to photographic equipment — hot, damp air made salty by the nearby sea. John Dominis minimized the corrosive effect of this atmosphere by keeping his camera in a strong plastic bag and removing it just long enough to shoot the picture.

Dust and Rain in the Tropics

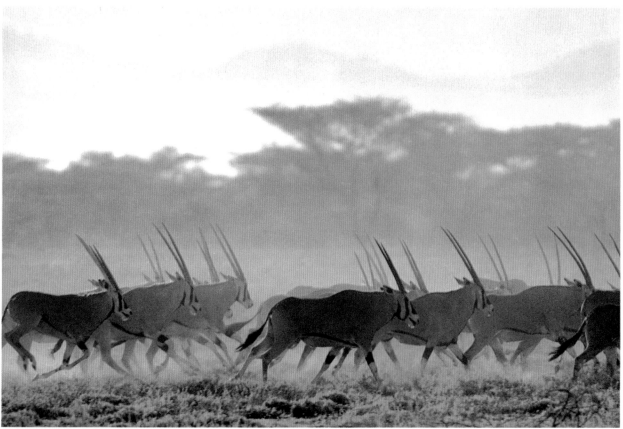

JOHN DOMINIS: *Oryx in Kenya,* 1969

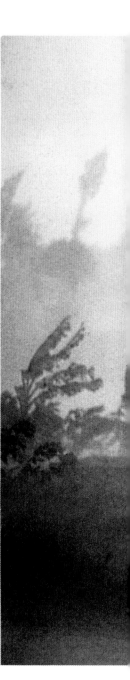

Galloping across the parched grasslands of Kenya, a herd of oryx fills the air with fine, lingering dust. John Dominis turned the choking cloud to his advantage by positioning himself so that the sun was in front of him, backlighting the dust and producing a soft, luminous background almost like fog. He used a long 600mm lens and kept a considerable distance between himself and the skittish antelopes, but dust kept getting inside his camera anyway, and he had to clean it out every night with brushes and an air stream squeezed from a rubber bulb.

Water buffaloes and their youthful tenders calmly endure the whip of rain during monsoon season in Java. The downpour lasted only two minutes, but it proved costly to the photographer, Co Rentmeester. Although he carried an umbrella, wind-blown spray knocked his exposure meter out of action by causing a short circuit and also corroded his shutter so badly that he had to throw the camera away.

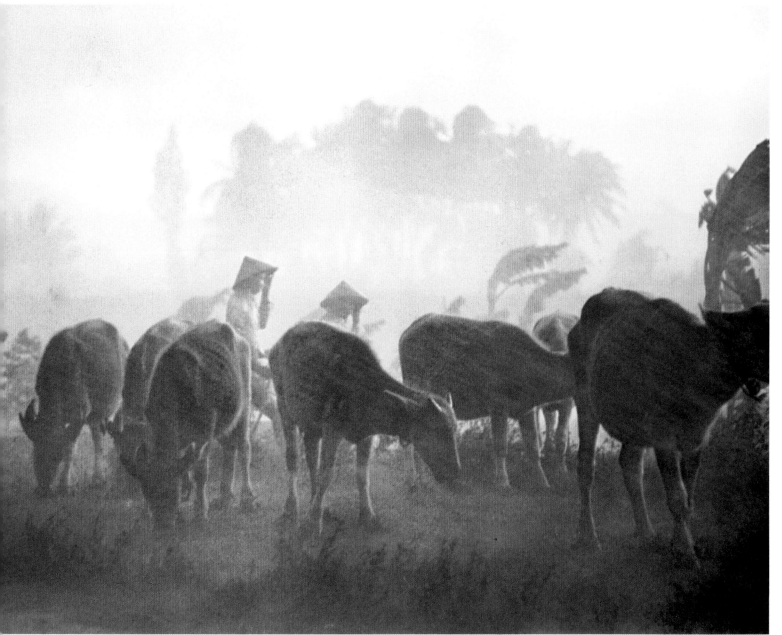

CO RENTMEESTER: *Java Monsoon*, 1970

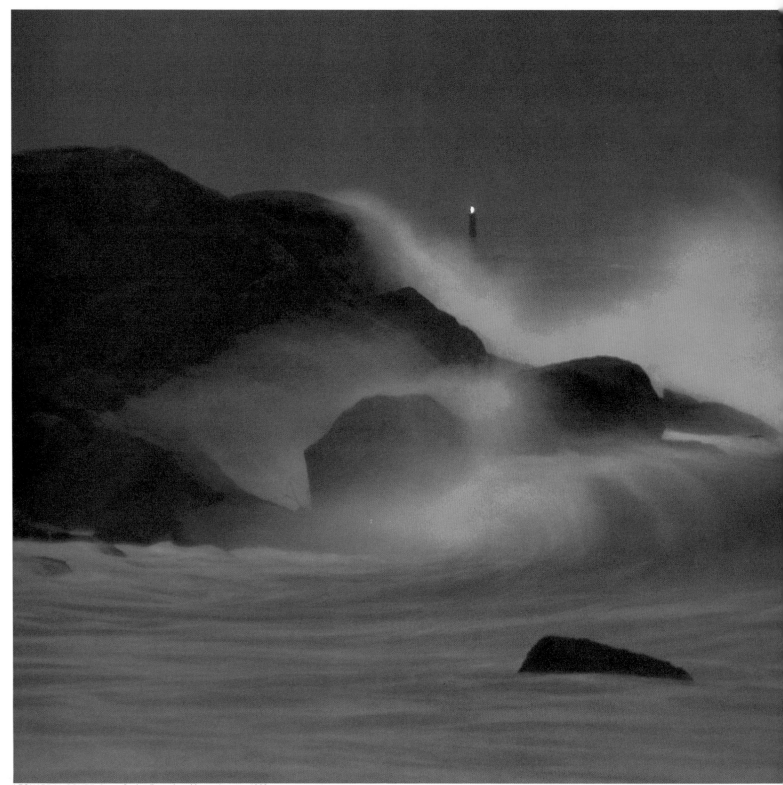

LEONARD McCOMBE: *Storm Surf at Cape Ann, Massachusetts,* 1962

The Spray of Pounding Surf

Storm-driven waves tear at the granite headland of Cape Ann, Massachusetts, as a lonely beacon in the background warns ships to stay clear. Leonard McCombe shot this picture of the sea's savagery an hour after sunset, using a tripod to steady his camera on the rocks. He protected his 200mm lens with an ultraviolet filter, wiping off spray just before he released the shutter. Then he quickly covered the camera with a plastic bag that kept out the corrosive spray.

Dazzling Light, Frigid Cold at the Poles

A whole new set of difficulties lies in wait for photographers who venture into the polar regions of the earth. Not only do low temperatures solidify camera lubricants and make film brittle enough to break if it is not advanced slowly, but the quality of the light is changed so much by snow and the low sun that exposure calculation is particularly demanding. Yet photographers travel to the Arctic and Antarctic in ever-greater numbers—for the simple reason that there is a surprising amount of activity there to be documented.

A million people live in Arctic lands, and unusual birds and animals abound. Mining is a thriving industry in the frigid reaches of northern Canada. And tankers *(right)* and pipelines are thrusting into the icy Arctic realm to bring back oil from a pool underlying northern Alaska.

The Antarctic is an even more fearsome place. With an average altitude of 6,000 feet, it is the highest and coldest of all continents, its land and surrounding seas burdened with 90 per cent of the world's ice. Yet more than 10 nations have established major camps in this lifeless, frozen land, for Antarctica holds important clues to global weather patterns, geological processes and the history of the planet. Photography plays an important role in all these scientific investigations, and also enables the world at large to see the work in progress. Even amateur photographers can now venture into this bleak region; travel agencies offer tours to Antarctica.

Crunching through ice floes in the Arctic Ocean, the heavily reinforced tanker Manhattan nears the last leg of a voyage that tested the practicality of shipping oil from Alaska to the East Coast by a northwest passage. To get this picture from a viewpoint close to the ice-choked water, John Olson attached his 35mm camera to a 20-foot pole, held it over the side of the ship, and triggered the shutter with a cable release. He had already had lubricants removed from the camera to prevent the shutter from slowing down or jamming in the severe cold. And before he went back indoors, he sealed the chilled camera inside a plastic bag so that moisture from the warm interior air would not condense on it.

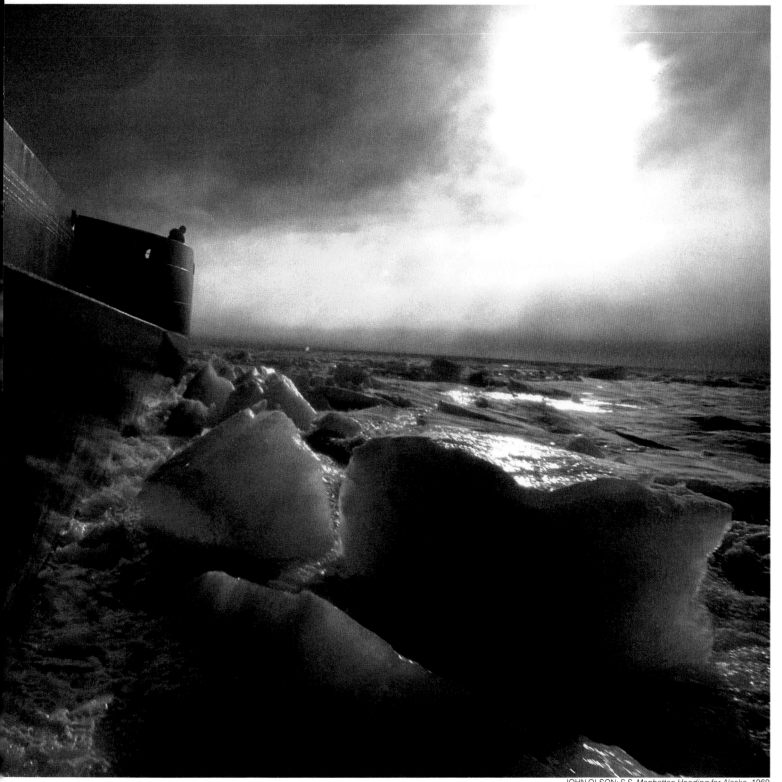

JOHN OLSON: *S.S. Manhattan Heading for Alaska,* 1969

Exploiting Antarctica's Brilliance

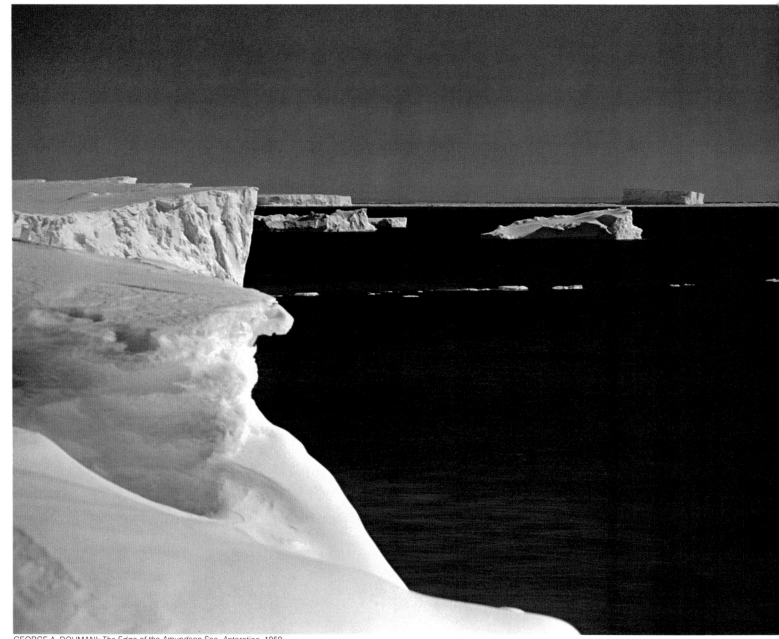

GEORGE A. DOUMANI: *The Edge of the Amundsen Sea, Antarctica,* 1959

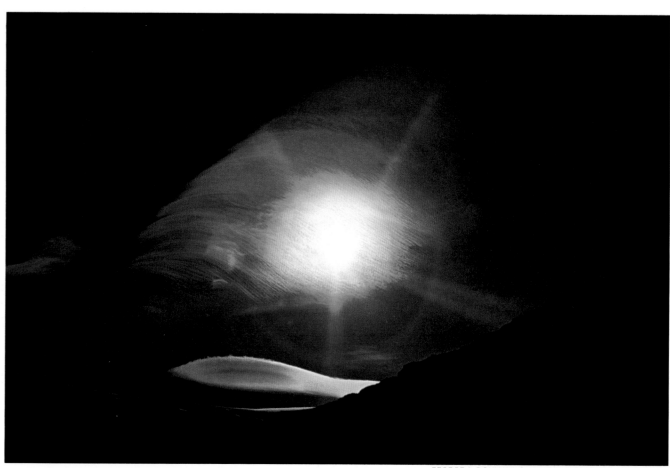

GEORGE A. DOUMANI: *Optical Effect of Clouds, Antarctica,* 1962

An ice shelf at the edge of Antarctica gleams gloriously white in the picture at left, taken by George A. Doumani, a geologist and glaciologist as well as a photographer. Using an ultraviolet filter over his lens, he blocked the great amount of ultraviolet radiation that the ice reflected from the sky, and thus reduced the bluish tinge such rays induce in color film. He also underexposed slightly to deepen the blue of the sea and show off the white ice to even greater advantage by heightening contrast.

To capture the unusual rainbow effect often observed around clouds laden with ice crystals, Doumani gauged exposure by pointing his meter directly at the Antarctic sun, then blocked the sun out of the camera's view by shooting from beneath a rock overhang. In effect, he was underexposing by several stops, thus suppressing the whiteness of the clouds and allowing the delicate rainbow colors to show up clearly. His meter was able to handle the direct rays of the sun because they were weakened by traveling a long distance through the atmosphere; in Antarctica, the sun never rises more than 50 degrees above the horizon.

Antidotes for Sub-zero Wind and Snow

Helicopters were grounded and scientists huddled inside their tents at Byrd Land Camp in western Antarctica when Navy photographer Robert R. Nunley ventured outside to take this chilling picture. The temperature stood at –30° F. and the wind was blowing fiercely. Under such conditions the slick metal of the camera would have instantly frozen to the skin of his face as he looked through the viewfinder of his camera, but Nunley averted this danger by covering up the metal with canvas tape. To keep the fine, blowing snow from penetrating the camera, he periodically cleaned the outer crevices with an ordinary typewriter-eraser brush.

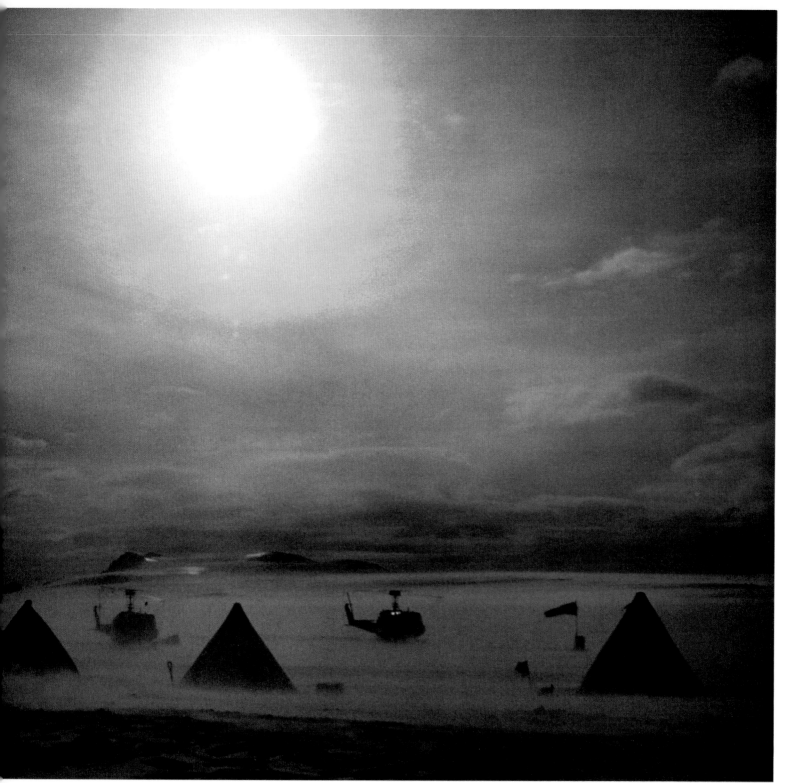

ROBERT R. NUNLEY: *Byrd Land Camp, Antarctica,* 1967

Perils of the "White-Out"

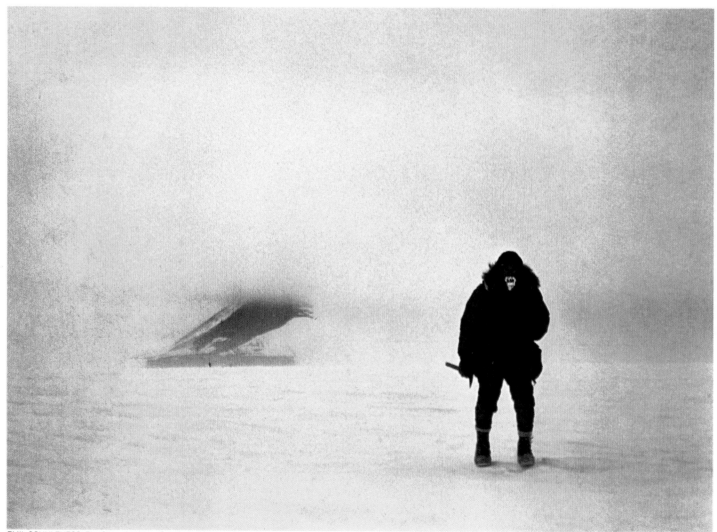

EMIL SCHULTHESS: *The Start of a White-Out, Antarctica,* 1958

A weary geologist, his beard caked with rime, returns from an expedition at the beginning of an Antarctic "white-out"—a perilous, disorienting condition when the reflection of light from the cloud cover and snow is almost exactly equal, and land and sky become indistinguishable. Focusing on the scientist's face with his winterized rangefinder camera, and shooting at 1/100 second and f/5.6, Emil Schulthess framed him against the rapidly disappearing horizon.

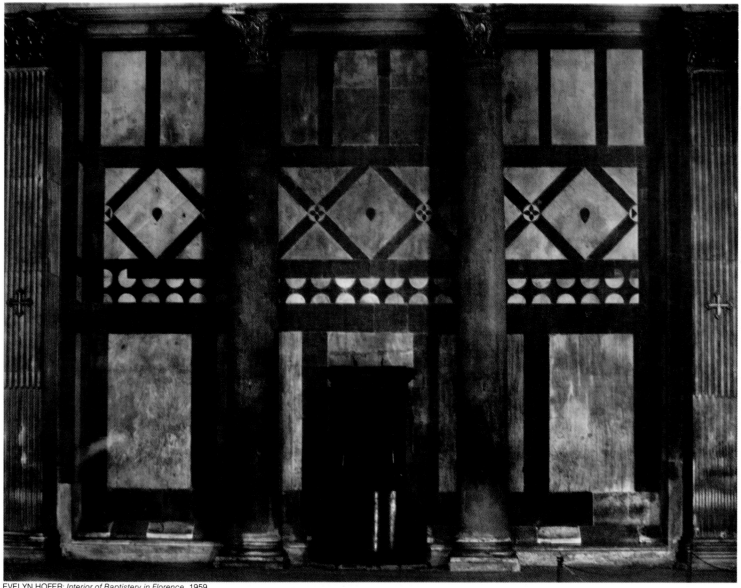

EVELYN HOFER: *Interior of Baptistery in Florence*, 1959

How to Get the Impossible Picture

It is often said of problems that everybody has them—an undeniable but not very comforting sentiment. In photography, to be sure, one does not have to be a world-roaming adventurer to encounter difficulties. Problems lurk in the most routine situations, where there are no glamorously extenuating circumstances, such as Amazonian heat or Antarctic chill, to help explain away a failure.

Photographers constantly find themselves trying for interesting kinds of pictures, only to find that various difficulties undo their esthetic intentions. A scene shot through a window, or toward the sun, or into a mirror holds out the promise of special visual excitement, but the picture is very likely to turn out to be marred by distracting reflections, cascading splotches of light, or unexpected blurriness. If a photographer poses a person against a beautiful landscape and then steps close to get a good-sized portrait, the background may well be lost in a blur—and just knowing that the picture was there will make the loss seem all the more disappointing. Or a picture may fall short of its potential because the photographer did not know how to deal with a background that was too busy, too bright, or the wrong color.

It is perversely logical that the most tempting pictures are often the hardest to get. Yet photographers need not accept this with a shrug, or curb their ambitions. When Evelyn Hofer took the picture on the preceding page of the 1,000-year-old Bapistery in Florence, she was undaunted by crowds blocking her camera's view of the architectural masterpiece. She deftly solved the problem by making a very long time-exposure. Dim light, slow film, a small aperture and heavy filtration all reduced the light reaching the film so much that she could use a 20-minute exposure, during which time the relatively rapid movements of the tourists were not recorded. However, she was not totally successful. One ghostlike streak can be seen in the lower left-hand corner of the picture. It was caused by a visitor who was apparently so transfixed by the architecture that he stayed several minutes in one spot.

Rather than staying put for a long time, however, most photographers will find mobility one of their biggest advantages in working with troublesome settings. By walking around a subject—a statue or a tree, say—a photographer can usually find a position from which distracting backgrounds are eliminated. Shots taken from a kneeling position will silhouette the subject against the clear, neutral background of the sky. A bird's-eye view may give an inkling of the subject's general environment—for instance, locating the statue in a tiled courtyard or the tree on a lawn—while holding back other details of the surroundings in a tantalizing way. And if the subject is mobile too, any setting can be maneuvered into submission, for the photographer will not have to give up a particular angle of view in exchange for ridding the scene of some obstacle.

The camera itself provides all sorts of means for dealing with troublesome surroundings. The most important are the familiar options of aperture size, shutter speed and focal length of the lens. Consider, for instance, the problem of taking a portrait in a city street, a setting with plentiful variety and vitality. In the mind's eye of the photographer, the person in front of his camera is an attention-drawing presence, and he expects the camera to render the subject that way. But the anticipated center of interest may not materialize in the photograph. The person may appear diminished and anonymous in a welter of signs, passing cars and hurrying bodies.

Yet these distractions might have been easily nullified. The photographer could have found a quieter backdrop by walking around his subject or posing the person in a carefully chosen spot. He could have set the camera diaphragm at a wide aperture, reducing depth of field and blurring the background. He could have selected a slow shutter speed so that the cars and passersby would be blurred while his motionless subject remained sharp (provided the camera was braced against a wall or car to prevent shake). Or he could have used a long lens with a narrow angle of view and shallow depth of field that would catch only a small part of the bothersome background.

This is not to say that a dynamic background should be divorced from a portrait on grounds of incompatibility. The urban setting may say something quite revealing about the person being portrayed, in which case the photographer may want to pursue different tactics — freezing the intricate motions of the city with a fast shutter, extending the depth of field with a small aperture, and perhaps pulling in a sweep of view with a wide-angle lens.

Photographers do not have to rely on technique alone to overcome difficulties. Handy aids can often solve a problem. A simple reflector, such as a sheet of white poster board, will reduce harsh shadows on a subject illuminated by a strong light source. A polarizing filter will cut down on reflections from glass or water, including those from water droplets in the air. Without these reflections the sky becomes darker and bluer while haze disappears. At the same time, manufacturers are pressing toward a state of affairs in which no situation can be said to be impossible. Film exposed in low light can be pushed — underexposed but then given a compensating development — without significant loss of quality. Automatic electronic flash units have eliminated time-consuming calculations that once were needed when using flash outdoors. And figuring out filtration for color film with an off-beat light source — a bluish mercury vapor lamp in a parking lot, for example — is simplified with a special color meter.

Equally significant improvements have been made in lenses. Some can scoop a very wide-angle view with almost no distortion; others can be swiveled to get great depth of field with a large aperture or can be racked upward to keep a building's sides from appearing to converge. And on many modern lenses, microscopically thin coatings allow a photographer to shoot directly into the sun without finding unexpected spots of light disfiguring his picture.

Erasing the Foreground

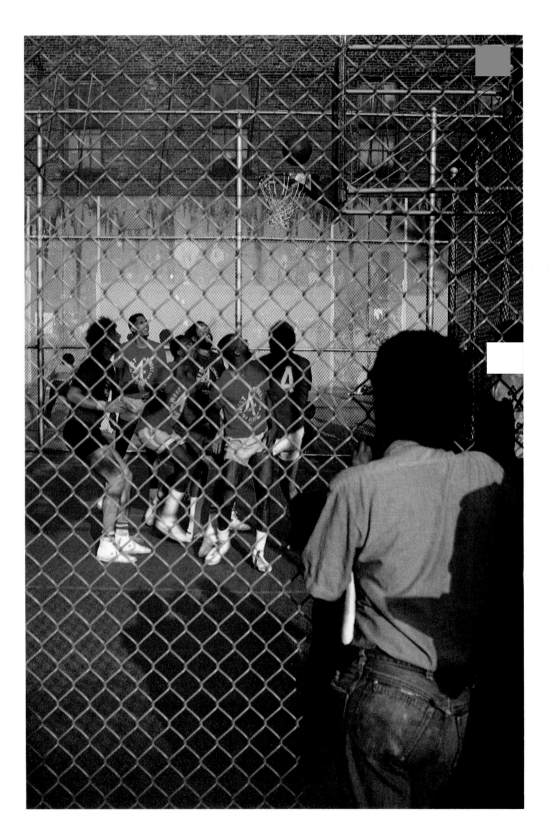

Many a potentially interesting photograph seems impossible to get because the subject is obscured by some intervening obstacle. A photographer standing at a window and trying for pictures of children playing outside may find his view obstructed by a window screen. Many sports and playground activities, such as the basketball game shown on these pages, take place in areas enclosed in mesh fences. And animals are most easily found behind bars in a zoo.

These barriers can be wiped out of the picture by simple focusing changes. If obstacles are sufficiently blurred, they will not show. A long-focal-length lens, which has limited depth of field at short distances, makes it easier to throw foreground subjects out of focus. But even with a normal lens, much of the heaviest foreground obstruction becomes an almost invisible blur when the aperture is opened wide, or when the photographer moves close to the obstacle, and focus is adjusted for the distant subject.

In some cases the photographer may prefer to retain a sense of place or to make a point by keeping in his picture a soft suggestion of the obstacles in the foreground. For example, he might want to show the hazy leaves of the blind in which he hid to photograph wildlife, or show the bars of a circus cage to emphasize that the lion tamer is right inside with the dangerous animals.

The subjects of this picture—basketball players in a New York City park—are in sharp focus, but are partly obscured by the mesh fence enclosing the court. Photographer Enrico Ferorelli took the picture to demonstrate what happens when the camera is placed far enough away to include both fence and players. He used a normal 50mm lens with a small enough aperture—f/8—to provide sufficient depth of field to keep both the foreground fence and the background players sharp.

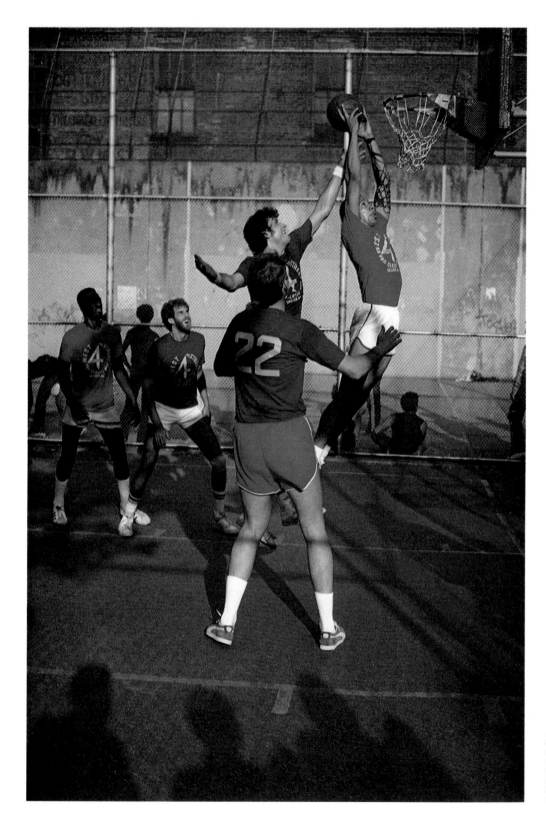

In this picture, photographer Ferorelli maintained his focus on the players but decreased his depth of field by opening the aperture to f/2. He also moved to within a couple of inches of the fence. Although some of the small links of the fence were still in front of the lens, they were thrown so completely out of focus that they have disappeared altogether.

Diffusing Distracting Backgrounds

When a busy background spoils a normal composition, there are two simple means of dealing with the difficulty. First, the background can be thrown out of focus by decreasing depth of field until only the subject is sharp, clearly delineated in the foreground. A long-focal-length lens, because of its severely restricted depth of field, when used to photograph objects near at hand can help to blur a distracting background, but simply increasing the aperture without changing lenses will have a similar effect.

Second, the photographer can shift his position to change the angle of the shot, so placing himself that he can picture his subject against a less cluttered background. On a busy street, he might move to a point where the background consists solely of a blank wall; in the countryside he can avoid the distraction of a background tree by turning to set his subject against an open field. Choosing a high angle, so the background is plain ground or pavement is another stratagem.

But a common dodge is simply to drop to one knee, shoot from a low angle and silhouette the subject against the sky—the technique that freelance photographer George Haling finally used to obtain the picture he wanted *(opposite, far right)* of a New York traffic sign.

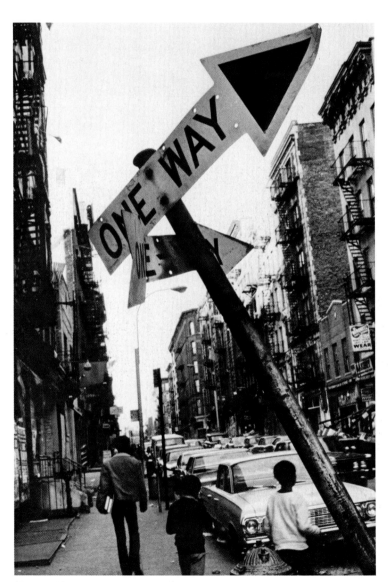

Sharp detail far down a bustling city street is caught in this picture shot at f/32, an extremely small aperture that gives great depth of field. But so clear a background distracts the viewer from the subject: a sadly smitten traffic sign.

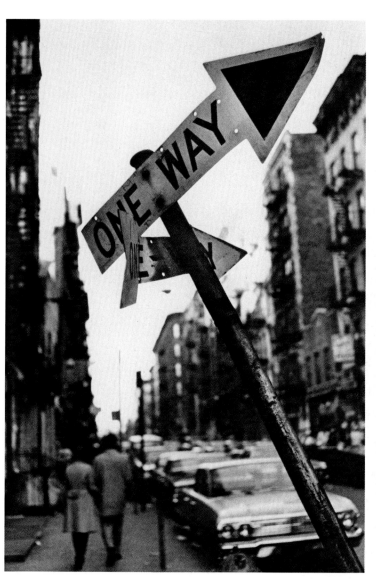

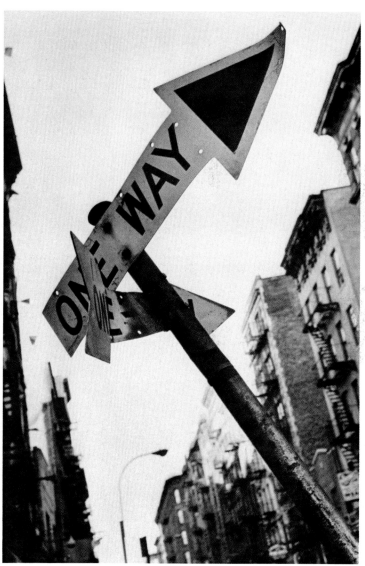

When the lens was opened to f/4, depth of field was so reduced that even the parked car a few feet away from the battered sign was thrown out of focus, and the design formed by its tormented arrows is sharp in comparison.

Changing the angle and shooting upward made the sign's outline stand out as the background virtually disappears. The buildings, fairly sharp at a moderate aperture, approximately f/12.5, now serve only to frame the sign against the sky.

Ducking Flare

Flare—a loose term that denotes bright spots on a picture caused by light reflections on the surface of a lens, on the inside lens elements or in the camera body itself—is normally avoided by obeying a hoary bit of advice: Do not shoot directly into the sun or any other light source.

This advice is not always easy to follow, and often it will not solve the problem. If, for example, a photographer is shooting a seaside scene, brilliant light will enter his lens from various sources—from reflections off the water, from the white sand, perhaps from the metal parts of beach gear, as well as from the direct rays of sun angling in. Any or all of these sources can produce flare.

A light source can cause flare even when it is out of the field of view of the picture—oblique rays are bent into the camera by the front surfaces of the lens. The wider the aperture the more opportunity for such unsuspected light to enter and to spread. Thus, the photographer who is shooting under conditions in which he suspects flare may occur should use a lens hood, and stop down for as small an aperture as possible.

It also helps to reduce the number of filters and to avoid lenses with many elements, such as zooms. Lens elements with antireflection coatings also reduce flare. Modern lens elements, which have up to 11 microscopically thin layers coated with mineral compounds, do a better job of controlling flare than older lenses, which have fewer layers or obsolete coatings, as the pictures here demonstrate.

Shot with a 20mm lens that had obsolete antireflection coatings, the late-afternoon sun flares into a glaring ball between two New York City skyscrapers. Sunlight reflecting between surfaces of the lens elements causes the flare. A relatively wide aperture, f/3.5, which allows more light to enter the lens, increases the problem.

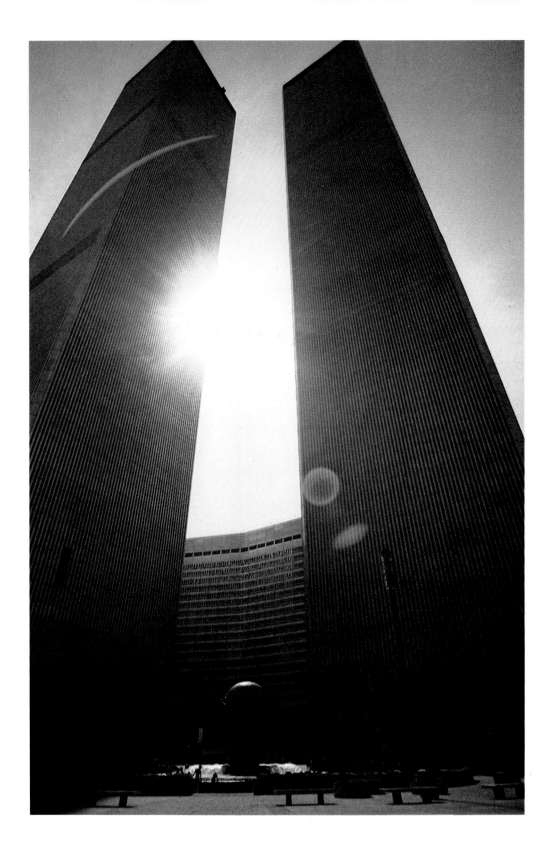

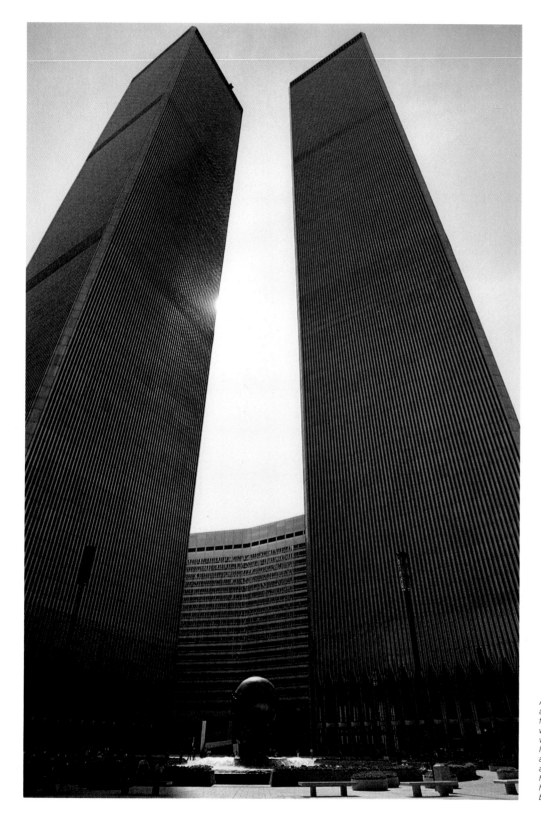

A 20mm lens with 11 layers of the most advanced antireflection coatings greatly reduces the amount of flare because each layer cuts reflections of specific wavelengths of light; together, they keep most of the visible wavelengths from bouncing around between lens elements. The photographer also made other adjustments to reduce flare. He used a smaller aperture—f/11—he employed a lens hood as well as his hand to block extraneous light and he changed his camera angle slightly so that part of the sun is behind the building at left.

55

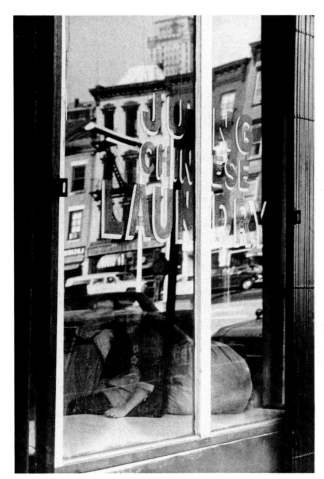 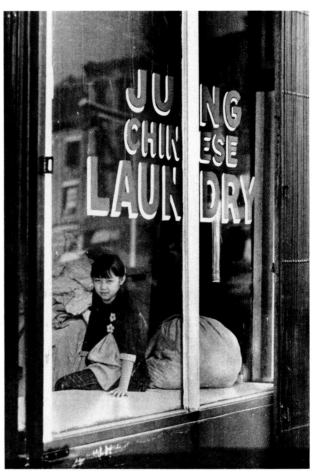

Freelance Bob Walch dextrously manipulated a polarizing filter to control the reflections that make nonsense of the picture at left above. He eliminated just enough reflection in the picture to the right to clear up the lettering inside the window, the condensed steam running down it, and the smiling child, still leaving the dim image of the buildings to maintain a sense of place.

There are various ways to overcome the distraction of surface reflections when photographing an object behind a pane of glass. One of the best methods depends on the fact that all reflections from any such nonmetallic surface as glass consist of polarized light—light rays that vibrate only in one plane. The reflection can thus be reduced by a polarizing filter, which blocks off the rays in a single plane of light. It is easy to swivel the filter around until the plane it blocks coincides with the plane of the reflected rays, thus trapping the reflections while leaving the subject clear in the viewer.

When taking a picture through a window, a polarizing filter is most efficient if it is held at an angle of about 35° to the surface, because it is at that angle that maximum polarization occurs. The light lost

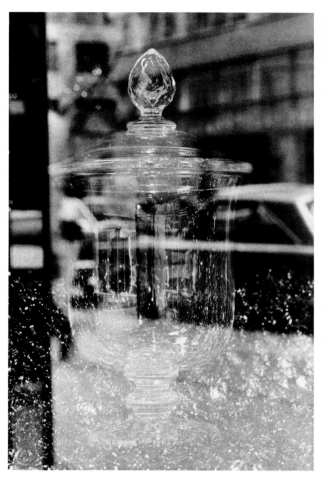

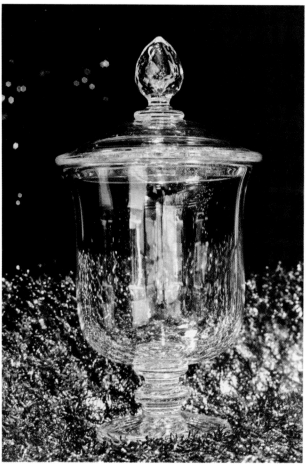

during filtration must be compensated for by additional exposure — usually 1 1/3 stops. But most in-camera meters, which measure light after it passes through the filter, will indicate the loss.

Without a polarizing filter, the most obvious technique is to move around until obtrusive reflections are at a minimum. But this works only when the camera angle is unimportant, and even this technique will not always work — especially on bright days. Another method, mainly good for small subjects behind the glass of a window or showcase, is to move close to the glass — even to the point of touching the front of the lens housing to the glass — so that the photographer and camera shield the window, preventing the formation of reflections that the camera can catch (above).

In the first shot (above left) the crystal bonbonnière in a display window is barely discernible beyond dazzling reflections from the street. By moving in close to the plate glass (right), the photographer screened out the reflected car and buildings, while the covered candy dish, as seen in this cropped enlargement, still gleamed with its own reflections, lit from angles he had not blocked.

Shooting through the Looking Glass

The first thing to keep in mind when photographing an object and its reflection in a mirror is the optical law that light from an image in a mirror has to make a double journey: It must travel from object to mirror, then from mirror to eye or film. This doubles the apparent distance between the reflection and the object being reflected, raising focusing problems if both are to be included in the picture *(right)*.

Depth of field is again the factor that controls success with such photographs. Changing to a lens of shorter focal length gives greater depth of field, but may introduce distortions in the size of the image, particularly in close-ups.

Retaining the normal lens but stopping down its aperture is a simpler way to increase depth of field and is frequently sufficient, provided allowance is made for the range of sharp focus. At distances of less than five feet, focus the camera midway between the reflection and the real object. At medium distances—five to 15 feet—focus on a point about a third of the apparent distance between the two. Such a focus makes the most of the available range of sharpness.

The three pictures at right and opposite of a bouquet in front of a mirror show the traps of shooting an object with its reflection—and how to avoid them. All three were taken in natural light, from a sunny window, with a single-lens reflex camera, using a zoom lens set at 90mm. In the first two shots (right and center) a wide aperture, f/5.6, so restricted depth of field that when the camera was focused on the bouquet, the mirror image appeared as a misty blur, and when the focus was set for the reflection, the flowers were blurred. Decreasing the aperture to f/16 enlarged the depth of field, and carefully adjusting the focus—bringing it closer to the foreground than the background—made all parts of the scene come out sharp (far right).

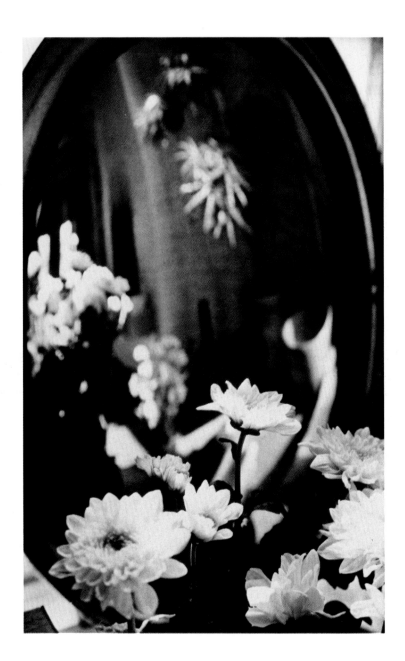

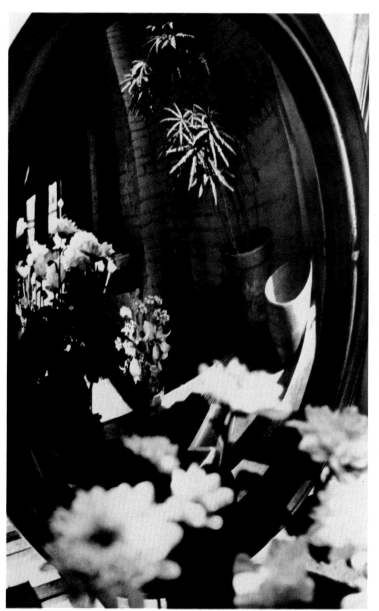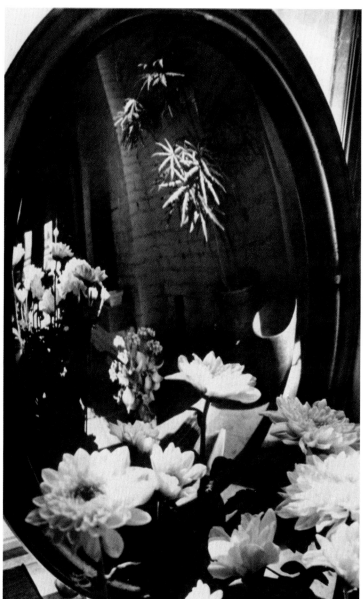

Improving Indoor Portraits

Indoors in the comparatively weak light from a lamp or window, getting a natural-looking picture with a hand-held camera is a challenge. Even if the photographer uses high-speed film and opens his lens to its widest aperture, his meter will often dictate a shutter speed so slow that only the steadiest hands could keep camera motion from blurring the scene.

The solution is to underexpose the film and compensate for underexposure during development—the technique called pushing. To push a roll of film the photographer treats it as if it is two or even three times more sensitive than the speed rating recommended by its manufacturer and sets a higher rating on his light meter. Typically, a high-speed ISO 400/27° film is pushed to 800/30°.

The film must then be specially processed, usually by giving it an extended development time that converts more of the silver crystals to image-producing silver metal. The extended development increases contrast and graininess somewhat, but that is a small price to pay to be able to photograph a dim scene.

Besides dimness, lamplight or window light has another deficiency; it comes from one direction, creating harsh shadows on parts of the subject. The simplest corrective measure is to angle a reflector—a large white poster board or even a bedsheet—so that light bounces into the shaded areas. Alternatively, a subject can be posed next to a white wall—preferably a wall opposite a window.

High-speed (ISO 400/27°) film and the lens's widest aperture, f/2, was not enough to properly record this dimly lit interior scene. When the photographer used the meter-recommended shutter speed, 1/30 second, it was not fast enough to prevent blurring from camera motion (top). When he set a holdable 1/60-second shutter speed, the picture was underexposed (bottom).

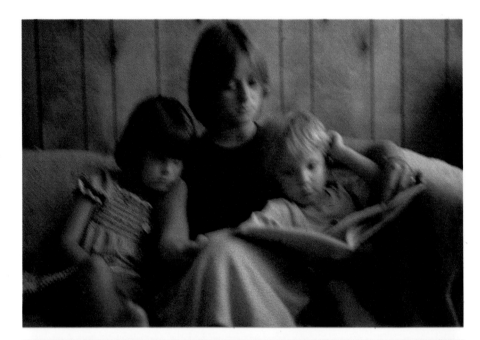

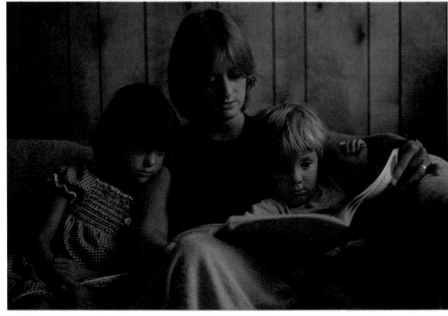

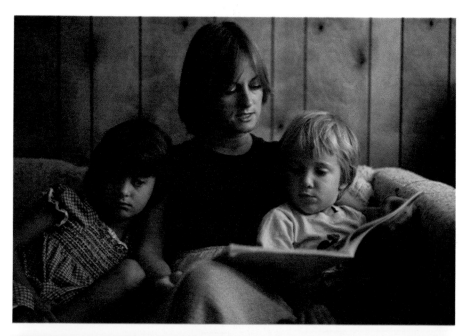

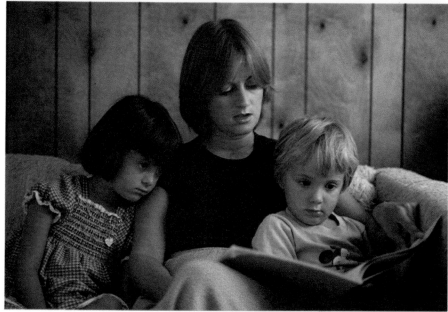

Switching to a new roll of ISO 400/27°-rated film and pushing it to ISO 800/30° permitted the photographer to use a 1/60-second shutter speed and get an image that is correctly exposed as well as sharp (top). But the strongly directional nature of the window light creates unattractive shadows on the subjects. Highlights are further enhanced because pushing boosts the bright tones in film without affecting the dark ones. These shortcomings were corrected by using a reflector to bounce light into the shadows (bottom).

Supplementing Sunlight with Flash

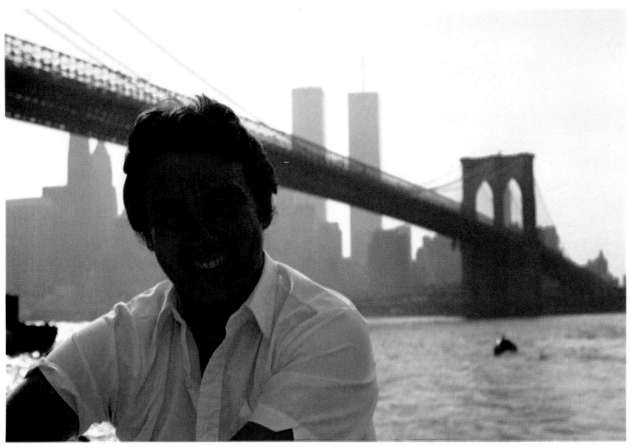

When the photographer took this shot of a subject posed against the Brooklyn Bridge he chose an aperture setting of f/8 at 1/125 second: This was the reading that his camera's built-in meter indicated would give correct exposure. The results of this averaged reading, however, are far from desirable because the bright sky caused the meter to recommend an incorrect setting. The subject has been darkened into a silhouette by underexposure while the background has been bleached out by overexposure.

An electronic flash unit is a surprisingly helpful tool out of doors. When intense, direct sunlight increases the contrast between the highlights and shadows in a scene, a strongly backlighted subject is apt to be underexposed, while the background will be overexposed and washed out *(above)*. Similarly, if sun hits a subject from above or the side, shadows and glaring highlights may result.

A flash unit will eliminate these problems by throwing light into the shadowed areas to fill them in. The output of most electronic models can be controlled to give a pleasing balance between flash and sun-illuminated portions of the picture. With too much light from the flash, the subject will be unnaturally bright or even bleached out. With too little, shadows will remain.

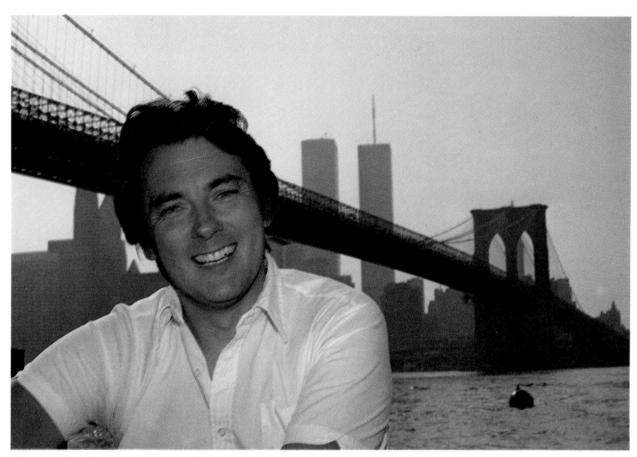

To determine the proper exposure for a fill-in flash picture, the photographer must match the speed rating on the flash to the speed rating of his film and set the shutter speed of the camera to synchronize with the flash—usually 1/125 second or less. Aperture is determined by taking a meter reading of the brightest portion of the scene.

Flash-to-subject distance, which deter-mines the amount of light falling on the subject, is calculated by referring to the guide dial on the flash unit, or by dividing the guide number of the flash unit by the f-stop. This setting, however, may cause too much light to strike a nearby subject. If less light is needed, the photographer can reduce the power of the unit to a half, quarter, eighth or only a sixteenth of full capacity, as in the example above.

For this dramatically improved shot of the same scene, the photographer made two crucial changes. First, he measured just the bright sunlighted part of the scene which indicated that the aperture should be stopped down to f/11 to prevent the background from washing out. More importantly, he used a flash unit to light up the shadowed subject. After calculating the amount of fill light that would illuminate his subject, he reduced the output of the unit to 1/16 of its full power so that shadows are not eliminated but are rendered more realistically. The shutter speed remained at 1/125 second; it was the only one that could be synchronized with the flash.

Compensating for Troublesome Lighting

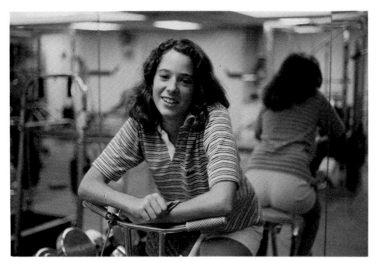 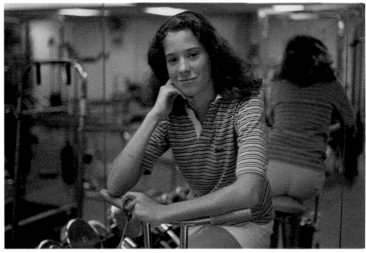

When daylight-balanced film was used indoors in a health club illuminated by a cool-white fluorescent tube, the resulting picture showed a green cast (above, left). When film type and light source were compared by a color meter (below), the +13 reading in the window indicated that better color balance could be achieved with a single filter—a magenta filter of medium strength. Magenta, green's complementary color, blocks green light. The photograph taken with that filter (right) has a much more natural appearance.

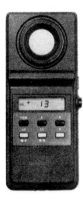 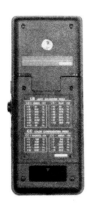

Below its circular light sensor, a color meter has a window to display its readings (far left). Controls under the window are used to enter information about film type, to instruct the meter to take a reading of a light source's color temperature, and to elicit information from the meter about what filtration will be needed to produce colors that appear normal. This information appears as a number in the display window; to convert the number to a filter recommendation, conversion tables are printed on the back of the meter (near left). The +13 reading from the gymnasium scene above indicates that a magenta filter of a specified density is required to achieve pleasing color results.

Most photographers who use color regularly know that each of the most common light sources for photography—the sun, household bulbs, fluorescent tubes—has a distinctly different color. These differences, which scientists can measure using a scale of Kelvin degrees (the sun at midday, for example, is 5,500° Kelvin; a 100-watt household bulb is 2,900° Kelvin) are rarely noticed by the human eye, but they can cause color shifts in a photograph unless the film has been bal-

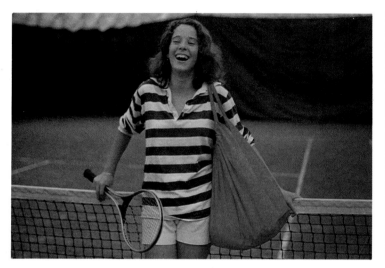 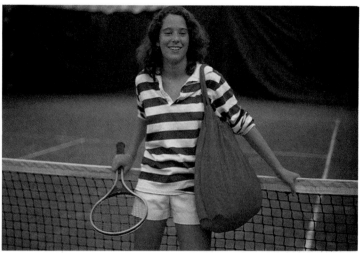

anced by the manufacturer to give natural results with one light source.

If the film is employed with another light source, color shifts will result. A shift toward orange, for example, will usually occur when film that is balanced for daylight is shot indoors; a shift toward blue results when indoor film is exposed in the sun *(page 208).*

Even more dramatic are the shifts that occur with fluorescent light *(above, left)* or sodium vapor lamps *(opposite, left).*

Because there are no special films available that are color-balanced for these light sources, filters must be used. They block out some wavelengths and transmit others to achieve natural-looking results. Selecting filters is tricky, however. Each light source requires its own filtration and a photographer often has no way of finding out the exact color temperature of the light source.

A variant of the light meter, known as a color temperature meter, helps solve the

problem. It contains three light-sensitive cells that measure each of the three primaries—blue, green and red. Once the photographer punches in the film type he is using, the meter will measure the wavelength of light reaching it from the light source and compare those readings with the ability of the film to record them. Then the meter will recommend filtration that will produce natural colors. In some cases, the meter will even recommend that another film type be used.

Shooting over a Crowd

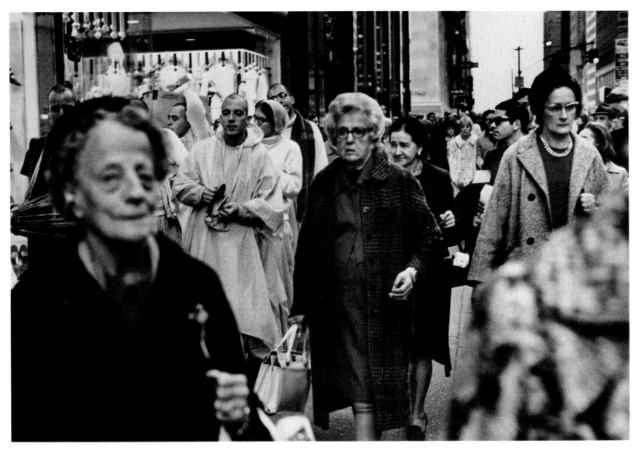

When shooting in a crowd—whether at a sporting event, at a parade or merely on a busy street—the photographer often is unable to get an unobstructed view of his subject. A vantage point above the activity is the ideal solution, although it is not always available. There is another option: The photographer can simply hold his camera up at arm's length and shoot over the heads of the crowd.

Certain cameras lend themselves to this procedure because of their viewing systems. Thus, although a photographer working with a rangefinder camera can only aim in the general direction of his subject and shoot blind, he is at no disadvantage if he has a twin-lens reflex: Its ground-glass viewer enables him to hold the camera overhead, upside down, and see the picture he is taking.

Many single-lens-reflex cameras can be easily adapted to work in much the same way. On some SLRs, the ground-glass focusing screen remains locked in place when the prism is removed and can be used as a viewer just like that on a twin-lens reflex. On other SLRs, the prism and ground glass come off together. In that case, an attachment called a waist-level viewer—simply a ground glass with pop-up metal sides that serve as light shields *(opposite)*—can be slipped into place to serve the same purpose.

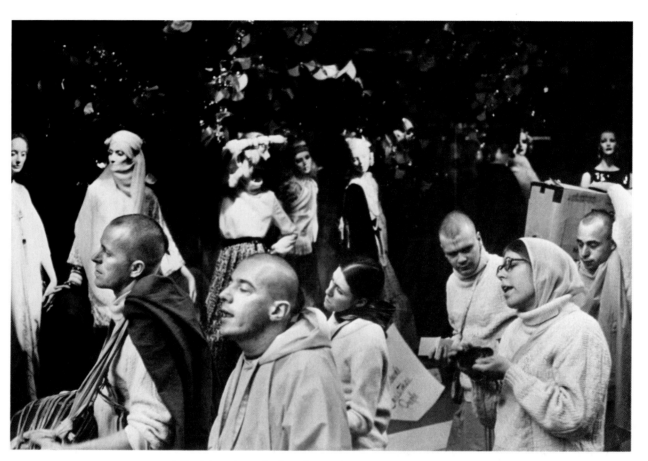

In the photograph opposite, the exotic group of ascetics at left is nearly lost among the more ordinary passersby. The photographer could not halt the pedestrians in order to shoot the group alone. To compose and focus the clear view above, he put on the accessory waist-level viewer shown at right, which made the viewing screen visible with the camera held an arm's length away. He moved out to the curb to avoid being jostled, raised his camera overhead, then looked up into the ground glass to see — and shoot — over the intervening crowd.

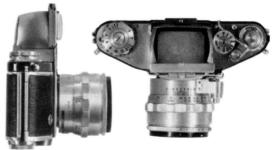

Recording Wide Views with Minimal Distortion

A wide-angle lens provides an expansive view as well as great depth of field, but those advantages are often accompanied by distortion—especially with ultra-wide-angle lenses that have focal lengths of 21mm or less on a 35mm camera.

The most disturbing liability in wide-angle design is "barrel distortion," which makes horizontal and vertical lines converge sharply at a picture's edges. This effect is most noticeable when a special wide-angle lens called a fisheye is used. The fisheye lens has an immense field of view—170° or more—but, as the picture at near right shows, it exacts a high price in distortion. The problem, however, can be almost completely eliminated by using another type of ultra-wide-angle lens. This type creates a virtually distortion-free picture *(far right),* but encompasses a slightly reduced field of view.

No matter which type the photographer selects, he must remain on guard against other distortions that are caused by all ultra-wide-angle lenses: a tendency to exaggerate the size of near objects at the expense of far ones and, consequently, a tendency, when the lens is tilted upward, to make vertical objects appear to be falling backward.

The 16mm fisheye lens shown below embraces a sprawling angle of view, but it was entirely inappropriate for this shot of the National Cathedral in Washington, D.C. because barrel distortion made the structure's 301-foot-tall Gothic tower appear curved.

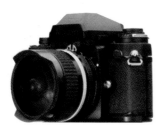

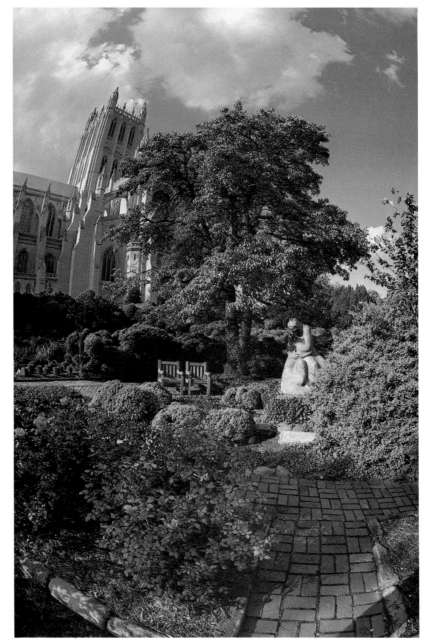

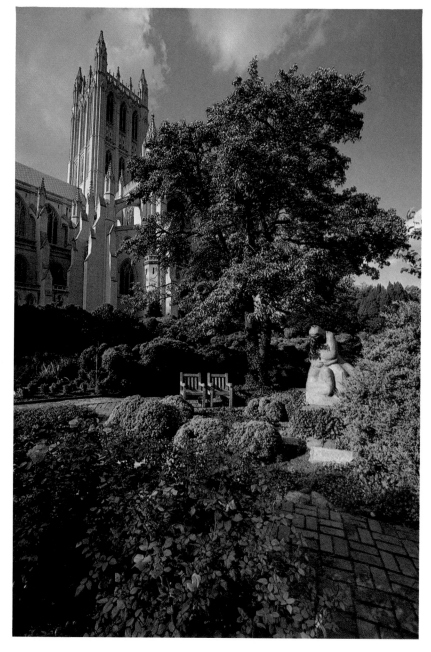

The 15mm lens below covers a smaller angle of view than a fisheye — 110°. But it also bends lines less. Only at the top and bottom of this picture is there any distortion: The rose bush appears elongated and the top of the cathedral's bell tower soars upward.

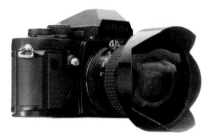

Solving Problems with Shifts and Tilts

There are few special wide-angle lenses for 35mm SLR cameras that can be adjusted to pivot or move up and down relative to the film plane. These movements, called shifts and tilts, are familiar to users of view cameras; they can solve many common problems by giving the user added control over his picture.

When shifting, the lens remains parallel to the film plane but is cranked up or down with a manual control on the side of the lens. Since the lens is designed to cover an area that is larger than the film frame, the image falling within the frame changes as the lens moves. Usually this capacity is used to photograph a building without angling the camera upward, a practice that always causes the structure's lines to slope in. Tilting the lens keeps the camera parallel to the building—and to the film—ensuring that all the building's lines remain parallel in the final picture.

Shifting can also produce a matched panorama on two adjacent film frames, or get rid of undesirable foreground obstructions, such as the photographer's reflection at right.

When tilting, the lens pivots from side to side in its mount, changing the alignment between lens, film and subject. If a subject is at an angle to the camera, tilting the lens will bring more of the subject into sharp focus *(page 72)*. Conversely, tilting the lens so that it is less parallel to a subject will cause blurring.

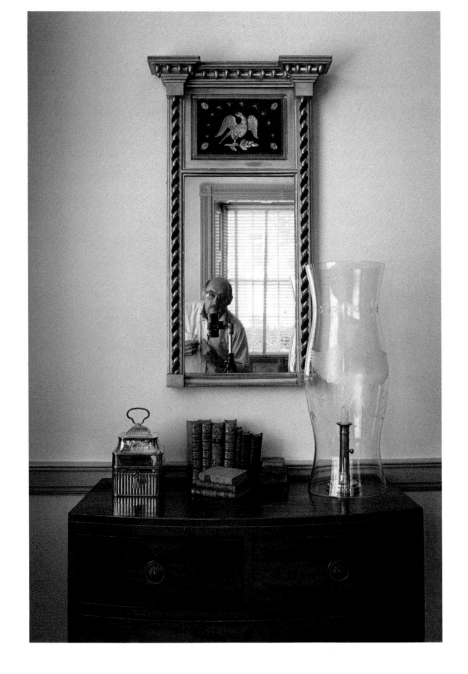

When the photographer took this straight-on view of a mirror without shifting his lens, there was no way he could avoid including his own reflection in the mirror. Had his angle of view changed enough to eliminate the reflection, the attractive symmetry of the interior would have been destroyed.

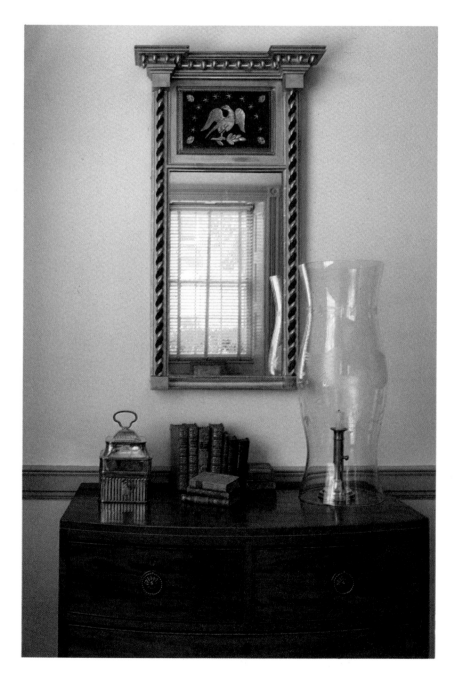

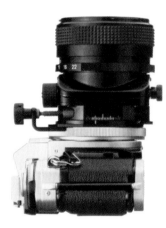

Shifting the lens to the right permitted the photographer to get this straight-on shot without his reflection. First, he moved the camera and tripod about six inches to the left of the mirror, where he was no longer reflected by it. Then he turned the threaded screw mechanism projecting from the left of the lens mount (above) and racked the lens five millimeters to the right, reading the amount of shift from a scale visible on the lens barrel. This changed the position of the lens enough to eliminate the photographer's reflection in the mirror. It also changed the perspective of the picture, but barely enough to be noticed.

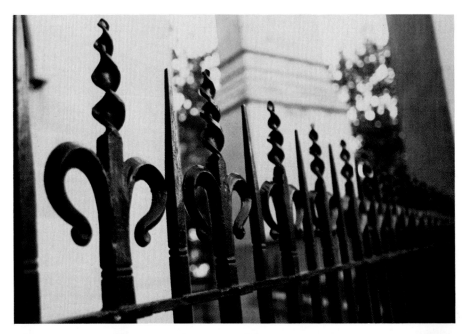

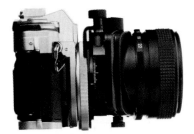

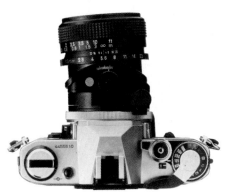

In shooting a decorative fence, the photographer confronted two problems (top right). First, the fence was so high he had to angle the camera upward, which distorted the perspective. Second, his large aperture—f/2.8—had a shallow depth of field that threw most of his subject out of focus. To correct the first problem, the photographer set the camera parallel to the fence, and then adjusted the shift mechanism on the lens barrel (above, top) eight millimeters upward to take in the whole fence. Then he used the tilt mechanism (above, bottom) to pivot the lens five degrees to the left. This increased the depth of field and the sharpness of the image (bottom right).

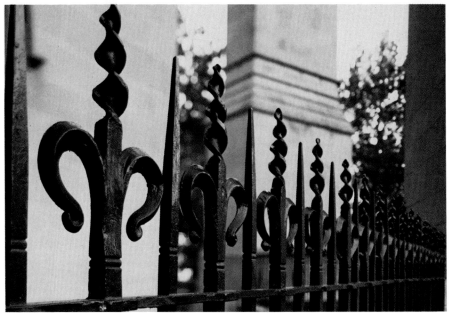

Problems of the Professional 3

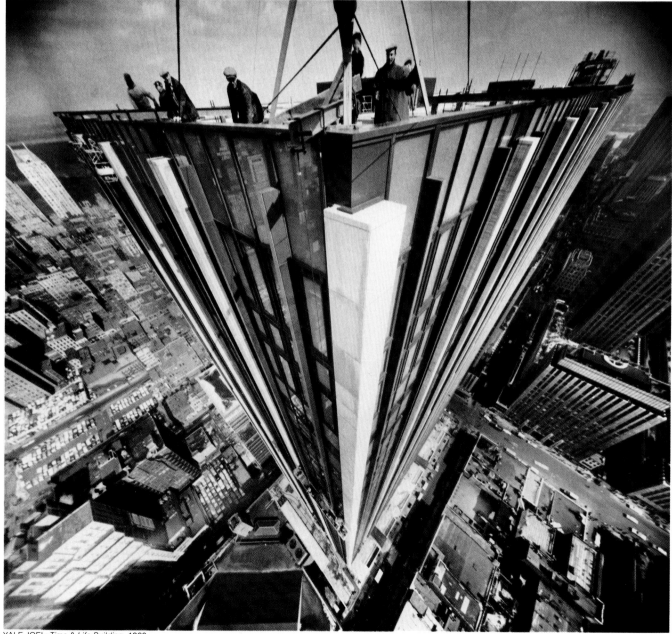

YALE JOEL: *Time & Life Building*, 1960

Triumphs of Inventive Gadgetry

Photographers in pursuit of striking pictures often find that special gear helps them get the shots they want. Al Schneider, head of the Equipment Section of the Time-Life Photo Department has had more than 30 years' experience in helping professionals solve their special problems. Sometimes, Schneider says, "the solution to the problem turns out to be so simple it's almost funny."

When *Life* photographer Yale Joel wanted to get a unique view of the newly completed Time & Life Building in midtown Manhattan shown on the preceding page, he came to Schneider for help. His equipment consisted of a view camera with an extremely wide-angle lens and a shutter that was tripped by air pressure from a rubber bulb. But for the bird's-eye view he had in mind, Joel found it necessary to suspend the camera out over the corner of the building with a 15-foot pole, and the bulb could not transmit enough pressure at that distance. Al Schneider's solution to the problem: Replace the bulb with an ordinary bicycle pump.

Sports Illustrated's Tony Triolo used an even less expensive gadget to get the dramatic picture of a diver on a springboard reproduced on the opposite page. To combine a blurred time exposure and a sharp, stop-action image in a single picture, he employed a simple switch with a very long name: a double-pole double-throw momentary contact switch. Set one way, the switch could start a motorized camera; set the other way, it could fire a motion-stopping electronic flash *(diagram, bottom right)*.

To photograph the diver, Triolo illuminated the scene with flood lamps and set the shutter of his motorized camera on BULB for a time exposure. He connected the camera to the double-pole double-throw switch so that when the circuit was closed to the camera, it would hold the shutter open. When the diver was ready, Triolo threw the switch forward to open the shutter; this recorded her run to the end of the board and her leap as a blur. When she reached the high point of her spring, he reversed the switch to fire the flash and cut off the current holding the shutter open. An instant after the flash, the shutter snapped closed, freezing the diver at the zenith of her dive.

In some circumstances, instead of using a moving subject to suggest action, a photographer must create the impression of motion where there is none. In principle, this is easy enough to do: Simply pan the camera while the shutter is open. But to get a believable image, the panning must be done smoothly and at an even rate— not so easy, unless the camera is mounted on a tripod with a motor-driven head.

Several years ago, when Yale Joel wanted to use the panning technique to get some out-of-the-ordinary pictures of motorcycles, he asked Al Schneider for a motorized tripod. "I told him the equipment would be very expensive," Schneider recalled, "since it had to be especially machined and geared."

Joel returned a few days later with an ungainly rig put together with a few

The double-pole double-throw momentary contact switch shown below can be used to create two versions of motion in a single photograph: time-exposure streaks or blurs, and a sharp, motion-freezing image. As diagramed at bottom, it controls both a motorized camera and an electronic flash unit. With the camera shutter set at BULB, turning the switch to connect the terminals to its left holds the shutter open and creates a blurred image; when flicked past the center (OFF) position over to the right-hand terminals, the switch stops holding the shutter open and fires an action-stopping electronic flash unit just before the shutter has had time to close.

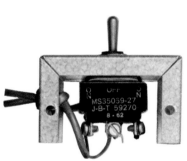

double-pole double-throw switch

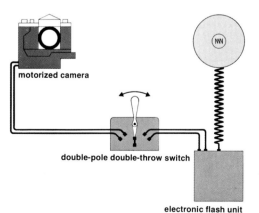

motorized camera

double-pole double-throw switch

electronic flash unit

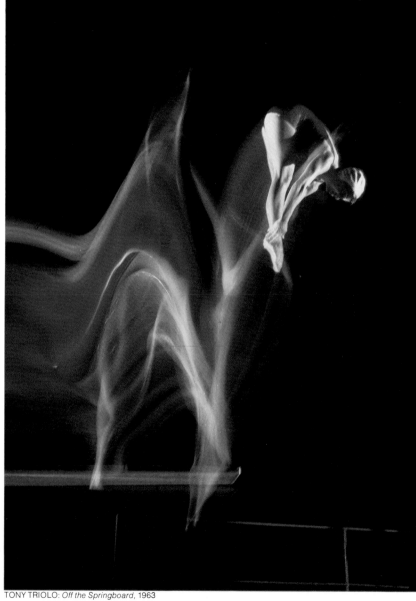

TONY TRIOLO: *Off the Springboard,* 1963

dollars' worth of old parts *(diagram, right)*. "He had dug up an old sewing machine motor," Schneider recalled, "and fixed it so it would turn a belt that slowly rotated a tripod head. It looked like a real Rube Goldberg contraption, but it worked like a charm."

To get the photograph opposite, Joel brought a motorcycle into the studio. He asked a model to sit on it and to lean forward as if she were roaring along a road. (In fact, the bike was resting on its parking stand—although the stand did not show when the picture was printed in *Life.)* Then he set his shutter on BULB, lit the subject with a photoflood and switched on the motor so that the camera, which had been aimed at a spot ahead of the model, slowly panned toward her. He held the shutter open as the camera panned, producing a blur of illusory movement on the film.

Just at the moment that the camera was pointed at the model, Joel dimmed the floodlight, set off a flash bulb and immediately closed the shutter. The flash registered the model's image strongly on the film and froze her motion—which was in reality the camera's motion. "The nicest touch of the picture," Schneider said, "is the whirling of the front wheel. Since the parking stand lifted the wheel off the ground, Joel was able to give it a good spin for verisimilitude before he began his complicated exposure."

Verisimilitude was not the problem when it came to photographing the launching of the space shuttle *Columbia* in April of 1981. For *Time* magazine photographer Ralph Morse, the experience was altogether too real: By special arrangement with NASA, Morse had been allowed to position six remote-control cameras only 200 yards from the shuttle's launching pad. After the launch he found the cameras almost completely destroyed and thrown as far as one-half mile away by the force of the blast-off. "We didn't expect that much of a blast," Morse said afterward, but added that "we didn't just burn cameras up; we had a definite plan."

The plan was a calculated gamble that—at least this time—did not pay off. Morse's idea was to shoot the launch from an entirely new vantage point, to capture views of the spacecraft as it emerged from roiling clouds of steam colored by the flames of the rocket exhaust.

"I asked myself," Morse said afterward, "what made the shuttle launch different from the other launches I had covered. The difference was all the power that the huge thing was going to need to get off the ground—so much power that they were planning to dump 300,000 gallons of water onto the pad during lift-off to cool down the blast. If you could position a camera to show the heat and that water, then you could show what was really different about this launch—the power. So I wanted a camera right up there shooting up through the billows of steam at the shuttle as it went up."

In seeking a close-range location that would afford maximum drama, Morse

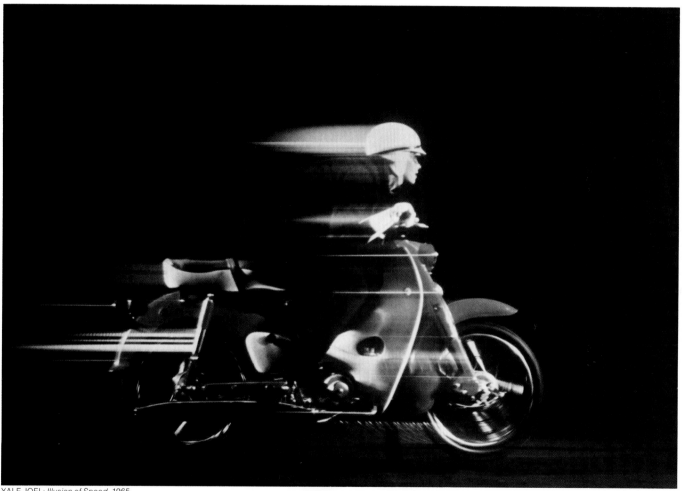

YALE JOEL: *Illusion of Speed,* 1965

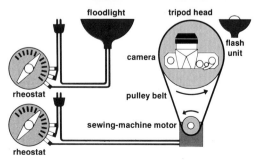

floodlight

tripod head

camera

flash unit

rheostat

pulley belt

rheostat

sewing-machine motor

The model who seems to be racing along on her motorcycle in the picture above was not actually moving — but the camera was. Yale Joel used the rig diagramed at left to get the photograph. A rheostat, connected to the sewing-machine motor, allowed him to control its speed as it turned the tripod head on which his camera was mounted. The camera was pointed in front of the motorcycle when he began the time exposure. When the panning camera was aimed right at the model, he dimmed the floodlight with a second rheostat, fired a flash bulb for a bright stop-action image, and closed the shutter.

79

was drawn to a massive trough along which the cataract of cooling water would cascade away from the launch pad during blast-off. He anchored four motor-driven cameras to concrete posts that had been positioned in the trough by NASA, and placed two more next to the trough on wood posts he drove into the ground himself. Next, he set up three different remote-control triggering systems to be sure that at least a few of the cameras would be clicking at the moment of lift-off. Two of the six cameras were connected to light-activated triggering units *(diagram, below)* similar to ones Morse had used for previous space shots. The units were focused on the rocket's exhaust area through telescopes; the exhaust flame, magnified by the telescopes, would activate the units and start the motor-driven cameras.

But NASA officials had cautioned Morse that because of the shuttle's new fuel mixture, the flame of the exhaust might not be visible as it had been in the past, so he and his assistants also set up other triggering systems. Two cameras were linked to a burglar-alarm switch, similar to one Morse had installed in his own house, that was sensitive to vibration. The switch was attached to a sheet of aluminum that would ripple violently in the shock waves from the rocket engines. Two more cameras were connected to a sound-activated switch that was connected to a powerful remote microphone—a parabolic disk such as those used by television sound men to pick up voices on a football field— which was aimed at the rocket exhaust.

Unfortunately, all these seemingly fail-safe preparations came to naught because no one had foreseen how powerful the blast of water and steam would be. Instead of submitting rolls of dramatic shots of the *Columbia* rising from clouds of red steam, Morse and his assistants spent the hours after the launch gathering the remnants of his devastated equipment. The only camera with any salvageable film was one of the light-activated ones; from it came the contact strip opposite. But these pictures were not used in *Time's* story on the shuttle; the magazine ran another Morse photograph taken by a backup

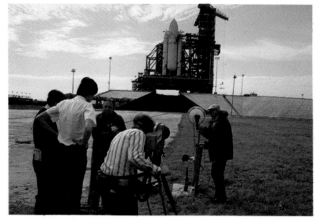

Barely 200 yards from the space shuttle Columbia's launch pad, Time photographer Ralph Morse (third from left) and assistant Al Asnis (far right) hook up two pole-mounted cameras to a sound-activated switch that was connected to a high-powered disk microphone. Morse positioned four other cameras at about this same distance from the pad, hoping to obtain unique, close-up views of the lift-off.

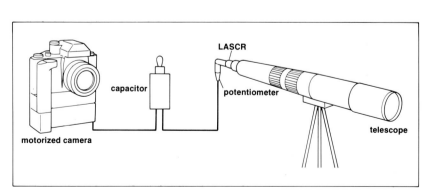

The only one of Morse's six close-range cameras that produced any usable images was triggered by light from the space shuttle's exhaust. A 600mm telescope, focused on the base of the rocket, beamed light from the exhaust into a special switch—a light-activated silicon-controlled rectifier (LASCR)—that transformed the light into an electrical impulse, which triggered the motorized camera. Attached to the LASCR was a device called a potentiometer, which prevented current from being transmitted until it reached a predetermined level of intensity. Another device called a capacitor was installed between the potentiometer and the camera for prelaunch testing. It was used to absorb the current from the LASCR before it reached the camera and to return the LASCR to its open position, ready for another test or for the launch itself.

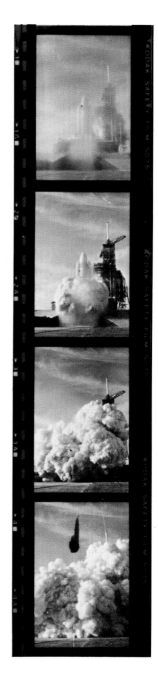

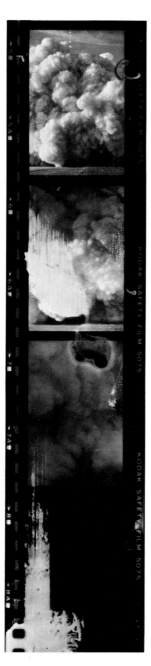

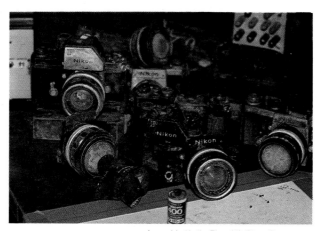

Assembled in the Time-Life Photo Department after it was recovered, Morse's equipment betrays the effects of the blast. All six cameras were ruined, and the only film to survive was used to make the contact strip reproduced at left.

These eight frames were all that came of Ralph Morse's elaborate efforts to take close-range photographs of the space shuttle's launch. The motor-driven camera clicked off only eight shots before it was engulfed by a cloud of steam and sand. The murkiness of the first frame is caused by an improvised lens cap—a plastic coffee-can lid—that Morse used to protect the lens before the launch. It was designed to pop off as the camera's motor advanced the film past the first frame. On other frames, splotches of magenta (bottom left) and blue (right) appear where emulsion came off the film back. Coils of film were virtually melted together by the blast and had to be unstuck before the film could be developed.

remote-control camera he had stationed in the normal press photographic area a quarter of a mile from the launching pad. It was triggered by a direct wire hook-up into NASA's own computer system.

Despite the spectacular fiasco, Morse did not regret the experiment. "The question is, do you gamble or don't you in a situation like this?" he said. "The answer is yes, if you want to make good pictures."

Morse was attempting to cope with a paroxysm of man-made violence, but a comparable level of photographic ingenuity may also be needed just to capture everyday occurrences in nature. Bruce Dale of *National Geographic* faced such a challenge. Assigned to photograph plants and animals that adapt to life in arid climates, he had to contrive an elaborate bit of gadgetry to record the behavior of a familiar desert character.

Dale was at work in Death Valley, California, when he noticed a bird walking toward him. It approached to within 10 feet, ran away and came back with a stick that it dropped near Dale's van before running off again. Later it returned with a cigarette butt. Later still it came back with a lizard, jumped into the van's open window and perched on the back of a seat, the lizard dangling from its beak. The bird was a ground cuckoo, sometimes called a chaparral cock and most commonly known as a roadrunner. This one seemed to have developed a crush on the photographer: Its offerings were all part of a male roadrunner's normal courting behavior.

Dale became so intrigued with the bird that he decided to make a thorough photographic study of roadrunners. He sought out a bird ethologist at the University of Northern Iowa, an authority on roadrunner behavior. Together they worked up an elaborate device that would enable Dale to lure the birds close enough to be photographed.

Atop a six-inch-high scale model of an Army tank that was operated by remote control, they mounted a motorized 35mm automatic-exposure camera with a 16mm fisheye lens, a stuffed roadrunner equipped with a miniature radio-controlled motor that would wiggle its tail, and two tape recorders. One tape recorder played male roadrunner mating calls, the other had a tape of female mating calls—"A lot of barks and coos," is how Dale described them.

From the tank's remote-control box, Dale was able to maneuver the vehicle, operate the tape recorders and camera, and wag the stuffed bird's tail. He put the elaborate decoy out on the desert, retreated a discreet 50 yards and started the female tape. Almost immediately a bird jumped out of a bush and ran up to the decoy to offer it a stick.

Love interest promised rewarding pictures, but the photographer also was interested in recording the behavior of the birds during less romantic situations. One of the methods he used was to confront the roadrunners with rattlesnakes—their natural enemies—and photograph the reaction. "There are

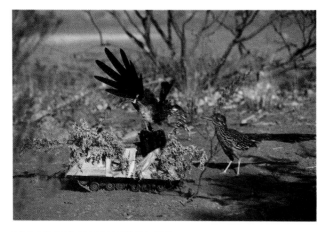

A live male roadrunner approaches a decoy that has been fitted with a tail-wagging electric motor and given voice by two tape recorders playing roadrunner mating calls. The decoy is mounted on a battery-powered, maneuverable model tank along with a motorized automatic-exposure camera. Photographer Bruce Dale operated the apparatus by radio control.

legends of roadrunners building corrals of thorns around rattlesnakes," Dale said later, "but we wanted to see what would really happen when the two animals came together in a natural setting."

When Dale released a rattler near the tank-decoy, the snake sought shade under the tank. When he then played one of the mating-call tapes and a roadrunner appeared, the photographer backed up the tank to reveal the snake and began taking pictures with the tank-mounted camera.

Sometimes the bird reacted as expected, attacking the snake with lightning jabs of its sharply pointed beak. But on other occasions, the roadrunner did not follow the script: It ignored the snake and attacked the stuffed decoy instead.

The mating and territorial habits of desert creatures are not the only unpredictable developments Dale has had to deal with in his quest for unusual pictures. Like Ralph Morse with the *Columbia* launch, Dale has learned that plans involving complicated equipment can easily go awry.

For a *National Geographic* picture essay on air safety, Dale needed a dramatic photograph to counterbalance the technical illustrations in the story. He came up with the idea of positioning a camera outside a jetliner in such a way that it would look down on the body of the plane and show its position during take-off and landing, when most accidents occur. After discussion with several airline manufacturers, he succeeded in persuading Lockheed to help with the project.

Using a model of the selected jet, the L-1011 TriStar, Dale made preliminary shots to determine exactly where his cameras should be placed to ensure dramatic pictures. He decided to mount two cameras high above the fuselage of the plane, near the top of its vertical tail fin. This promised an exciting perspective from a spot that remained relatively stable during flight. The cameras were to be motor-driven 35mm SLRs with automatic exposure control, 250-frame exposure backs and 16mm fisheye lenses that had 180° angles of view. They were attached to either side of the tail fin and enclosed in specially designed windproof aluminum housings. One was mounted perpendicular to the tail fin; the other was canted at a 30° angle so that when the plane banked to the right, the camera would show a level horizon *(top diagram, page 84)*.

The take-off was planned for a late afternoon, with a return in the early evening. Dale therefore loaded one camera with slow ISO 64/19° film for daylight shots and the other with ISO 200/24° film for pictures taken after sunset. The triggering device for the shutter releases was a set of cables that ran from the cameras down through the tail fin and along the fuselage to the cockpit, where Dale would be sitting *(bottom diagram, pages 84-85)*.

Because it was such an expensive proposition, there was to be only one flight, from Lockheed's test-flight airbase at Palmdale, California. When Dale had finished mounting the cameras on the plane and was about to seal them in their housings, he radioed the cockpit to test-fire one of them. "I held my ear to the camera to make sure it was working," Dale said. "It went 'click' as it was supposed to — but at the same time I heard the second camera go 'click-click-click-click-click.'" After making some adjustments, Dale told the cockpit to trip the second camera. The same thing happened in reverse: "The second camera went 'click' and the first just ran away."

"The mistake in retrospect," Dale said, "was using three wires instead of four. All of our tests worked when the cameras were off the plane. But metal cameras on the metal surfaces of the airplane created electrical interference because of the common ground wire. It was a variable we hadn't counted on." At the time, however, Dale had no leisure to speculate on what was going wrong. It was nearly 5 o'clock in the afternoon, so he had to propose some immediate changes to save the shooting session. Dale had one of the Lockheed engineers sit in the tail section of the plane, just below the cameras, and operate the shutter releases manually.

During the flight, Dale sat in the cockpit and told the engineer over the plane's intercom when to trigger the shutters. Fortunately, this bit of teamwork succeeded in producing dozens of extraordinary views of the jetliner taking off and landing. The masterpiece was the one at right — taken in level flight but with the canted camera, because the level camera was out of film. It appeared as a three-page foldout in an issue of *National Geographic* magazine.

Photographer Bruce Dale mounted a camera on each side of a Lockheed TriStar's vertical tail fin with a bracket built to withstand high-speed flight. One camera, seen here in its housing, was placed to show a level horizon when the plane was level. The other camera, shown with its housing removed, was canted at a 30° angle so the horizon would appear level when the plane banked to the right.

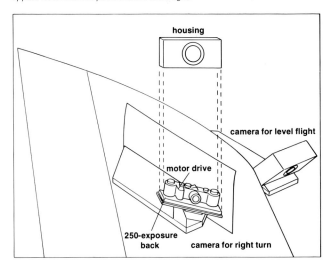

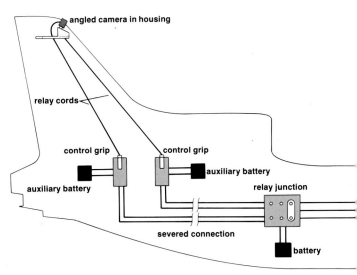

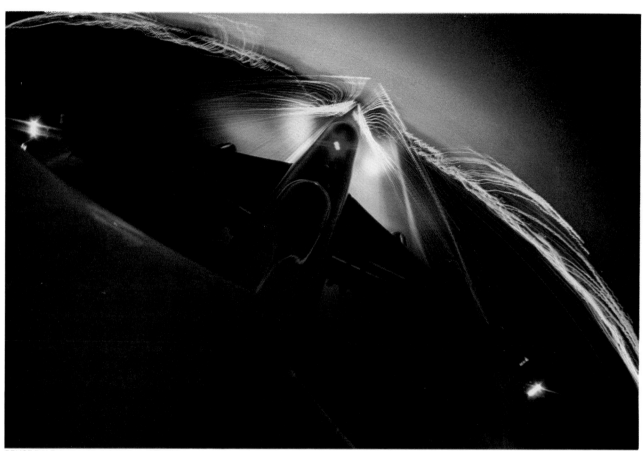

BRUCE DALE: *L-1011 Night Landing*, 1976

"A happy accident" is what Dale calls this spectacular shot of the TriStar about to land. Light was so low when the picture was taken that the aperture-priority automatic camera selected a 23-second exposure. This caused the runway lights to form a golden V in front of ragged trails of green and yellow made by other lights on the horizon.

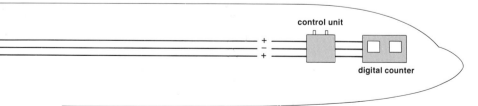

control unit

digital counter

The elaborate—but faulty—relay system designed by Dale and Lockheed's engineers included 220 feet of cable, a digital film counter, a control unit and a relay junction that connected the controls to the grips that triggered the cameras. Electrical interference required drastic last-minute changes: The cables were severed, and an engineer sat in the plane's tail and operated the control grips manually as Dale issued instructions by intercom from the cockpit.

The Experts' Ingenuity

Photographers have been performing visual sleight of hand ever since the days when the earliest practitioners of the craft used to join several daguerreotypes together to simulate a single panoramic shot. This trickery was well intentioned— a healthy refusal to admit that certain kinds of pictures were not feasible.

Today the impulse to do the impossible is stronger than ever, and the list of ingenious ploys seems endless: Multiple exposures and sandwiched transparencies add new layers to reality, time exposures record light patterns not easily perceived by the eye, and remote-control rigs and special lenses give stunning views that no human observer could ever see.

All of the photographers whose work is shown on the following pages have used these innovative techniques and tools not merely to turn out photographic novelties, but to create beautiful, informative pictures by solving formidable technical problems—often problems posed by editors who may not be aware of the difficulties involved.

For example, Michael Nichols, on assignment for the magazine *Geo,* needed to illuminate the unearthly darkness of a deep cave shaft. He could not use conventional electronic flash units or elaborate flash synchronizers because dampness in the cave would have corroded vital electrical contacts. Instead, he resorted to the old press photographers' standby, powerful Number 5 flash bulbs, which can fire when their contacts are moist, and he synchronized them by the simple expedient of leaving his camera shutter open and having his fellow spelunkers fire the bulbs manually.

The techniques employed to record the striking images on the next 14 pages vary widely, but all were carefully thought out in advance, sometimes before the photographer encountered the subject. "Without setting foot on the ship," says Harald Sund, who took the shot of a supertanker on pages 88-89, "I figured out what I wanted to do with it; then when I got there I figured out how to do it."

Sund's dramatic picture became the first two pages of a *Life* photo essay on giant ships, and the other photographs shown in this section received similarly prominent display when they were published—in each case because the photographer was a thorough professional who sought a practical way to realize his idea for a spectacular picture.

Like glowing ornaments, two light-bearing spelunkers dangle partway down a 125-foot shaft in Ellison's Cave in northern Georgia. To light up the shaft's impenetrable blackness, the photographer gave the cavers manually operated flash units fitted with powerful bulbs the size of lemons. He positioned the men so that one bulb would illuminate the top half of the shaft and the other the bottom half all the way to the floor. After adjusting his lens aperture to a setting he knew from experience would work with the bulbs in the cave, he opened his shutter, aimed blindly into the gloom and counted to three. At that point, the men below him fired their flashes and exposed this image of subterranean splendor.

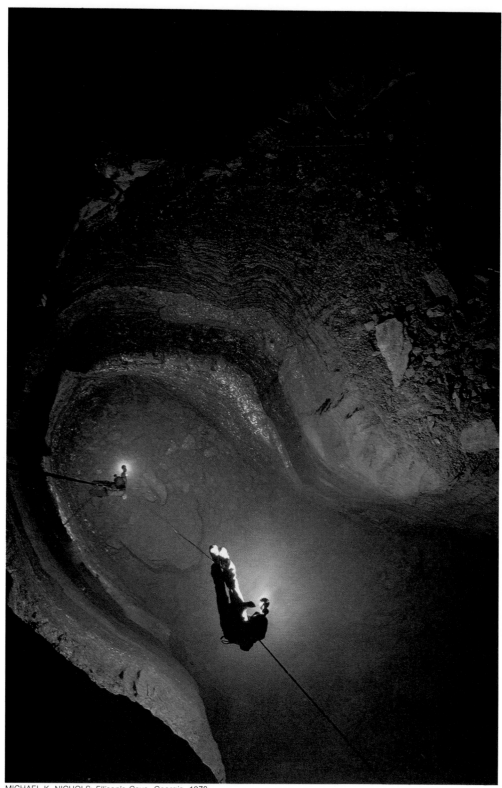

MICHAEL K. NICHOLS: *Ellison's Cave, Georgia,* 1978

Supertanker, Super Picture

To obtain this imposing view of the quarter-mile-long deck of the French oil-tanker Bellamya, Harald Sund employed a 20mm wide-angle lens with a 94° angle of view, and placed his camera as far forward as he could—on the tanker's forward observation tower. Sund wanted to achieve three objectives: to keep the ship in sharp detail, to show the sea as a blur and to deliberately alter the color balance of the film to yield muted twilight tones. A 7-second-long exposure ensured the color shift and blurred the sea. To keep the rolling tanker in sharp detail, Sund anchored his tripod-mounted camera to the deck. The image recorded on the film was so sharp that railing supports can be counted on both sides of the deck.

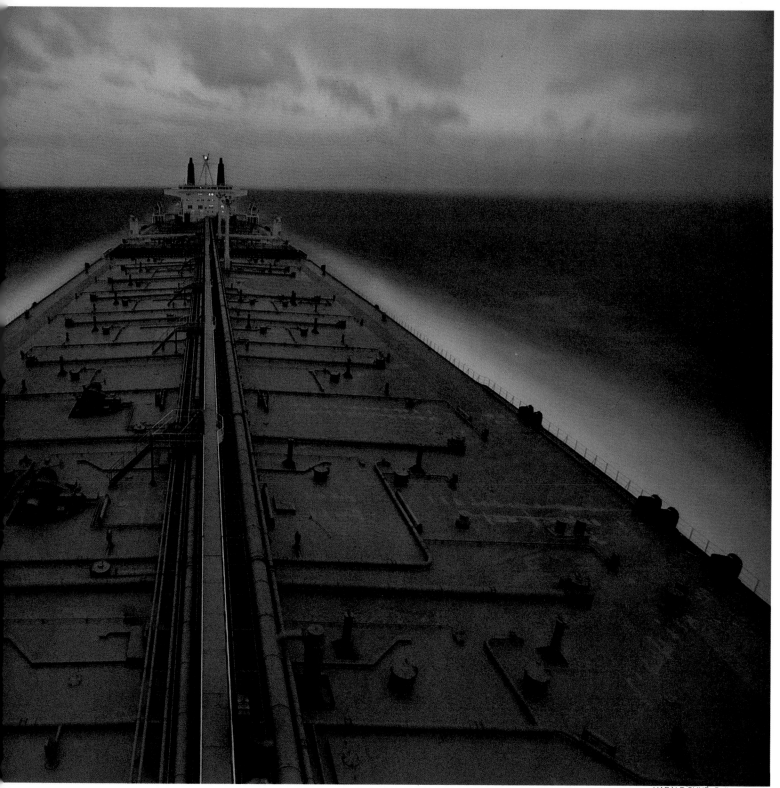

HARALD SUND: *Bellamya,* 1979

Tracing the Motion of the Heavens

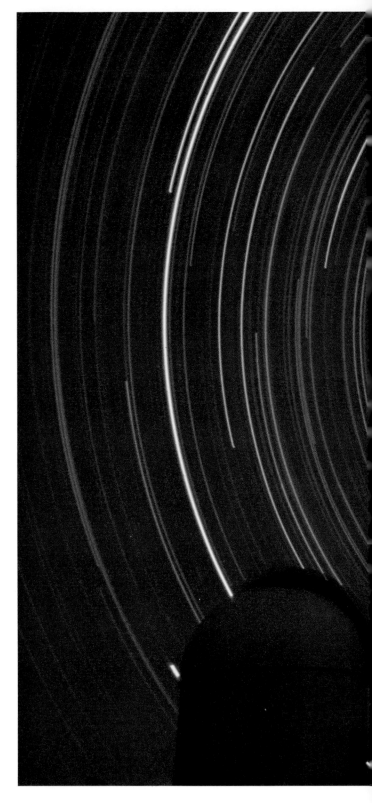

Precise placement of the camera and a long exposure yielded this spectacular pattern of circular star trails. Douglas Kirkland took the picture on a clear, moonless night on the grounds of Las Campanas Observatory in the Chilean Andes. He aimed his camera due south and locked his shutter open for seven hours. As the earth rotated on its polar axis, the circular paths in which the stars are seen to move from an earthly perspective were traced on the film. The sky's unnatural hue is the result of a shift in color that occurs when color film is exposed for more than a few seconds. For this shot Kirkland chose a film that he knew would shift toward magenta.

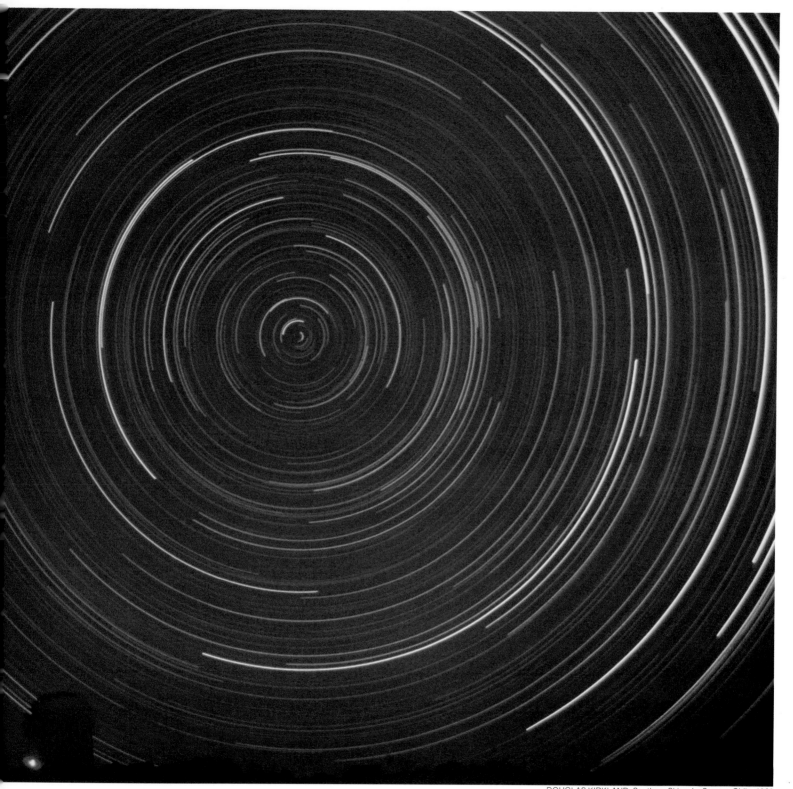

DOUGLAS KIRKLAND: *Southern Skies, La Serena, Chile,* 1980

Creating a Mood by Combining Views

Harald Sund wanted to take a picture that captured the twilight beauty of the Pacific Northwest shoreline. But from his vantage point there was no way he could include both the rising moon and the coastal rocks in the same shot. He solved the problem by making a double exposure. He first took a ½-second exposure of the moon, using a 300mm telephoto lens to magnify its size. Then, after pressing in the camera's film rewind button, which allowed him to cock the shutter without advancing the film, he took an 8-second exposure of the coastline on the same frame. The rapid movement of the pounding surf caused it to be recorded as a blur.

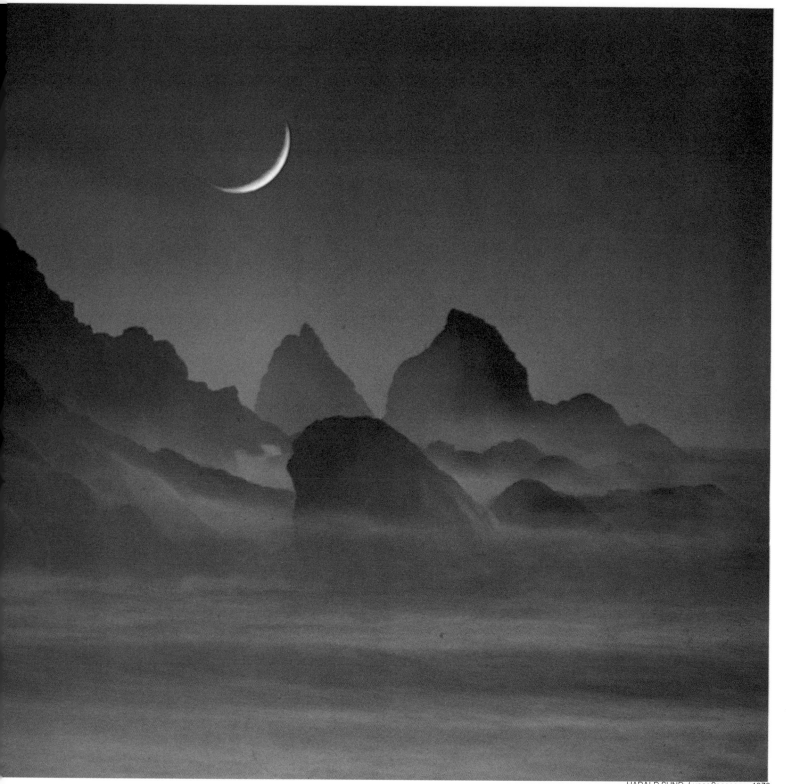

HARALD SUND: *Lunar Seascape*, 1973

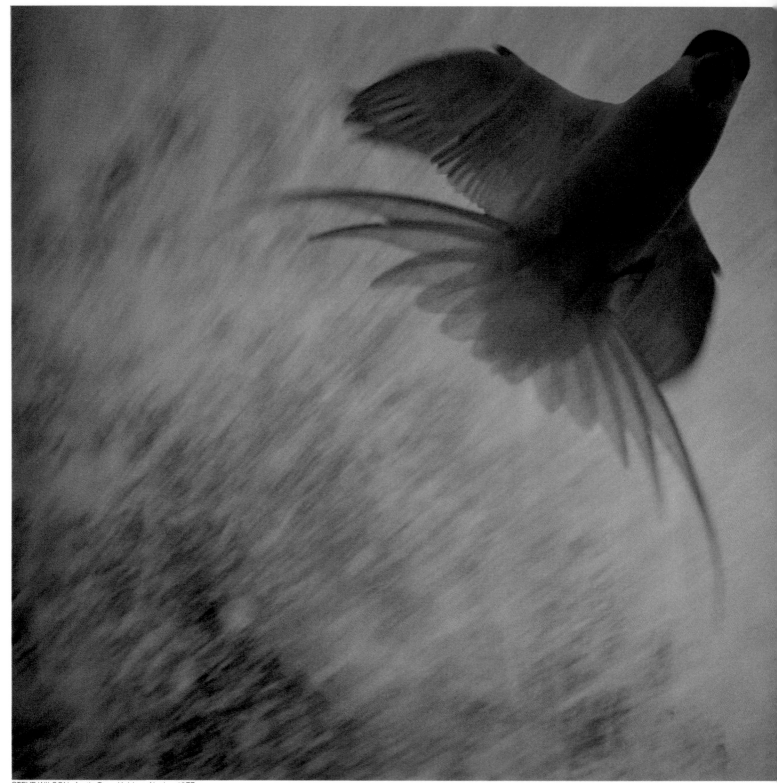

STEVE WILSON: *Arctic Tern, Valdez, Alaska,* 1977

Adding a Background by Sandwiching Slides

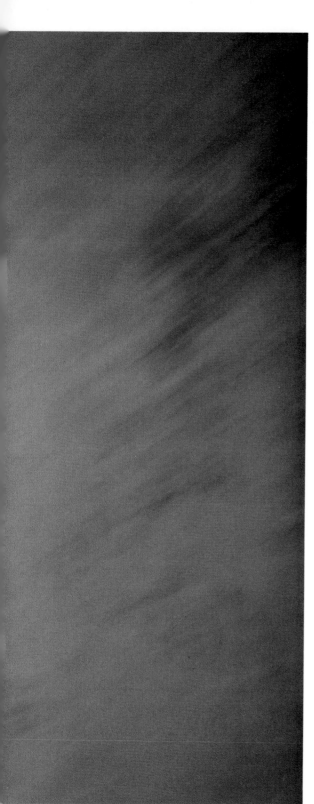

Steve Wilson found it impossible to come up with a camera angle that let him get a close-up of an arctic tern wheeling over the surf. So he took two separate pictures on transparency film and superimposed the resulting slides. First the photographer deliberately stirred up a flock of terns. As one bird flew within a foot of the camera, an ultra-wide-angle 15mm lens exaggerated and slightly distorted its shape; a shutter speed of 1/1000 second froze motion. Two hours later, Wilson shot the background, using a slower shutter speed to blur the waves. He overexposed the second shot to produce a pale slide that would merge more easily with the image of the tern.

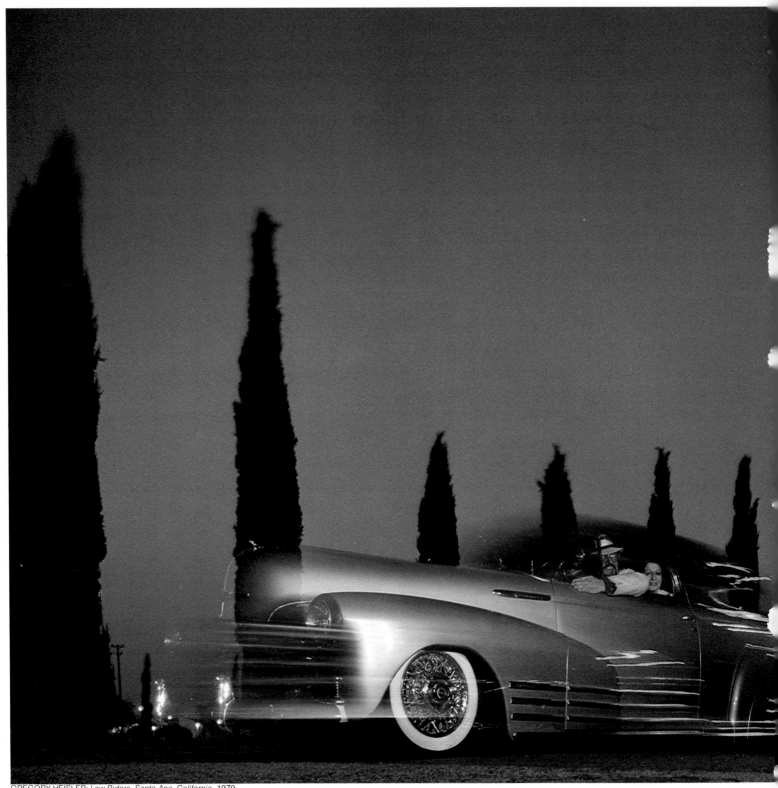

GREGORY HEISLER: *Low Riders, Santa Ana, California,* 1979

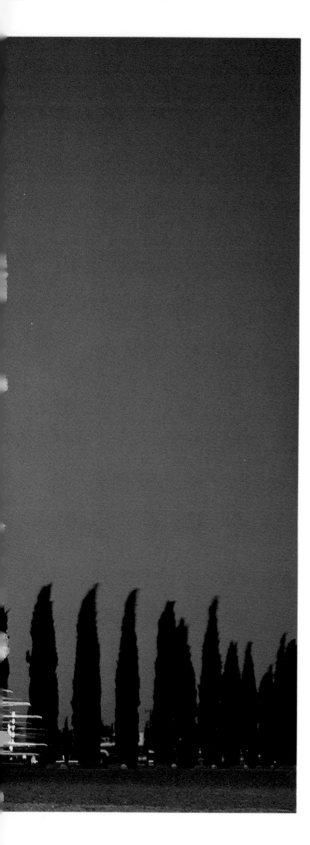

Flashy Results with a Time Exposure

Electronic flash was judiciously combined with a long exposure time to create this photograph of two Californians in their 1947 Fleetline Chevrolet. Shooting at twilight so he could leave his shutter open for two seconds without overexposing the film, Gregory Heisler carefully posed his subjects. Then, as he set off two battery-powered electronic flash units and started the time exposure, he had the driver back up at about two miles per hour. Where car and riders were illuminated by the flash, their image is sharp; where ambient light provided the illumination, as in the front fender, the image is blurred. Some background features, such as the second tree from the left, were recorded on film vacated by the backward-moving vehicle, making the front of the car seem transparent.

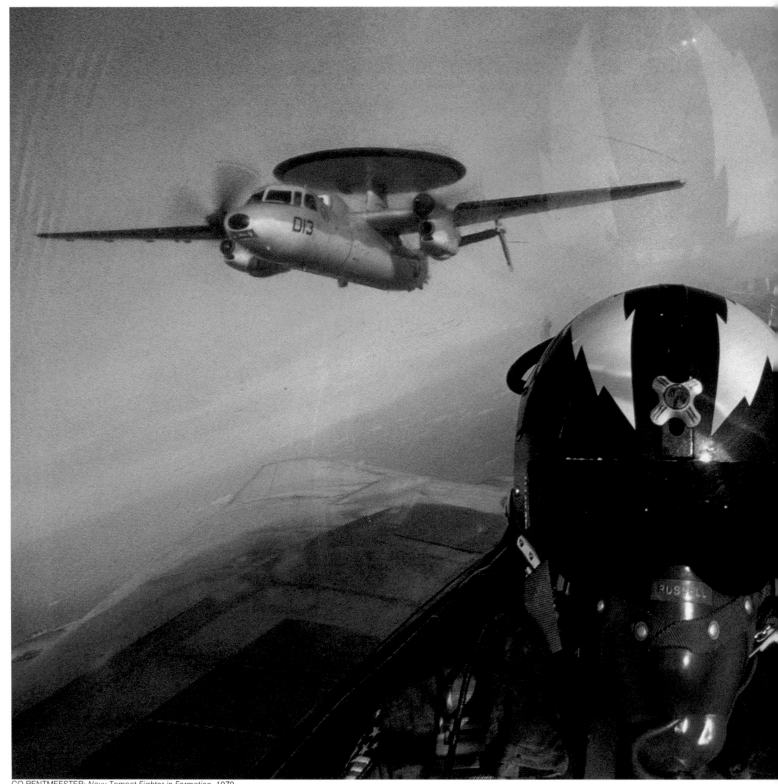

CO RENTMEESTER: *Navy Tomcat Fighter in Formation*, 1979

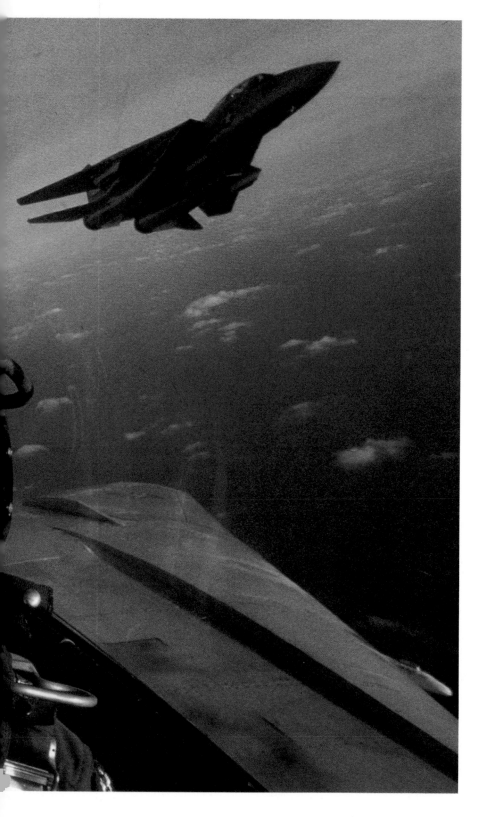

To produce this extraordinary photograph from the cockpit of a U.S. Navy F-14 Tomcat fighter plane flying in formation with a surveillance plane (left) and another F-14 fighter (right), Co Rentmeester acted as backstage engineer rather than on-the-spot snapshooter. He mounted a camera with an 18mm lens on the back of one F-14 pilot's seat, preset its exposure and distance controls, then waited below. The radio systems control officer triggered the shutter with a remote-control release.

Low Comedy with High Technology

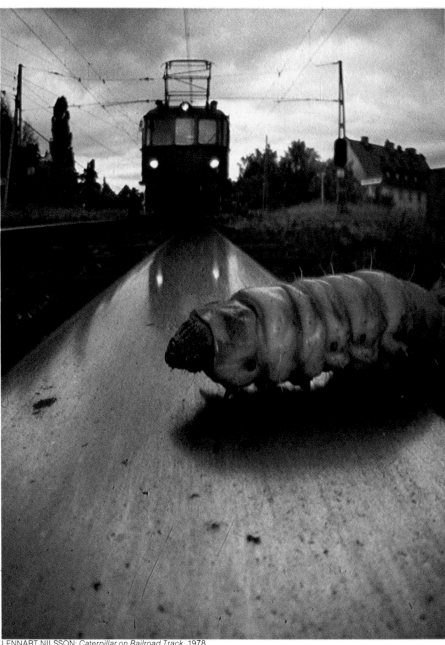

This close-up of a caterpillar appearing to crawl across a railroad track was taken with a lens that has a focal length of only 4mm. The lens, which can focus without noticeable distortion on subjects only inches away, was specially designed for photographer Lennart Nilsson, who uses it primarily to make magnifications of medical and scientific phenomena. But noting that the lens can also keep distant objects in relatively sharp focus because of the enormous depth of field its short focal length provides, Nilsson used it to take this playful shot.

LENNART NILSSON: *Caterpillar on Railroad Track, 1978*

Mechanical Failure **4**

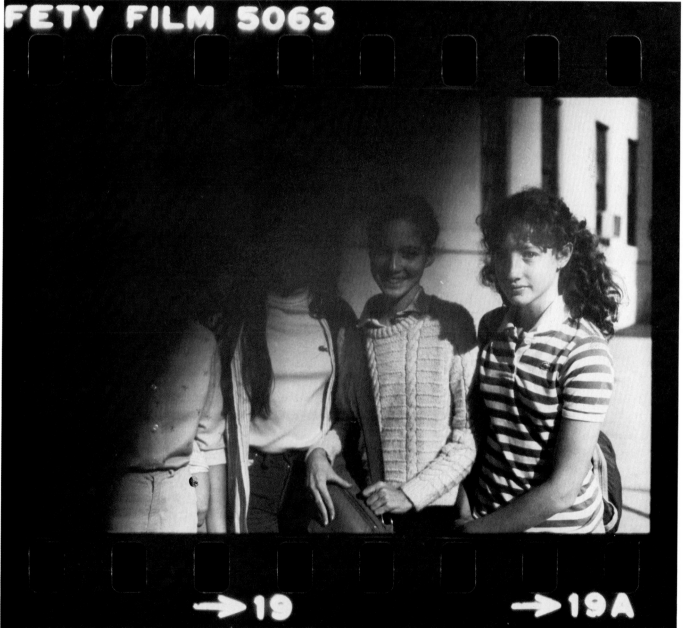

FETY FILM 5063

→19 →19A

Shutter malfunction

Techniques of Troubleshooting

In February 1968, as debate raged throughout the nation over American bombing raids in Southeast Asia, *Life* photographer Co Rentmeester arrived at a United States air base in Guam with a satchelful of sophisticated camera equipment. His plan was to fly aboard a B-52 bomber on a mission over North and South Vietnam, and to take pictures as the jet dropped its bomb load on Communist supply lines and ammo depots. To catch the bombs at the very moment that they spewed from the belly of the aircraft, he fitted remote controls to a motorized camera and installed it in a wing. Sixteen hours of painstaking work were needed to attach the camera and to lead its triggering cable through the wing to the cabin where he would sit. It hardly seemed worth it in the end. He flew three high-altitude missions, but each time, despite winterizing, his camera froze. Only by mounting a second motorized camera in the warmer bomb bay and by shooting when the bay doors opened and the bombs were released, did Rentmeester manage to come back with the kind of picture he was after.

Camera malfunction is probably the photographer's blackest nightmare. Whether the trouble lies with the expensive, specialized equipment of a professional like Rentmeester or with an amateur's standard gear, the effects in lost time and wasted pictures can be heartbreaking. Many things can go wrong. In the camera, the metal springs that close shutters can lose their tension, causing a partial loss of image as in the example on the preceding page. A sharp jolt can wreck a focusing system by knocking lens elements out of alignment. Parts can deteriorate from long use. The mechanism that simultaneously advances the film and cocks the shutter can wear out, resulting in multiple exposures. The retractable mirror in a single-lens reflex, situated directly behind the lens to allow the photographer to focus, can fail to pull back when the shutter is tripped, so that the image never reaches the film and no exposure takes place. Continuous vibrations from an automobile or airplane can shake parts loose in a camera. *Life* science photographer Fritz Goro, shooting pictures of an archeological dig in Guatemala in 1963, produced several rolls of light-struck negatives. A tiny fitting in the base of his camera had vibrated loose during the helicopter flight to the dig, so that sunlight streamed into his camera like the beam from a miniature flashlight. If Goro had not backed up his initial pictures by taking additional shots with another camera, his assignment would have been a total failure.

Many such disasters become apparent only after the pictures have been processed, and close study of prints is often the best way to detect malfunctions. But the professional tries to prevent trouble by periodically testing his equipment. Before setting out on an assignment he may aim his camera out a window and focus on a distant building to make sure that the image is sharp when the focusing scale indicates infinity. By opening the back of the camera, looking through the lens and clicking the shutter, he can see whether the shutter opens and closes smoothly. He makes sure that the batteries in cameras, flash units and light meters operate effectively. After loading a 35mm camera, he can tell whether the film will run through smoothly by clicking off a few frames, and seeing if the rewind knob turns as he cocks the film-advance lever. For a more exhaustive check-out, working photographers send their cameras to a repair shop. Some publications maintain their own. *The National Geographic* magazine, for example, considers testing so important that it asks photographers to turn in their equipment for a thorough checkup after each assignment. And some manufacturers send teams of experts from the factory to major news events, such as space shots and political conventions, to offer free testing and repair service to the professionals on assignment there.

Repairmen rely on a battery of complex optical and electronic equipment to ensure the accuracy of their tests. Shutter testers indicate exactly how long a shutter stays open at each setting, as well as how long it takes the shutter curtains to open and close. Battery testers determine the strength of flash batteries, and a lamp with an opal-glass screen and a dial for regulating light intensity allows technicians to make certain that light meters register correctly for all degrees of brightness. But such special equipment is not really necessary for most tests. Much information can be discovered at home by an amateur with no more equipment than a few charts, a tape measure, several rolls of film, phosphorescent tape and a magnifying glass.

Do-it-yourself tests like those that follow, applied either to the camera itself or to pictures made with the camera, can reveal most common defects. They are invaluable for detecting hidden faults in newly purchased cameras and lenses, particularly if the equipment is bought secondhand. And they also provide a convenient way of checking out a favorite old camera, indicating if it should go to the repair shop before a once-in-a-lifetime photographic opportunity is lost.

How Sharp Is a Lens?

The heart of a camera is its lens. Finely constructed shutters, precise focusing systems, lightproof, sturdy housings—all will be of little help to the photographer in search of fine pictures if his camera is lacking a good lens, or if the lens has somehow got out of adjustment. Camera manufacturers are so particular about the quality of their lenses that they often take as much trouble testing them as they do making them.

Before a new lens design goes into production, the manufacturer sometimes spends weeks testing a prototype, probing it with light rays and laser beams, feeding hundreds of statistics into computers for evaluation. Later, as lenses leave production lines, they are tested again to make sure they conform to the same high standard as the prototype.

In spite of this, no lens is ever perfect. The most carefully constructed lens will have certain built-in aberrations because of the peculiar ways in which light rays travel through curved pieces of glass. Images will be sharper at certain apertures than at others, and they will usually be sharper at the center than at the edges. Some lenses will produce clearer images with blue light rays than with yellow ones, and some are particularly likely to pick up unwanted flashes of reflected light, or flare. Though none of these faults can be eliminated entirely, lens-makers rely on testing to make sure they are kept to a practical minimum.

One basic test evaluates lens resolution—the ability of the lens to render detail; it can be carried out by the amateur, as described on pages 108-109. The test determines how many lines per millimeter the lens can distinguish at a prescribed distance from a target. There are a number of versions. One pattern, for example, was developed for the U.S. Air Force to test lenses used in aerial reconnaissance, where good detail is essential.

But all versions of the resolution test are carried out in much the same way, by photographing a wall chart covered with a number of carefully designed test patterns. Each test pattern (one example is shown on the opposite page) consists of groups of lines of different sizes separated by varying widths of blank space. The developed negative is examined through a magnifying glass. The groups of larger lines will appear sharp, but some of the smaller groups will blur into each other. The smallest group that the lens is able to separate into clearly defined lines and blank spaces will be a measure of its resolving power.

Many variables besides the quality of the lens may affect the results of the resolution test. The film used and the process by which it is developed both influence the sharpness of the negatives. More significant, perhaps, is the fact that the test may uncover defects in the camera body or the focusing system. An uneven lens mount, a pressure plate at the back of the camera that does not hold the film firmly in the focal plane, or an inaccurate range finder all create a telltale blurring in the lines of the test patterns.

A test pattern, designed during the Korean War to check the resolving power of Air Force camera lenses, is shown enlarged two and a half times. It consists of 24 groups of lines of diminishing size, with each group containing three vertical lines and three horizontal ones. A number of such patterns arranged on a wall form the target for the resolution test. The numerals next to each line group refer to a table that lists the resolution in lines per millimeter.

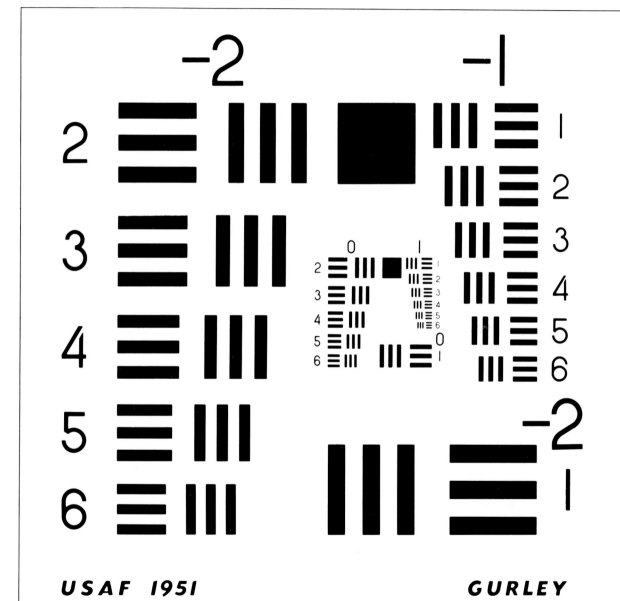

Simple Tests for Lenses

Using a resolution chart to test the sharpness of a lens requires the utmost accuracy and care. The camera must be properly placed, lighting must be precise, and the film must be developed in a specified manner. But an amateur, following the right procedures, not only can determine a lens's resolving power, but can check it for various types of distortion and aberration as well.

The first step is positioning the camera and chart. (Opposite, at left, is a negative of one standard chart, consisting of 16 test patterns arranged in a cross.) The camera must be placed securely on a tripod at the standard distance from the chart: 26 times the focal length of the lens. Thus, the front of a two-inch (50mm) lens should be 52 inches away from the chart; a six-inch (150mm) lens should be 156 inches away.

The camera should be loaded with a high-resolution film, such as Panatomic-X, and a series of exposures should be made, one at each f-stop, while the shutter speed is adjusted so that the exposures remain constant. After exposure, the film should be carefully developed in a fine-grain developer.

Results of the test must be read directly from the negative through a magnifying glass. Using an enlarger to make a print would add another variable—the enlarger's lens—and thus could give misleading results for the camera lens. With the Photo-Lab-Index chart shown here, resolution in lines per millimeter is indicated by numbers next to each group of lines in the test patterns. To obtain the lens's resolving power, read the smallest group of lines in each test pattern that the lens is able to differentiate clearly.

Test results can tell more about a lens than just its overall sharpness. Almost all lenses have an unavoidable defect called spherical aberration. This means that they tend to form sharper images with light rays that come through the center than with rays that enter through the edges. Therefore, the negatives taken at smaller apertures, where the edges are blocked off by the diaphragm, will show less spherical aberration than negatives taken at wide-open apertures. On the other hand, resolution problems such as diffraction become worse at small apertures, so a careful examination of the negatives is needed to reveal which apertures will produce the sharpest pictures in a given lens.

Other defects may show up on the negatives. The test patterns at the corners of the chart may be fuzzier than the ones near the center, indicating that the sharpest image the lens forms is curved slightly. Astigmatism—inability of a lens to reproduce horizontal and vertical lines equally well at the same time—shows up because the lines in each test pattern run at right angles to one another.

Finally, a glance at the three long lines that frame the edges of the chart may show that the lens distorts images. If the lines bow inward the lens suffers from what is known as pin-cushion distortion; an outward bowing means barrel distortion *(opposite, top)*.

Standardized test charts, which give an accurate, numerical reading of the lens's resolving power, are available at most camera supply shops. But even without a chart an amateur can estimate the quality of his lens by substituting another flat surface with right-angle lines, such as a brick wall *(opposite)*. While the results are not as exact, they provide clues to many of the same defects that test charts show.

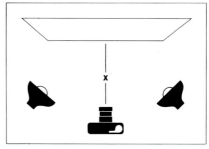

Accurate positioning of camera and lights is essential for getting good results from a test chart. The camera's lens must be centered exactly opposite the center of the chart, as shown above. If the camera is set at the slightest angle to left or right, or tilted up or down the smallest bit, the test will be misleading. Lights should be placed to provide even, glare-free illumination. In the arrangement shown here, two 15-watt frosted bulbs set in satin-finish reflectors are placed on either side of the camera at an angle of approximately 45°.

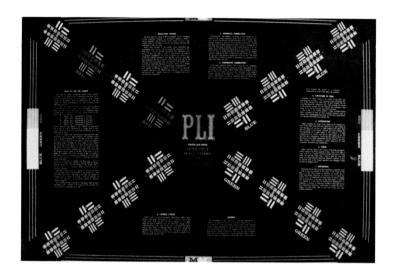

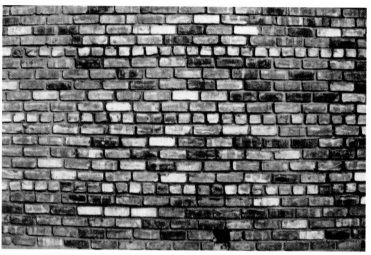

The test results for one lens, obtained from both a Photo-Lab-Index chart (left) and a brick wall, show barrel distortion. The parallel lines on the top and bottom edges of the chart, and the upper and lower rows of bricks, are bowed.

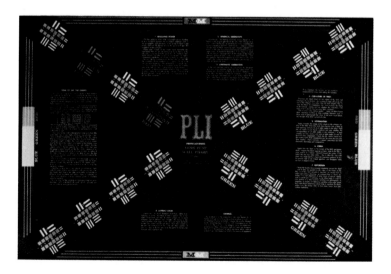

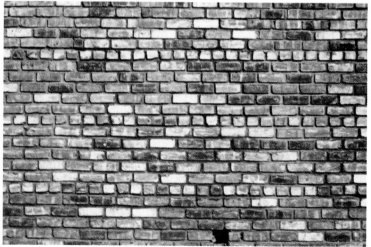

Another test from a different lens shows no sign of distortion. This particular lens also seems to have a greater resolving power than the lens tested at the top, since details in both the chart and the brick wall appear to be much sharper.

How Precise Is a Shutter?

While shutters on modern cameras are normally quite durable, they sometimes wear out. There are two common types of shutter. In one, the leaf type, thin metal blades slide from the center of the shutter toward its perimeter to open, and slide back to close. In the focal-plane type, by contrast, a pair of curtains with an adjustable opening between them sweeps across the film, from one side of the camera to the other.

Both types of shutter are operated by springs. With age, the springs lose their springiness, causing the shutter to move more slowly than it should. Thus at a setting of 1/500 second the shutter may stay open for twice that time, producing over-exposed pictures.

Other faults throw shutters off their timing. A complicated arrangement of gears and levers regulates the speed. If one gear works loose or wears out, the shutter may not function properly at a particular setting. The mechanism may become clogged with dirt, causing the shutter to move unevenly. In each instance exposures become erratic.

One way to test shutter mechanisms is to take a series of photographs of the same subject under the same lighting conditions, one at each shutter speed, while changing the f-stop so that the total amount of illumination reaching the film remains constant. If one frame is odd—significantly lighter or darker than the other frames *(opposite)*—either the shutter does not operate at that speed, or the diaphragm is out of adjustment at that f-stop. The diaphragm can be ruled out if, in a second test series shot with a different set of graduated shutter/f-stop combinations, another odd frame turns up at the same shutter speed that produced the first odd frame.

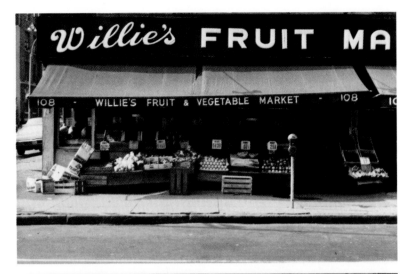

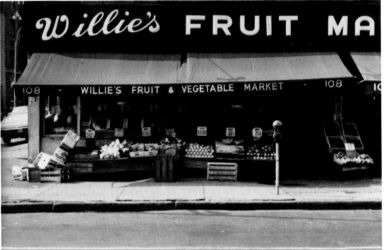

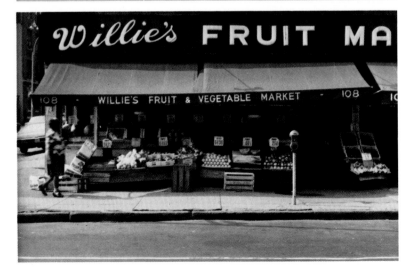

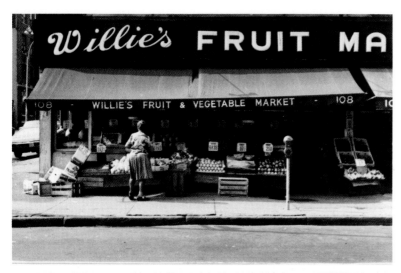

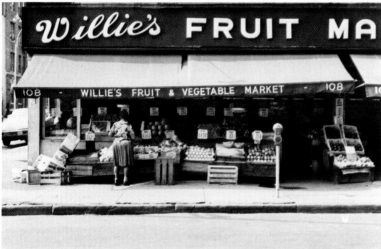

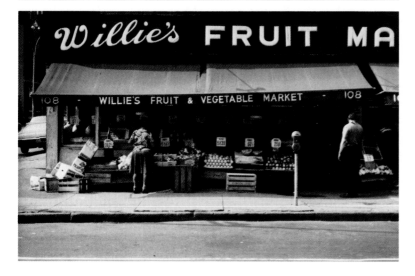

To check the shutter speeds on a camera, an evenly lighted street scene such as the one on these pages makes a good test subject. A series of pictures was shot at different combinations of shutter speeds and diaphragm openings, beginning with 1/30 second at f/16 (top, opposite), then 1/60 second at f/11 (center, opposite), and so on up to 1/1000 second at f/2.8 (bottom, this page). Since f-stop changes compensated for shutter-speed changes in each case, density of the resulting pictures should have been almost identical. But one, shot at 1/500 second at f/4 (center, this page), was obviously overexposed. To make certain that it was the shutter and not the diaphragm that malfunctioned at that setting, another set of exposures was made, beginning with f/22 at 1/30 second. The camera again overexposed at 1/500 (with an f-stop of f/5.6), clear proof that the shutter was the mechanism that needed repair.

Testing an Automatic Camera

Shutters and lens diaphragms of many automatic cameras cannot be tested by using the method shown on the preceding pages. On some of these cameras shutter speed cannot be set manually; on others it is impossible to set the aperture. In such cases, a test with varied amounts of light falling on the subject *(right)* will check shutter and aperture operation.

An aperture-priority automatic camera allows the photographer to set the aperture; the camera then selects a shutter speed. With such a camera, using a single aperture to photograph a scene lit at several levels of brightness tests the camera's shutter system as it adjusts to the changing light. A noticeable exposure variation in the processed photographs *(opposite, bottom right)* indicates a shutter problem.

Similarly, to test a shutter-priority automatic camera, use a single shutter speed under varying light. The test should be made with each of the camera's lenses to check each lens diaphragm. Exposure variation here indicates a problem in the automatic-aperture setting system.

In conducting a variable-light test, an evenly lit subject works best. A movable flood lamp provides the variable illumination. It is useful to test shutter and aperture operation over a broad range of light intensities. Here brightness was varied over a range equivalent to five f-stops, with each change of brightness amounting to a difference of a single stop. For each successive exposure, the lamp was placed at a distance from the subject that reduced the light reaching the subject by half. In such a test, relative brightness can be gauged by using a light meter, or simply by making each new light-to-subject distance 1.4 times as long as the previous one *(diagram, right)*.

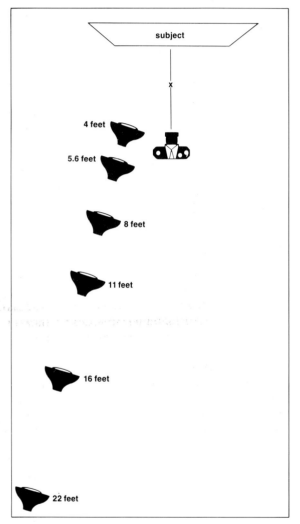

To test an automatic camera's exposure controls at various light levels, a subject is set up so that a single movable lamp can illuminate it at a range of distances and from the same angle. Illumination should be even, and there should be no shadows cast on the subject. A shortcut in setting the lamp at distances that vary brightness by a significant amount is to use common f-numbers for the distances in feet. If, for example, lamp-to-subject distances are 4, 5.6, 8, 11, 16 and 22 feet, then the subject will be lit half as brightly in each succeeding exposure.

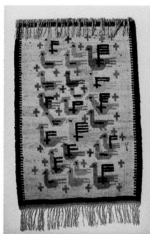

4 feet; 1/60 second

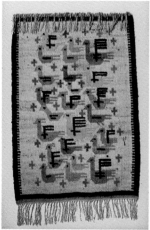

5.6 feet; 1/30 second

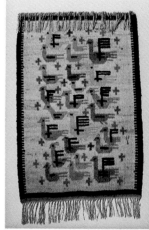

8 feet; 1/15 second

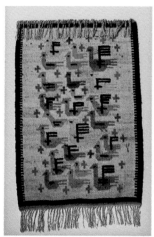

11 feet; 1/8 second

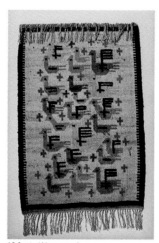

16 feet; 1/4 second

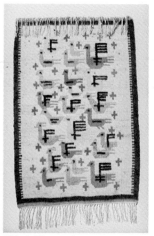

22 feet; 1/2 second

These pictures of a Polish wall hanging were made with an aperture-priority automatic camera set at f/5.6. The light came from a single flood lamp that was moved farther away after each shot (diagram, left). The shutter speeds indicated by the camera's meter for the six pictures were 1/60, 1/30, 1/15, 1/8, 1/4 and 1/2 second. The lightness of the picture at bottom right shows that the shutter speed that was supposed to have been 1/2 second was actually longer. This overexposure is bad enough to warrant having a repairman check the shutter system.

Checking Synchronization of Flash and Shutter

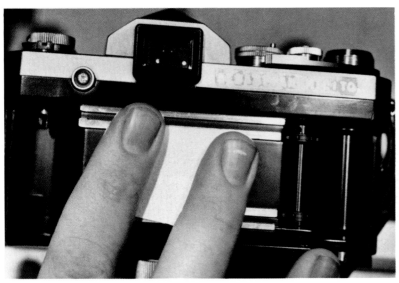

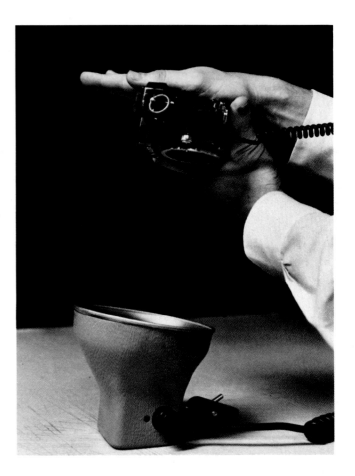

To test a focal-plane shutter for electronic flash synchronization, use luminous tape, which glows after it is exposed to light. Hold a piece of tape — measuring one and a half by two inches — with the fingers (above) or palm (right), luminous side toward the front of the camera, in the place where the film would normally be. Next, with the flash unit's synchronization cord connected to the camera and the shutter set at the camera's recommended synchronization speed, aim the camera at the unit and snap the shutter (right). Inspect the tape (opposite) to see if the frame was uniformly exposed.

Another part of a camera that must operate with extreme precision is the mechanism that synchronizes the shutter with an electronic flash unit. If the timing of either the shutter or the flash is off by as little as a few thousandths of a second, the result will be a loss of part of the image if the camera uses a focal-plane shutter, or an underexposure if the camera has a leaf shutter.

With either type of shutter, the electronic flash is designed to go off at almost—but not quite—the same instant that the shutter is tripped. A tiny moment of hesitation is purposely built into the synchronization device. This gives the shutter time to open up completely before the light reaches the film. The leaves of a leaf shutter, radiating out from its center, must be fully dilated; otherwise insufficient light will reach the film, causing the underexposure. To test such a shutter, simply set the diaphragm wide, open the camera back, aim at the flash unit and watch through the back of the camera as the shutter opens and the flash fires. If the synchronization is correct, a perfectly round bright spot will be seen.

The problem is different in a camera with a focal-plane shutter. Both of its curtains start out at one side of the window. When the shutter is tripped at the flash-sync setting, the first curtain moves across the window, opening it completely and firing the flash. Then the second cur-tain follows to close the window. But if the light unit fires too late—after the second curtain has started to move, covering one end of the frame—only a part of the film will be fully exposed and the rest of the negative will be blank.

A slow shutter speed (usually 1/60 second) is needed to make the curtain open completely and expose every part of the frame at once, admitting light from the flash to all sections of the film. For this reason, only at these slow speeds can a focal-plane shutter be synchronized with electronic flash.

A simple way to test synchronization of a focal-plane shutter is to take a "picture" of the flash itself (left). Instead of film, photographers use luminous tape, available at photo supply stores at nominal cost. In subdued light, with the camera back open, the tape is held in the spot where the film would normally be (opposite, far left), and the shutter is set at the speed recommended for electronic flash synchronization. The photographer shoots directly into the flash unit (left).

If the flash is synchronized with the shutter, it will leave an afterglow on the tape that fills the entire frame; otherwise the glow may be only a sliver (right). The glow will last for about 30 seconds. The fault could be nothing more than an error in setting the shutter to the speed for flash synchronization; but if that can be ruled out, the mechanism needs repair. □

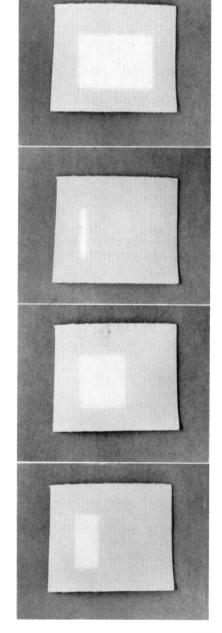

Light patterns on luminous tape reveal whether electronic flash and focal-plane shutter were synchronized or, if not, how drastically they were out of step. In the example at the top, where the light pattern covers the entire picture frame, the flash was properly timed to go off when the shutter was completely open. But in the other examples, the flash fired late, when the shutter was no longer fully open.

How the Pictures Show What Went Wrong

No matter how thoroughly a photographer checks his equipment in advance, the acid test of its performance is the picture it produces. A quick glance at a set of contact sheets is sometimes all that is necessary to reveal many of these mechanical failures. When prints are double exposed, unevenly shaded or marred by light spots or dark patches, a bit of armchair detective work can often determine exactly what went wrong.

Double exposures, like those opposite, are quickly spotted in contact sheets. Such mishaps are simply not supposed to occur with most modern roll-film cameras. Virtually all have a single lever that both cocks the shutter and advances the film to bring a fresh frame into taking position. Thus the shutter cannot operate unless the film has also been moved, theoretically protecting the photographer from an error that happened rather frequently in the past—forgetting to wind the film between shots. But if the mechanism malfunctions, so that the film does not advance a full frame when the shutter is cocked, double or overlapping exposures are inevitable, no matter how careful the photographer is.

Even if the film-advance device operates normally, too much tension on the film can also prevent it from moving. This excessive tension results occasionally if the film has been improperly packaged and does not roll smoothly out of the magazine or off the spool; too much tension may also be produced by the camera's own rewind device, which can jam and cause a drag that holds back the moving film. The same kind of drag can sometimes occur in wet weather, when moisture may condense on the pressure plate, which is designed to keep the film flat as it passes through the back of the camera; the moisture makes the film stick to the plate.

The evidence of the contact sheet can solve many other mysteries of what went wrong. Multiple exposures on the first few negatives and blanks everywhere else on the roll suggest that the film stopped moving completely, perhaps because its forward end slipped out of the take-up spool; a series of partially overlapping exposures, on the other hand, could signify slippage in the mechanism or drag on the film. If the prints show blank white areas, indicating the film was struck unintentionally by light, the extent and location of the light-struck sections may reveal how the leak occurred—around the edges of a bent back, through a hole in a focal plane shutter, past the incomplete protection of a faulty cassette.

The clues on contact sheets can lead a photographic detective to deduce that equipment is not broken but misused. Consistent overexposure or underexposure in prints may indicate an incorrect setting for film speed; blank corners reveal use of a misfit lens or an undersized sunshade. Such failures are mechanical malfunctions, too—a breakdown in the vital link between the human photographer and his responsive machine.

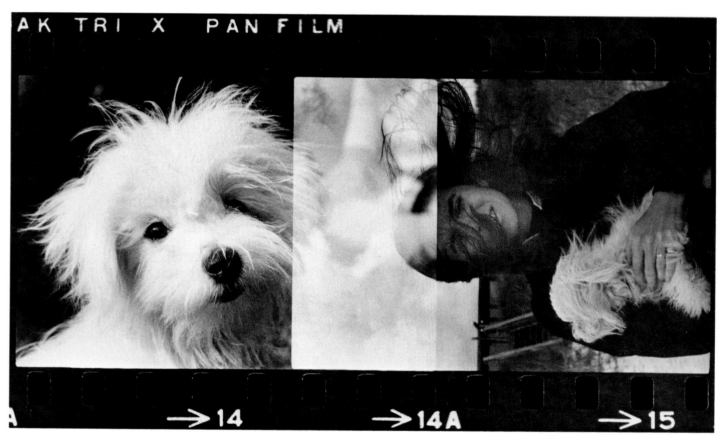

AK TRI X   PAN FILM

→14   →14A   →15

The overlapping exposures that showed up in this contact sheet seem to warn of trouble in the film-advance system of the camera. It was a camera in which a small button disengages the forward-moving take-up spool so that exposed film can be wound back into its cassette. But the photographer inadvertently misused it: He happened to press the rewind button as he cocked the shutter, thus allowing the film-advance mechanism to slip a bit so it only advanced the film about two thirds of a frame.

Vignetting—The Lost Corners

Interchangeable lenses, generally considered one of the most convenient features of many cameras, share a built-in hazard: In practice, not all of them are completely interchangeable. A lens may fit into the mount of a camera, yet chop off part of the picture—a phenomenon called vignetting, in which the corners of a picture are underexposed or blank because the lens forms an image that is too small to cover the entire negative. The problem may escape notice when the lens is being used—the corners of some cameras' viewing screens often appear dark anyway—but it quickly becomes apparent on the contact sheet.

Vignetting also occurs when a lens is used with a filter or lens shade that is too small for it *(right)*. The 28mm wide-angle lens on a 35mm camera, for example, "sees" everything in front of the camera included within an angle of about 75°. It needs a lens shade that flares outward sufficiently to avoid blocking any of this region. If the lens were fitted with a shade that is designed for a very long lens, which takes in a smaller angle of view, part of the image that the lens transmits would be blocked off.

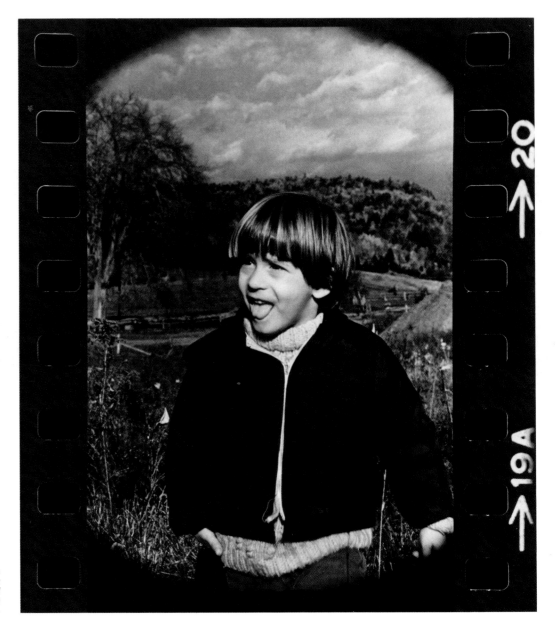

A picture without corners resulted when the photographer inadvertently fitted a long, narrow shade designed for a 105mm lens to his normal 55mm lens. The shade blocked out part of the image as effectively as blinders on a horse.

Dirty Lens, Smudged Picture

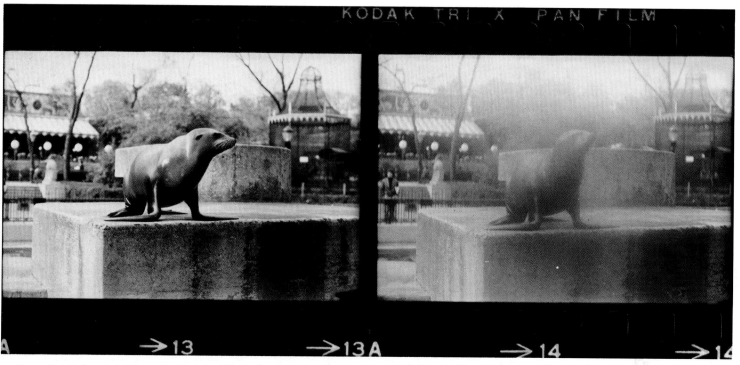

KODAK TRI X PAN FILM

→13   →13A   →14   →14

The print at the left clearly shows a seal basking in the sun at Central Park Zoo in New York: A fingerprint on the filter used during the taking of the next shot turned it and the seal into a meaningless blur. Although picture-ruining smears are easy to acquire and difficult to see, lenses and filters should be wiped off as seldom as possible, and then cautiously (they get scratched). Blow loose dust off before wiping. One of the best cleaning materials is nothing but a very old, freshly laundered handkerchief—the many washings in its past will have removed all lint that might otherwise stick to a lens.

Soot, grease marks, drops of moisture, lint from a handkerchief—all diffuse the light that passes through a lens or a filter, softening the focus of the image as it appears on a contact sheet. Sometimes photographers will deliberately cultivate this kind of softness for effect, by covering their lenses with a translucent cloth, a filter smeared with grease or a diffusion disk—a sheet of glass incised with tiny grooves. But most photographs require the clear, precise detail that results only from clean lenses and filters.

Attempts to clean the lens may cause more trouble than the dirt, however. Rubbing the lens with a rough cloth produces fine scratches that soften images as effectively as the lines of a diffusion disk.

Even when its front and back surfaces are clean, a lens may lose its sharpness because of internal dirt. In smoggy or humid climates, soot may filter into the interior through the focus- and aperture-adjustment rings. If internal dirt is suspected—the exterior surface is clean, and the lens and the focusing system are in order *(pages 106-109)*—a simple test should be made. Shine a pencil flashlight through the lens while examining it from the other side. If a layer of grayish scum can be seen on the interior surfaces, take the lens to a repair shop for cleaning.

Why a Shutter Obscures Part of a Frame

Nothing is more disappointing than to take only half a picture. Yet this is exactly what may happen when the focal-plane shutter of a camera does not act the way the photographer expects. In these sets of contact sheets, part of the image is lopped off because of shutter problems.

As the curtains that form the elements of most focal-plane shutters sweep from one side of the camera to the other, permitting light to enter through the space between them, they are rolled up on a rotating shaft, which must occasionally be readjusted by a repairman.

Sometimes the first curtain will bounce back slightly when it reaches the shaft, blocking light—a phenomenon known as first-curtain shutter bounce. This is what has happened in the top sequence, cutting off a small part of each picture.

At other times, a larger part of the picture may be lost because tension on the rotating shaft is too weak; the first curtain moves so slowly that the second curtain catches up with it before it has reached the far edge of the window. The opening closes prematurely, blocking light from an edge or a corner of the picture—as a contact-sheet inspection would reveal. This is the cause of the partial image on the contact strip on page 103.

The contact strip at the bottom, taken with an electronic flash, suggests that flash and shutter were out of synchronization or that the shutter speed was improperly set. Either fault *(test described on pages 114-115)* keeps the shutter curtains from opening fully to expose the entire frame during the flash—and either one causes loss of part of the picture.

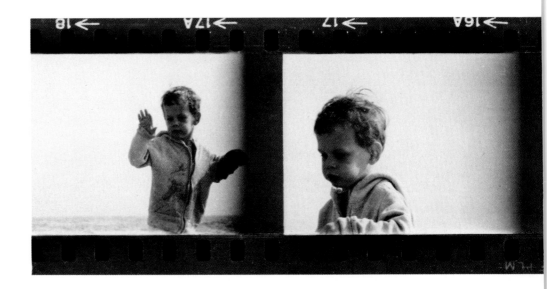

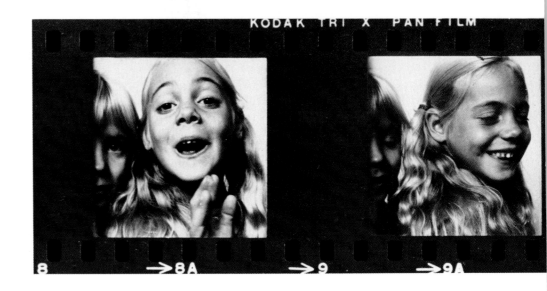

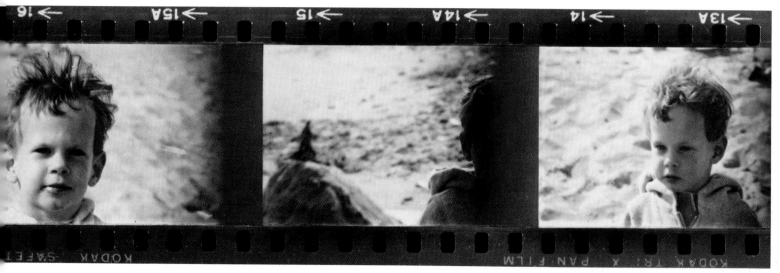

A focal-plane shutter that moved erratically blocked exposure along one edge of these portraits, taken at 1/125 second. Careful cropping could save four of the pictures.

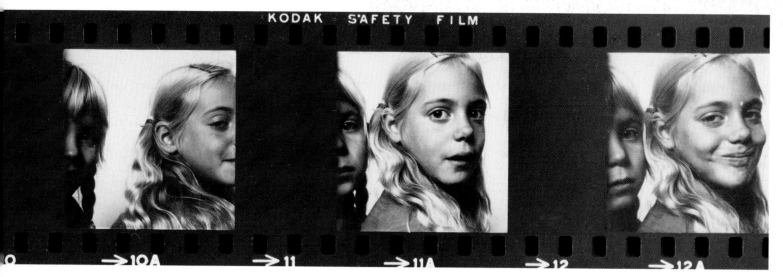

Partial exposures always result when focal-plane shutters are improperly synchronized with electronic flash. These pictures were taken at too fast a shutter speed.

Fogging—Pictures Spoiled by Light

Light makes a photograph but it can destroy one, too. If it leaks into the film compartment, it may fog or wash away the images on an entire roll, or ruin a considerable number of pictures on the roll. The top strip at right shows a candlelit scene at a New York nightclub, shot using a 35mm SLR with a slightly warped back. Light filtered through to bleach a scallop along the edge of the film. The fogged strip on the contact sheet reveals not only the existence of this light leakage but, by its location, suggests the source—the top of the camera back, since photographed images are always inverted within the camera.

The series at the bottom, taken to illustrate a book on rock musicians, shows an even more disastrous effect of light striking exposed film. The photographer, who was shooting during the rock session, became worried that film was not winding onto the take-up spool when he cocked the film-advance lever—a situation that would have caused double exposures *(pages 116-117)*. To be certain that he had a functioning camera for the rest of the session, he risked opening the back of the camera—and ruined a number of his pictures, as the contact sheet made abundantly and unhappily clear.

Many modern cameras now have indicators to show when film is advancing properly, but on most cameras, a glance at the rewind knob to see whether it turns as the film is advanced is enough to ensure that all is well.

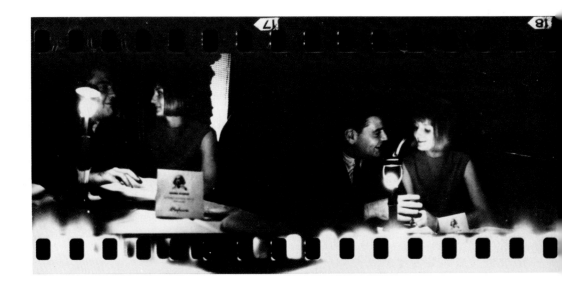

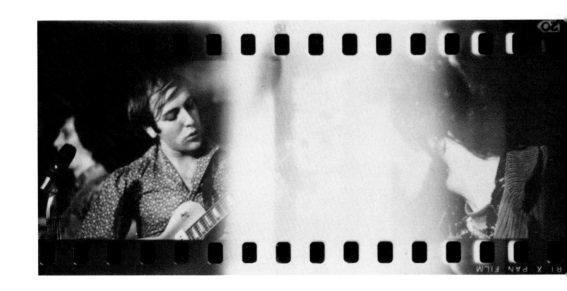

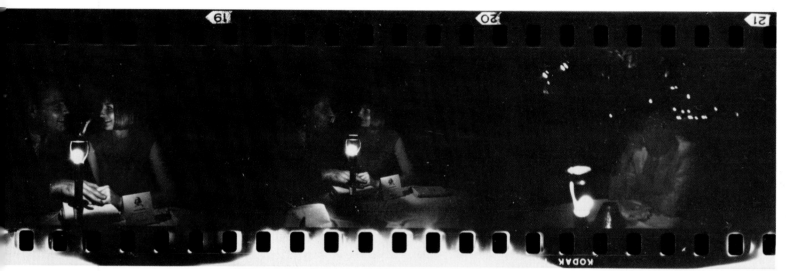

Even the dim illumination of a candlelit nightclub was sufficient to burn out the edges of a film sequence that had been photographed after the back of the camera sprang a light leak.

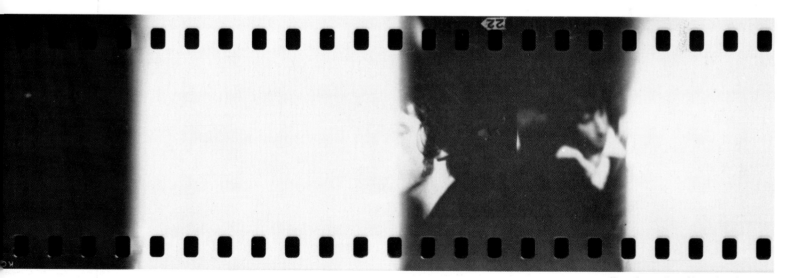

Alternating sections of burned-out film are the result of opening the back of a loaded camera. They occurred because the photographer checked to see if the film was jammed.

Disasters in the Darkroom

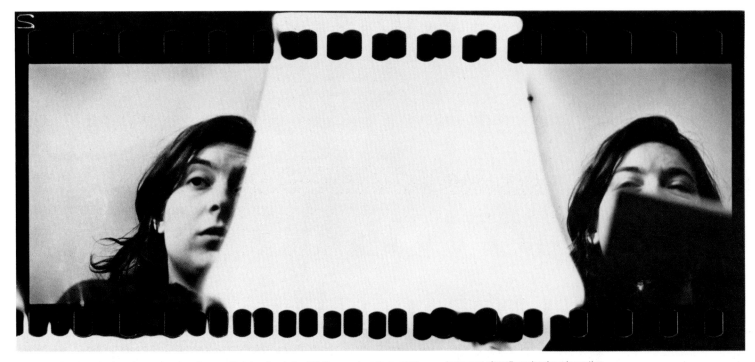

Mishaps in the darkroom can ruin pictures just as effectively as broken-down camera equipment. The whole process of developing and printing a picture demands the delicate, exacting care needed for preparing a soufflé. Chemicals must be fresh and properly mixed or negatives turn out underdeveloped or overdeveloped; temperatures must be correct to make the emulsion produce a properly developed image; timing must be precise to ensure the proper degree of development. Even a slip in loading film onto a reel for development or insufficient agitation can ruin a picture *(above and opposite)*.

Darkroom disasters always show up on finished prints. White spots are a common flaw. They may be caused by dust or lint on the negative, and darkrooms should be kept as free of dust as possible—even the walls should be wiped down regularly with a damp cloth. Dark splotches may result from air bubbles, which adhere to the surfaces of negatives when they are in the developer, thus preventing the chemicals from reaching the emulsion. Since air bubbles will form in developer when the film is being introduced, the tank should be tapped gently to eliminate them. Other defects, such as streaks and blank spots, can usually be traced to their sources with a little detective work.

A segment of totally undeveloped negative resulted when two parts of the film stuck together during the initial stage of development. The photographer's carelessness in winding the film onto the wire reel of his developing tank caused one loop of film to rest against the loop next to it, thus preventing the chemicals from reaching the emulsion at the area of contact.

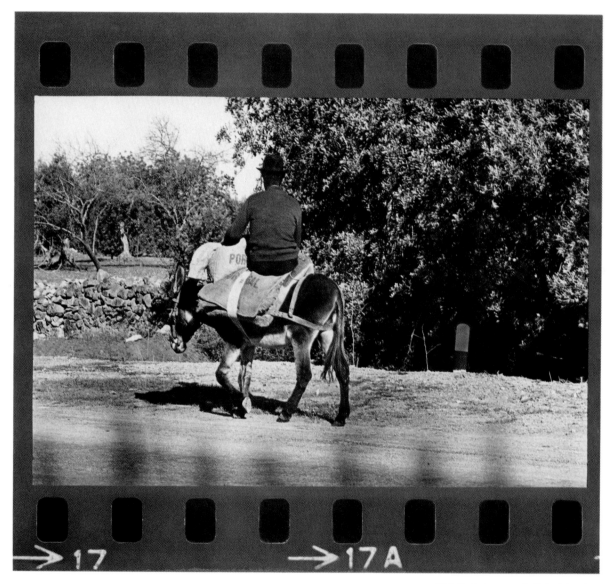

Dark streaks near sprocket holes (above) are caused by stale fixer and insufficient agitation of the developing tank. Enough fixer flowed through sprocket holes to halt development near the holes; but development continued on the rest of the negative.

125

Pitfalls of Color Processing

Errors in color processing can produce a much wider range of effects than similar mistakes in black-and-white processing because color film has three layers of image-forming dyes, each of which may be affected in its own way. Thus, improperly developed color negatives or slides may exhibit unnatural color shifts as well as defects of contrast and density that are common to badly processed black-and-white negatives.

Processing faults are easy to spot in slides, but with color negatives, which have an overall orange tint or mask, it is usually necessary to make contact prints before trying to identify problem sources. To distinguish errors in the negative from errors in the print, it is best to print a known standard negative on the same contact sheet as the new negatives. If the standard negative produces a satisfactory print, any faults visible in the other prints must lie in the negatives themselves—and may have been caused by incorrect processing.

Color processing is no longer the formidably intricate procedure it once was. Nevertheless, like black-and-white processing, it requires careful workmanship and rigorous adherence to manufacturers' specifications for such tasks as mixing chemicals, timing steps and controlling temperature.

Temperature control is vitally important for many processing chemicals. Unless costly thermostatically controlled equipment is used, the temperature of the developing solutions and some of the other chemicals must be monitored throughout development to ensure that the temperature of the darkroom does not cause the solution temperature to drift beyond the range specified by the manufacturers. If the solution temperature should move out of the prescribed range, it may not only affect the rate of development, but also may cause differing reactions in the three color layers and an overall color shift.

Contamination can be another source of problems. Chemicals should be mixed and added in the proper sequence. If powders are to be dissolved, the spread of dust should be minimized—emulsions often exhibit spots where tiny chemical crystals have settled and later reacted, leaving a colored speck. All equipment should be thoroughly rinsed and then air-dried or wiped with a clean cloth. Containers, particularly, should be dry before they are reloaded with film or paper; wet spots on the emulsion develop faster than dry areas and can appear as blotches in the final image.

Blotches may also result from sloppy handling. Some emulsions are sensitive to oils or chemicals on fingertips. The upper color layers are most susceptible. Cloth gloves help, but it is best to avoid touching the emulsion altogether.

The pictures opposite demonstrate the consequences of some common errors made in developing negatives with Kodak's C-41 processing chemicals. The images appear as they would on a contact sheet printed in exactly the same way as the correctly processed reference image *(right)*. In addition to the examples shown, troubleshooting charts issued by manufacturers are useful guides to sources of darkroom problems, since each color system has its own characteristic response to processing errors.

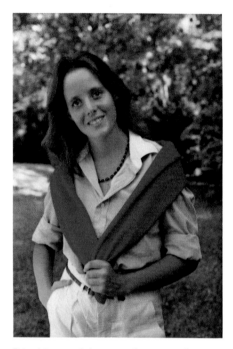

This print was made from a negative processed correctly in Kodak's C-41 chemicals. Outdoor portraits like this one, taken in even, shaded light, can be useful reference pictures for troubleshooting. When making such a reference image, have the film processed by a reliable laboratory. The negative can then serve as a standard for other negatives processed at home. Comparing this print to the ones on the opposite page—made from improperly processed negatives—will show the effects of various processing errors.

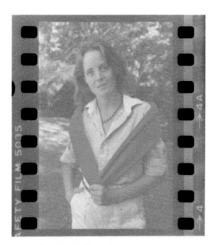

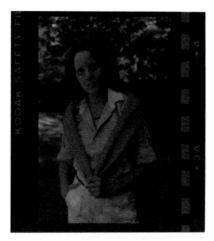

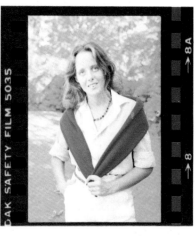

Fogging the film — inadvertently exposing it to light — produced this washed-out image. The negative was dark everywhere, and the print is correspondingly light. Even the edges, which should be dark, show the effects of exposure. Contrast is low because fogging most affects areas that received the least initial exposure. Thus fogging evens out exposure and reduces contrast.

Poor temperature control accounts for the darkness seen here. The temperature of the developer fell too low, slowing development and producing a thin, underdeveloped negative that yielded this murky print. If the film had been underexposed in the camera, only the image would have been affected, but here the edge markings are dark as well, indicating a processing error.

Careless timing produced this pale picture. The film was left in the developer too long; as a result, the negative became too dense and this print correspondingly light. The picture could be printed darker, but the increase in contrast caused by the overdevelopment would still leave the highlight areas washed out. Moreover, the color shift noticeable in the hair might not be correctable.

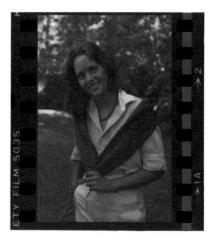

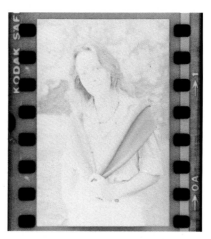

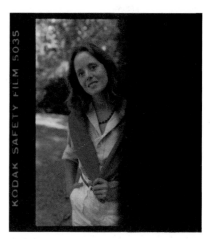

The milky bluish quality in this print results from fixer contaminating the developing solution. A few milliliters of fixer began to dissolve unexposed silver crystals in the top — yellow — dye layer of the negative, and thus to render them developable. Since the affected crystals were spread over the negative, development created a screen of yellow dye, which caused the fog.

This print is very light and has little color because the dense negative that produced it still contained silver. A correctly processed color negative has an image formed only of dye; the silver that helps create the image is bleached away in processing. Here, the bleach step was accidentally omitted. The negative could be salvaged, however, by bleaching and fixing it again.

This partial image resembles one made with an improperly synchronized flash (pages 114-115) — but flash was not used. The flaw is a consequence of using too little developer in the developing tank; the film was not completely covered. Trying to get away with less than the prescribed quantity of an expensive processing chemical usually proves to be a false economy.

127

Tracing Lines of Static

Professional photographers usually take pride in their talent for creating startling effects. But the bolt of lightning that appears to be striking the policeman on the sidelines *(right)* was a completely unpremeditated stroke—the chance effect of static electricity streaking across the film emulsion in the camera.

The picture was taken at Yankee Stadium in New York during a game between the Giants and the Pittsburgh Steelers, on just the kind of crackling-cold, dry December day that causes sparks to jump between fingers and metal door handles —and, sometimes, from camera to film. The camera was a motorized SLR that sped the film along at the rate of three frames per second, fast enough under cold, dry conditions to generate a sufficient charge for a spark.

Static electricity can sometimes blight film in a darkroom. Pulling undeveloped film away from its paper backing too rapidly can result in clusters of star-shaped static marks. Rubbing a hand along a strip of undeveloped film on a dry day may generate enough static to produce a row of black dots on the negative. It can sometimes be prevented from occurring in the camera simply by wiping the pressure plate with a solution of household detergent and water, and allowing the plate to dry before loading the film. □

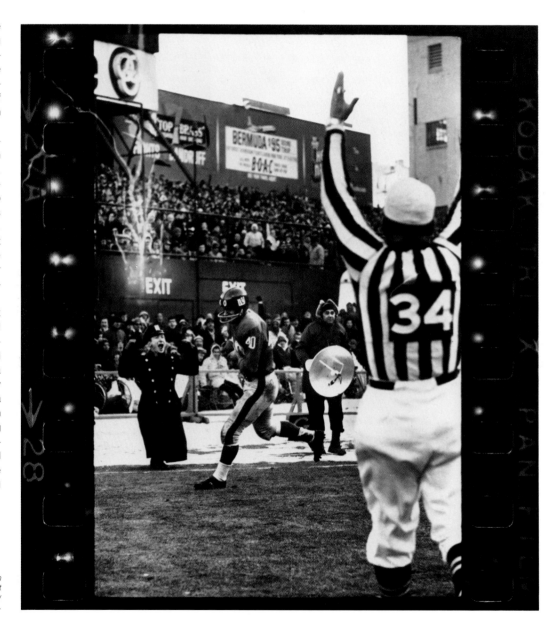

Catching the excitement of a Giants touchdown play, this shot registers dramatic currents that were not really there—a lightning flash caused by static electricity inside the camera.

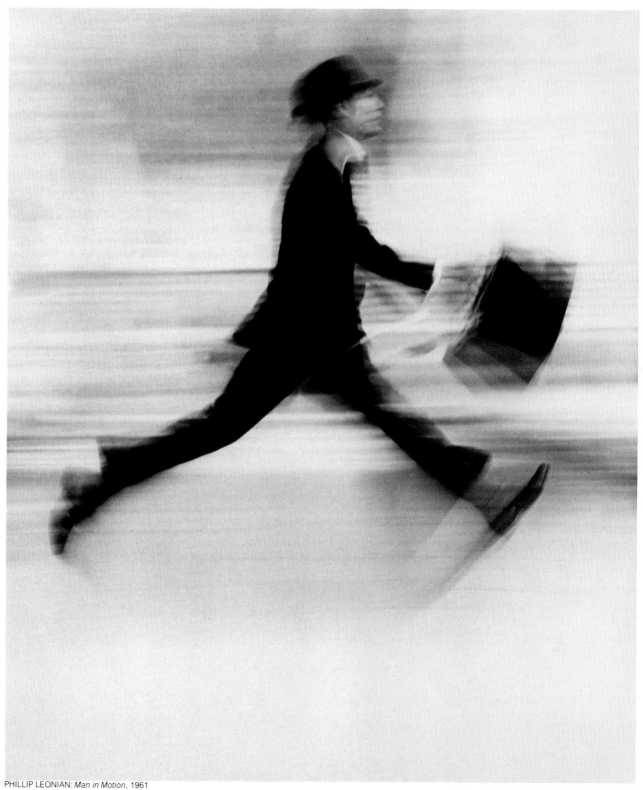

PHILLIP LEONIAN: *Man in Motion*, 1961

Making a Still Picture Show Movement

The businessman hurries along a busy New York City street, his stride wide, his briefcase swinging, his hat somehow remaining firmly on his head *(preceding page)*. His gait tells us that he is in a rush. But to add to the sense of action, the photographer has allowed portions of the body to blur. Through this simple effect, a routine study of a walking man suddenly becomes an ingenious demonstration of motion portrayed on film.

All around are similar opportunities for making ordinary subject matter into extraordinary pictures by the simple expedient of conveying action. Few things in the real world stand still. Trees sway, children run and wrestle on the lawn, friends talk and gesticulate, traffic rushes by. Some situations are packed with action. Not just sports, although these provide great pictures for photographers—amateur as well as professional—who know how to get the shots that re-create a game's excitement. Though all kinds of events that are part of everyday life are photographed endlessly, too often they are photographed poorly because the action that animates them is missed. The tumult of a child's birthday party, a trip to an amusement park, a dance in the recreation room, a family picnic, a cocktail party—all are picturemaking opportunities that call for special skill in conveying action if the pictures are to be more than routine.

One reason so many photographers fail to make the most of their opportunities to convey action is a mistaken belief that any kind of motion is the enemy of good photography. This prejudice is a hangover from the old days of slow film's bulky cameras and inadequate shutters. It seemed then that every other shot was marred by the blurred outlines of a squirming child or the suddenly turned head that fuzzed a smiling face. "Hold still," was the universal command from behind the camera. Such restriction is no longer necessary, because modern equipment does not demand rigid posing. The photographer who recognizes that fact and begins to seek and emphasize motion in his subjects will find a new dimension added to his picturemaking —but he will also find he has taken on a host of new problems. While they are varied, they all relate to one basic question: How can movement be shown in a photograph that does not move?

The answer to that question is simple and seemingly discouraging: It cannot be. No way has ever been found to record motion exactly the way the eye and brain perceive it. Even the pictures of movies and television do not move; they only seem to because of an optical illusion. The physical impossibility of recording motion has intrigued artists for many thousands of years, and they have worked out methods for conveying the idea of motion, if not the actual motion itself, in images—drawn, sculpted or photographed—that do not move. There are only three basic techniques:

1 Freezing the action, with every detail clear and sharp, suggests that the

eye has caught a quick glimpse of an object, isolating one instant from a continuous flow of movement.

2 A sequence of separate pictures conveys the pattern of movement, showing not one part of it but several parts as the motion progresses from beginning to end.

3 Blurring, which appeared rather late in the history of art, conveys an impression of speed because the eye, too, sees rapidly moving objects—such as a spinning airplane propeller—as a blur.

A most dramatic way of portraying action in photographs is by freezing motion. This technique produces the most familiar of the action shots—the runner breasting the tape at the finish line, the woodchopper in mid-swing, the party jokester with his head thrown back, laughing at his own story. The faces are easily recognizable, the pictures are unmarked by blurs, and such movements as arm-waving are caught in mid-motion but are nevertheless sharp. This fidelity to detail contains one drawback—it somehow lessens the realism of the picture. The human eye cannot pick up such detail from figures in motion. The camera sees better than the eye, its super-reality adding an air of unreality. But because stop-action photographs pick out detail the eye would miss, they can often be stunning in their visual impact, presenting an entirely new perspective on the world.

It is easy enough to make stop-action pictures when a high-speed electronic flash unit or a fast shutter speed can be used. The burst from a typical flash unit lasts no more than 1/1000 second, and sometimes much less—easily short enough to freeze the most energetic child jumping on his bed. And most 35mm cameras also provide shutter speeds of 1/1000 second, fast enough under certain circumstances to stop a 60-mile-an-hour car. But when such brief exposures are impractical, and they often are for one reason or another, action can still be frozen by a number of different techniques.

One of the most useful ways of stopping motion is to catch the action at its peak. Then it seems to be in motion but is actually stationary, and it can be frozen with even the simplest equipment. A child at the high point on a swing or seesaw is at the peak of his action; he has moved as far as he can go in one direction and comes to a momentary halt before beginning to move again in the opposite direction. Peak action is part of any rhythmic movement—a dancer at the top of his leap, a golfer at the beginning of his stroke, a boy at the highest point of his jump over a fence. Shooting at that instant not only seems to freeze the action but also produces exciting pictures because it captures a high point, the precise moment when energy is about to be released as the motion reverses its pattern. The face of a child perched on a swing just before the downward arc begins is alight with eager anticipation. The diver and the pole vaulter at the top of their upward thrusts reveal in their expressions and body control the utter intensity of their efforts.

To achieve good peak-action pictures, the photographer must train himself to anticipate the elusive moment when motion comes to its fleeting halt. The open shutter and the peak action must coincide exactly. A shutter button pushed slightly too early or too late produces unwanted blurring. With practice, the photographer learns to press the button slightly before the peak action. This allows for the split second it takes for the brain to send the message to the finger and the added fraction of a second for the camera's mechanism to open the shutter.

There is no peak to catch, however, in many kinds of action — a running boy, for instance, or a speeding car. Yet such continuous motion can also be frozen with slow exposures and simple equipment. One technique that works depends on the angle of the camera and the relative distance from the subject.

The greater the distance between the lens and subject, the less the shutter speed demanded to stop action. This is because the farther the moving subject is from the camera, the smaller its image on the film and the less the image can move as the subject moves. From 25 feet, for example, the picture of a running child would be blurred if shot at a shutter speed of 1/125 second. But this same picture taken at the same speed from 50 feet away will show an unblurred child. Thus, doubling the shooting distance greatly increases the capacity of the camera to freeze action.

As important as distance from the subject is the angle from which the picture is being taken. At 25 feet, a car speeding at 60 miles per hour straight across the camera's view can be stopped only with a shutter speed of 1/1000 second or faster. A slower shutter would produce only a long blur. Yet the speeding car, if photographed from head on, could be captured sharp and clear with a shutter speed of only 1/250 second. When the car streaks across the camera's field, the image shifts from one side of the scene to the other, creating the extreme blur of motion. From head on, or an angle up to about 45°, the car's image does not really move very much. Its motion is principally its fairly slight increase in size as it approaches. (Head-on shots, even of a car, are perfectly feasible and safe if made from a vantage point on a turn.)

When distance or angle cannot reduce image movement enough to stop fast action, turning the camera — panning — will do so. If the subject is kept continuously centered in the viewfinder by careful panning, its image will always stay in the same spot on the film and there will be no blurring. Panning is a fairly simple technique that becomes almost automatic if it is practiced regularly. The feet should be planted firmly on the ground to avoid jerking the camera, and the entire upper half of the photographer's torso should move from one side to the other, not the camera alone. The entire motion should have a flowing grace that keeps the subject exactly centered.

Panning produces pictures in which the subject appears sharp while the background is blurred; the subject is recognizable and the blur helps reinforce the illusion of motion. When used to freeze a running boy in the midst of his sprint, for example, the drama of stopped motion is retained while the blurred backdrop makes obvious the fact that the boy is actually running.

While a stop-action picture freezes a moment for the photographer, a series of such pictures can provide the history of an event. Sequence photographs, taken in rapid succession, can be made with almost any camera, even fairly simple ones, but they are easier to manage if the film-advance and shutter-cocking operations are combined in one device. Most modern camera designs include this feature; they can be operated manually in rapid sequence, since only two steps are necessary: pressing the shutter release, then advancing the film and recocking the shutter with a single swing of a lever. Better yet are battery-operated motor drives that automatically advance the film, cock the shutter and then release it in quick succession. The simplest of these motor drives, called autowinders, are built into some cameras and are available for many others as an accessory costing no more than most lenses. They can take up to two pictures per second. Professional motor drives, which are usually employed in conjunction with a special camera back holding rolls of film yielding 250 exposures, can cost as much as the camera itself but can be set to take as many as six frames a second.

Making a series of pictures works particularly well for photographs of children. A boy running across the lawn with the family dog, an incident that may cover only a few seconds, becomes a study of youthful exuberance. Children's portraits are easier to make this way, too, for the sitter can be permitted to move about as much as he wants while the camera clicks away. And few pictures of youngsters are more charming than a series that begins just as a two-year-old tentatively digs a spoon into some cake and ends when his face is smeared with chocolate.

While stop-action and sequence pictures halt action for closer inspection, their very clarity may belie the sense of motion. To simulate a feeling of action, many photographers deliberately blur pictures by using relatively slow shutter speeds. The shot of the busy businessman *(page 131)* is an example of a deliberate blur. It was made with a 2¼ x 2¼-inch SLR at ½ second while the camera was panned. The panning kept some of the figure sharp while the slow shutter speed gave partial blurring. The picture of the racing car on pages 152-153 is a similar example of deliberate blur. Only the lower portion of the driver's face is relatively sharp. The rest is blurred. Yet the images of both the car and driver are clearly distinguishable even though not graphically delineated, and a sense of hurtling speed is conveyed.

Deliberate blurring lends animation and excitement to any action picture. A bird coming in to land on a feeding tray can be stopped sharp with a shutter speed of 1/250 second—except for the wings, which will blur. When taking photographs of guests at a cocktail party or a wedding reception, the photographer might want to show the faces clearly but blur waving arms and hands to convey the liveliness of the affair. A combination of frozen and blurred action can be achieved by slowing shutter speed and anticipating the moment when guests are most active. For the best pictures, rehearsals may be necessary: The face of the hostess passing canapés, for example, should be recognizable, yet the arms and canapé tray might be blurred to show motion, and several tries may be needed to keep her head still while the tray moves.

Nowhere can a photographer find a better stage for action pictures than the playing fields of organized sport. The action is fast, colorful and played out close at hand, within full view. Few amateurs take advantage of this opportunity, although sports expert Neil Leifer maintained that they could rival the professional photographers. To begin with, the amateurs have more freedom to experiment, he pointed out, simply because they are unencumbered by assignments. This freedom enables them to shoot at will without the pressure of satisfying a picture editor or a client.

One amateur who became a weekend sports photographer is Robert Smith, an art director for a New York advertising agency. A lifelong camera buff, Smith began taking pictures of sports events at the high school near his home when his daughter, Wendy, became a cheerleader. He soon became intrigued with the potential of this special brand of action photography and began attending every football game the school played. The first problem was getting onto the field, where he could shoot without interference from spectators. The solution was easy. He had already taken a number of good pictures of the team from the front row of spectators; he made enlargements of these photographs and left them at the coach's office. When Smith stopped by the athletic department the next week to promise more prints of future games, he found waiting for him warm thanks and a season pass admitting him to the sidelines.

For an amateur, Smith's photographic equipment was elaborate. He used a 35mm SLR with a zoom lens that goes from 80 to 200mm, which served about 80 per cent of the time at the games. Its wide range of focal length permitted full-figure shots of the players no matter where they were on the field. A second SLR was outfitted with a 300mm lens that he used for long pass plays and kick returns. On sunny days he kept both cameras loaded with ISO 400/27° film and set at 1/500 second and f/16. He was in search of clear, unblurred pictures, primarily so that the boys on the team could easily recognize themselves, or at least spot their numbers. For this reason he never blurred deliberately.

Good sports-action pictures require a feel for the game. Smith learned enough about football—and saw enough games—to sense where the action was going to be. He roamed along the edges of the field and behind the end zone, going where he expected the next flurry of activity to take place. When he sensed a pass on a third down with eight yards to go, he stationed himself about 20 or 30 yards from the line of scrimmage, hoping the pass would come his way. If it did, he usually kneeled for his shot, for two reasons—to set the players against the uncluttered background of the sky, and to keep spectators behind him from screaming at him to sit down.

Like many photographers, Smith sometimes prefocused his camera. With shutter speed and aperture preset at his preferred 1/500 and f/16, he focused on a point where he thought the action would be—the goal line, for example—and then shot when the runner crossed the line. (Similarly, a photographer shooting a horse race might, before the start, focus on the starting gate, on the first turn and on the finish line, marking each of the focus points with a grease pencil on his lens-focusing ring.) Smith did not hesitate to use all of his film. Three or four good pictures from one roll of film is considered a respectable average in action photography.

The differences between what professional photographers want from a sports event and a skilled amateur like Smith are not that great. Primarily, the professionals are always searching for the different shot, the unusual angle, the fresh approach. Walter Iooss Jr., a *Sports Illustrated* photographer, likes the challenge of sports photography "because it's all been done before." Therefore, the photographer's job is to restate what has been done before with insight and imagination. To do so, Iooss relies heavily on telephoto lenses, either a 400mm or an even longer 600mm, which he uses with a motorized 35mm SLR. To hold these heavy lenses steady—essential because their long focal length exaggerates blur from camera movement—Iooss employs a unipod, a support that has only one leg. Iooss likes the mobility the unipod gives him, enabling him to swing his long lenses around the field so that he can train them quickly on the ever-shifting scenes of action. With his long lenses, Iooss can focus on one player, even on his facial expression, isolating him, or his small zone of action, from the playing field and the throngs of fans in the multi-tiered stadiums. So doing, Iooss—like many another professional and amateur today armed with knowledge, imagination and modern equipment—brings forth the many faces of action.   □

Sports Photography: A Game without Rules

Motorists on a New York parkway one fall day in 1969 were dismayed to spot what looked like a radar speed-trap apparatus; drivers quickly throttled back to the speed limit: 60 mph. That was fine with the man using the equipment, photographer Neil Leifer, for his rig was not radar but a special action camera, and to prepare it to photograph a downhill ski race for *Sports Illustrated* that winter he needed a steady supply of 60 mph subjects.

Leifer was trying to adjust the movement of film running past a slit inside the camera so that the film's motion exactly matched that of a car moving at the same speed, recording it clearly and sharply; then he knew he could get a similarly clear photograph of a similarly speeding skier *(page 150)* — whose downhill velocity also reached 60 mph, as he had discovered by checking with the ski coach.

Elaborate preparations merely for one picture? Perhaps. But the photographer must know both the game and his equipment to capture the action of sport. No all-purpose rules work.

Unusual pictures are made with gear like Leifer's, which makes a sharp photograph of a moving object while blurring the background. But the basic camera-lens combinations many amateurs use every day can also convey the essence of a sport, by freezing movement at a critical moment *(right),* catching action at its peak or by introducing deliberate blur with panning. And some of the most memorable sports photographs are ones that convert moments of fierce action into displays of beauty *(page 144)* or are taken after the action is over *(page 160).*

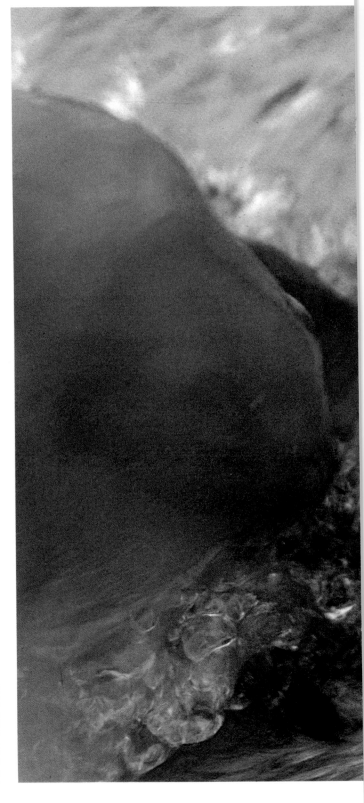

A close-up of Olympic swimmer Mark Spitz during a training sprint reveals the concentration of effort that was eventually to win him seven gold medals. Co Rentmeester used a 180mm telephoto lens from poolside to zero in on the swimmer's face but included enough of the surroundings to suggest the event. He chose a shutter speed of 1/125 second, which was fast enough to freeze the expression on Spitz's face but slow enough to let his arm and the churning water around him blur, suggesting his strong forward surge.

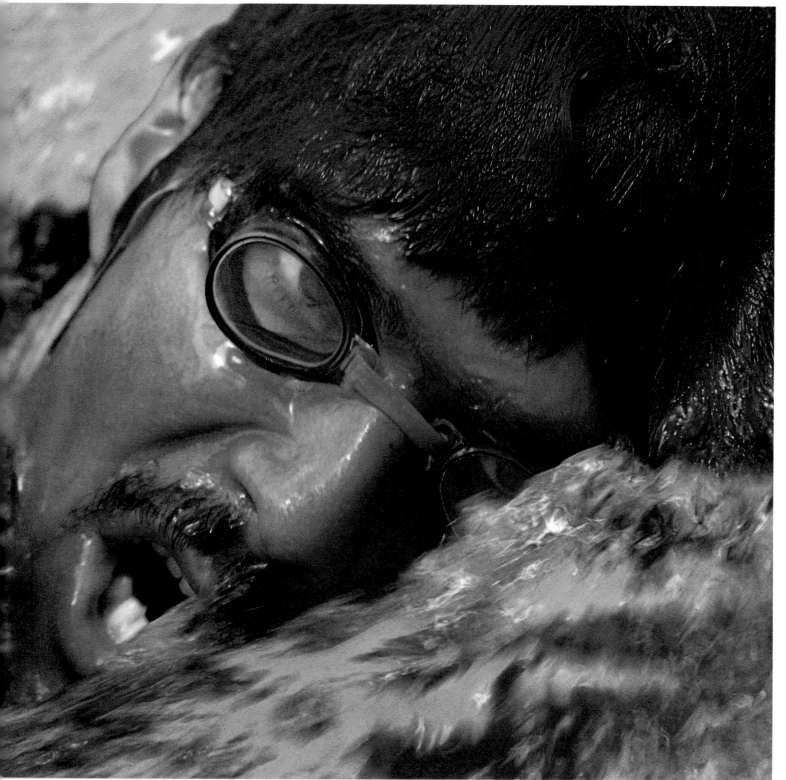

CO RENTMEESTER: *Mark Spitz in Training, Santa Clara, California,* 1972

The Critical Instant

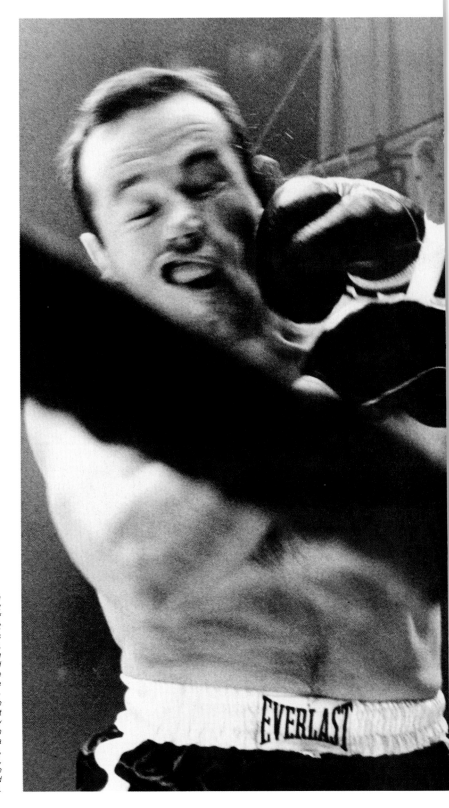

All the raw force of boxing is concentrated in this one slice of action: the precise instant that Ingemar Johansson's face was crushed out of shape by Floyd Patterson's right in a heavyweigt title match. Everything in the picture emphasizes the impact of the blow. Like converging arrows, Patterson's extended arm and a string of glaring ring lights point to Johansson's distorted expression, which is counterbalanced by the fierce determination of Patterson's own face. The photograph is the crucial one in a sequence — the others were discarded — made from ringside with a custom-made, motor-driven camera that shoots one picture after another automatically at any rate between 5 and 20 frames per second. With the ring lights providing the only illumination and a fairly slow shutter setting (1/150 second), Johansson's recoiling face is slightly blurred, intensifying the sensation of violent action. The powerhouse blows were more than Johansson could take; he was knocked out in the sixth round.

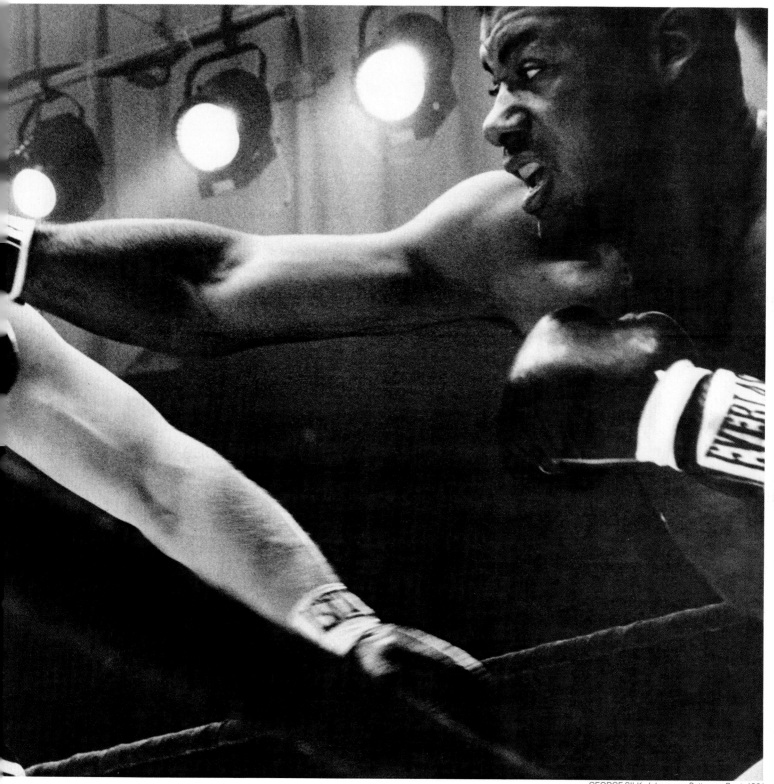

GEORGE SILK: *Johansson-Patterson Bout,* 1961

Anticipating Drama

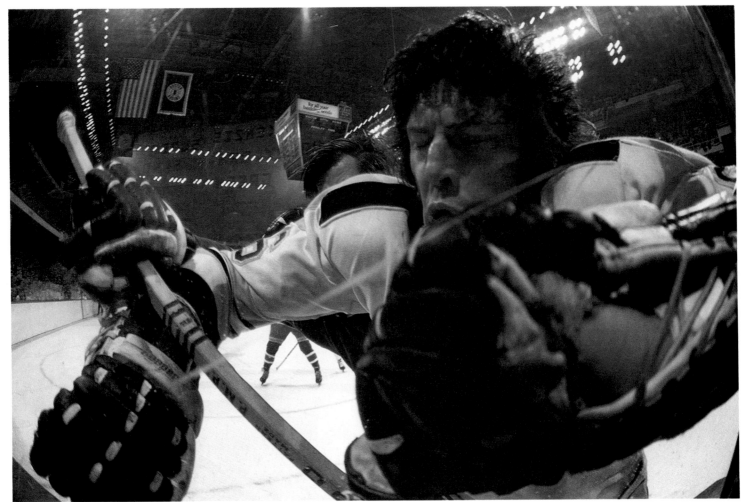

NEIL LEIFER: *Hockey at Boston Garden, 1972*

To get this extraordinary closeup of a Boston Bruins hockey player pinned against the boards by an opponent, the photographer took up a position just behind the plastic barrier that protects the spectators. He waited patiently until the two players chased the puck up against the barrier directly in front of him. Then with the pair struggling only 12 inches from his camera, he shot using an ultra-wide-angle 17mm lens, which not only exaggerated dramatically the size of their gloves but yielded enough depth of field to give a view of the arena behind them.

This spectacular spill on an English race course ▶ was captured because the photographer selected his vantage point carefully beforehand. After examining the cross-country course, he positioned himself at a particularly treacherous water obstacle because its slippery approach "meant that if the rider got into trouble, the chances were that an interesting picture would result." Using an 85mm lens on a 35mm SLR equipped with a motor drive, he fired six frames as the plunge occurred, getting this shot on the third. The woman rider suffered a broken leg; the horse was unhurt.

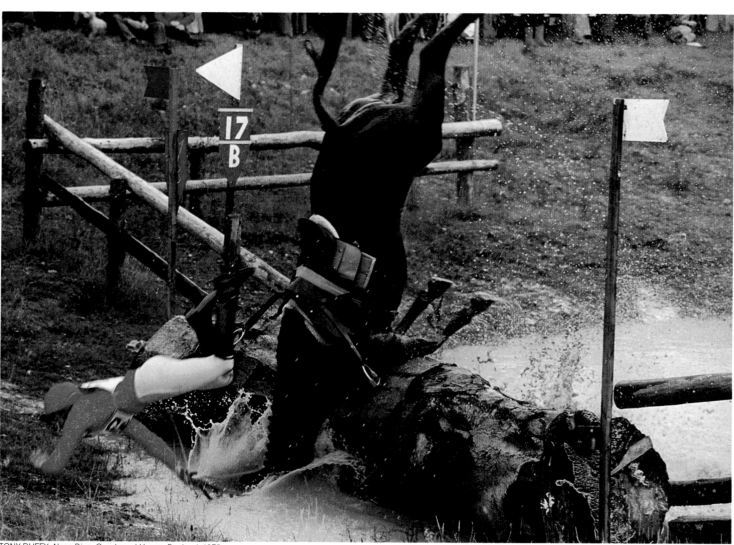

TONY DUFFY: *Nose Dive, Goodwood House, England,* 1975

Preserving Moments of Beauty and Grace

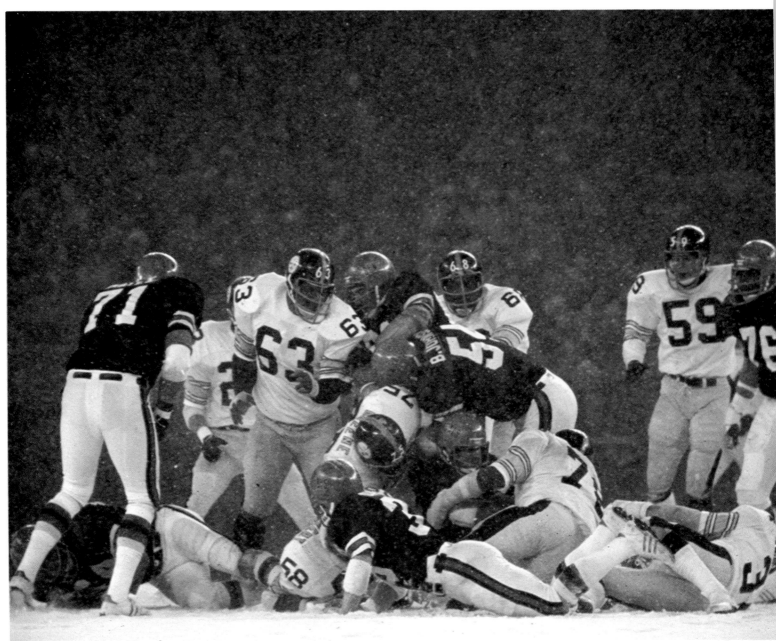

WALTER IOOSS JR.: *Pittsburgh Steelers vs. Cincinnati Bengals, Cincinnati,* 1976

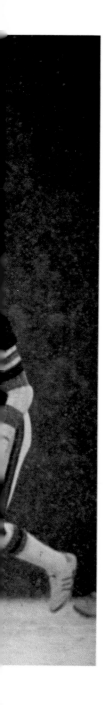

This beautifully composed, action-filled picture
was made after the play was over. On the
snow-covered field, huge linemen appear to be
battling their way through the snowflakes. To include
the field, players and spectators in one shot,
the photographer used a 300mm lens; he stopped
movement with a 1/500-second shutter speed.

Combining power and grace, Jodi Anderson
soars through a winning long jump at the 1980
Olympic trials. The photographer left the end of
the pit where others were shooting the event head-
on, and selected a site at a slight angle to the
direction of the jump, enabling him to isolate the
jumper against a neutral background. He
used the widest aperture, f/3.5, on his 400mm
telephoto lens to blur the background, making
the sharply focused jumper stand out dramatically.

ANDY HAYT: *Long Jumper Jodi Anderson, Eugene, Oregon,* 1980

A Race Frozen by Flash

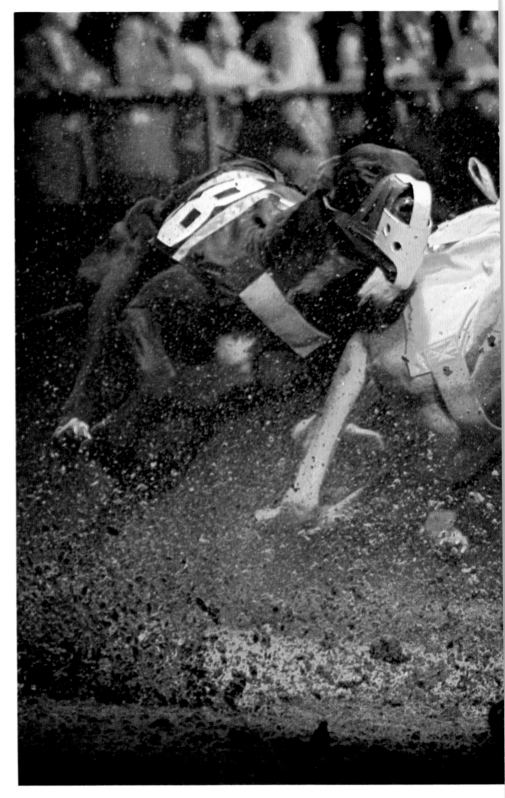

To dramatize the dirt-scattering frenzy of
greyhounds racing in Arizona, the photographer set
up a bank of strobes over the track and shot the
hurtling dogs from ground level. The strobes —
flashed just after the front runner had passed under
the bank — momentarily froze the dogs in frantic
mid-air pursuit of the decoy rabbit.

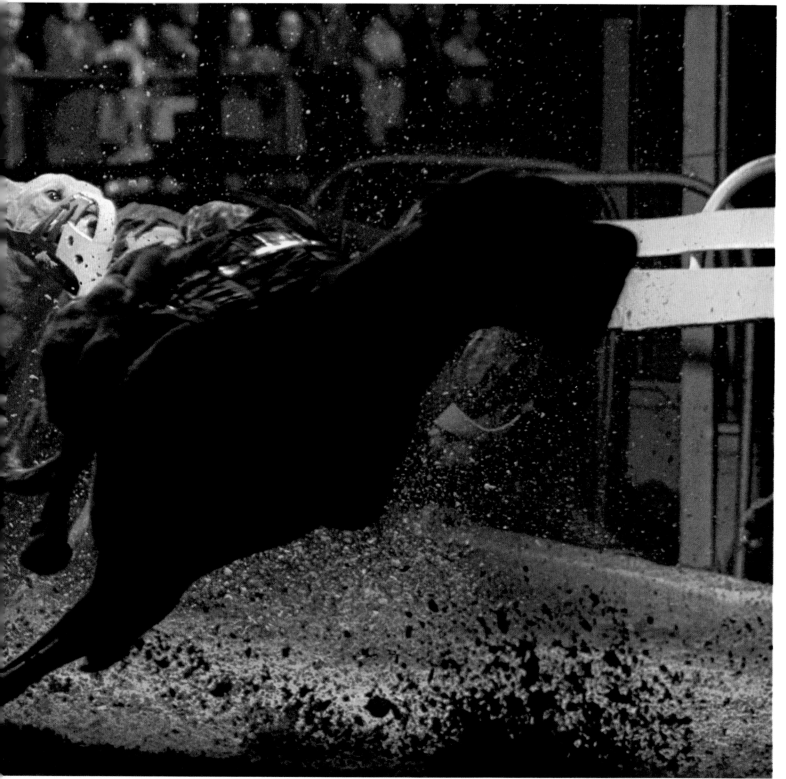

JOHN ZIMMERMAN: *Greyhound Race, Arizona,* 1962

Emphasizing Speed with Distortion

United States trackmen taking a hurdle during tryouts for the 1960 Olympics appear to be racing even faster than they are because their figures are so weirdly elongated. They were made to look that way on purpose by an adjustment of a motorized slit camera. Instead of setting the speed of its moving film strip to compensate for that of the action and thus freeze it totally, as is usually done, the photographer ran the film slightly faster, stretching the runners' images on the film as it moved past the slit. A 200mm telephoto lens, used from a relatively short distance, created additional purposeful distortion; its flattening effect so compressed the runners that they seem to interlock in one hurtling mass.

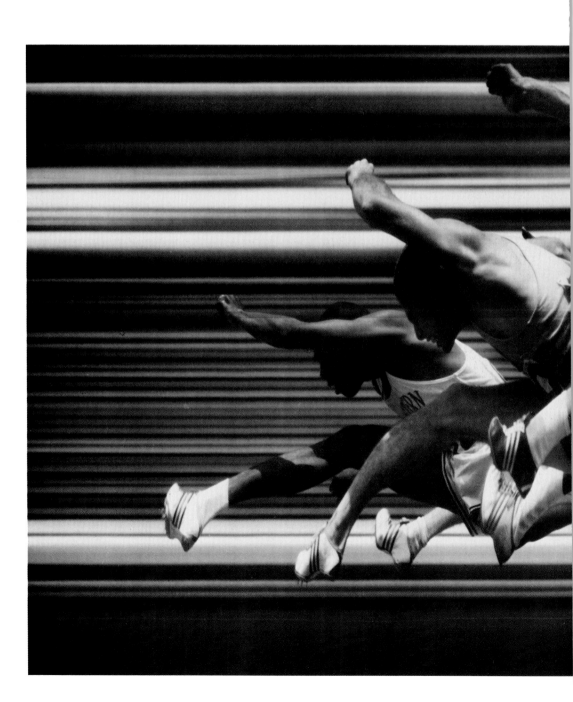

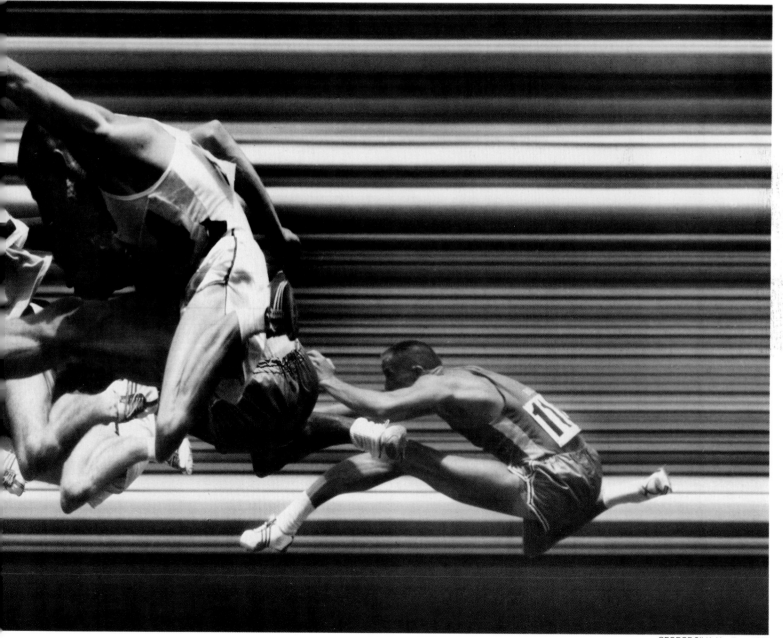

GEORGE SILK: *Hurdlers*, 1960
149

Showing Motion with Background Blur

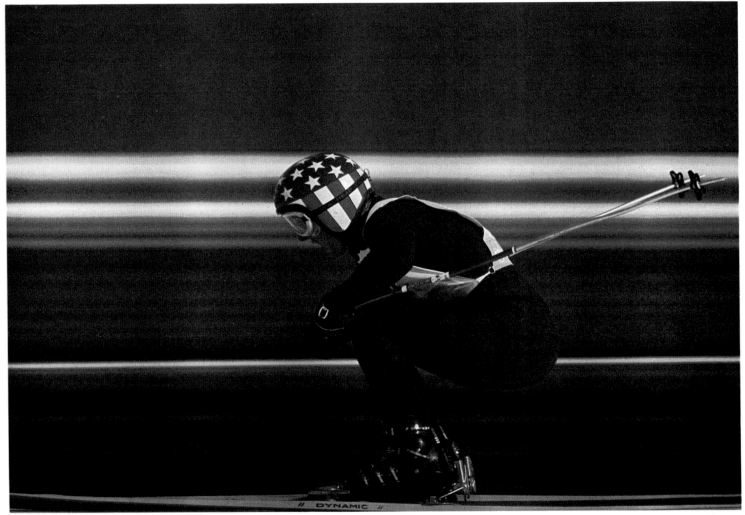

NEIL LEIFER: *Billy Kidd at Val Gardena*, 1970

*A 35mm SLR equipped with a .004-inch slit
shutter and a motor-driven film strip was the solution
to the problem of halting racer Billy Kidd on an
Italian slope. There was time to shoot only two
pictures, one of which is shown above, but it
was enough to produce a startling impression of
speed as the moving film sharply registered Kidd
against the background blur.*

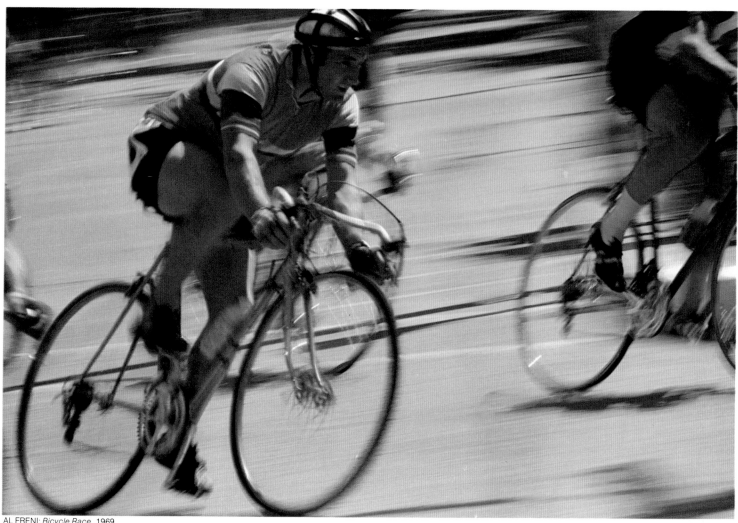

AL FRENI: *Bicycle Race,* 1969

Panning on the orange-shirted bicycle racer (left), the photographer neatly isolated him from most of the other contenders, a blur behind his sharp figure. He was tracked in the viewfinder until he reached a spot upon which the camera had been focused in advance; at that moment, the shutter was released. A slow setting, 1/60 second, made the whirling spokes a silvery blur.

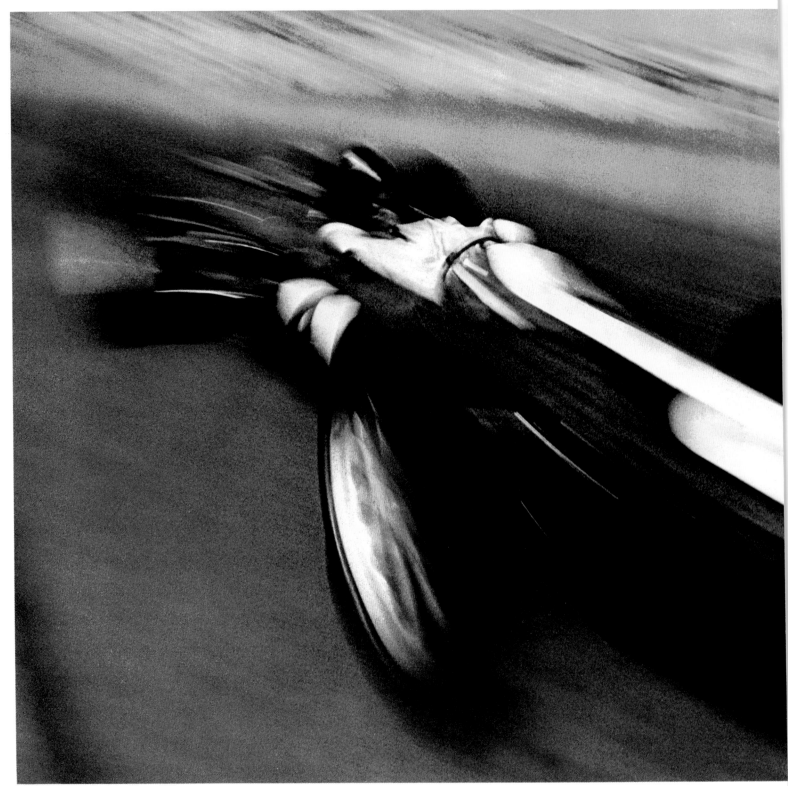

HORST BAUMANN: *The Lotus Winner*, 1963
152

Only three feet separated the camera from Jim Clark's Lotus as it sped to victory in Britain's Grand Prix. At 100 mph, the car produced the blurred image that was sought, suggesting the excitement and pace of the sport. The camera was panned with Clark's head, making it slightly sharper than the car hurtling past the blurred background of the track. To heighten the impression of speed a wide-angle lens exaggerated foreground objects and elongated the hood so that the entire car seems to lunge forward.

Suiting the Angle to the Sport

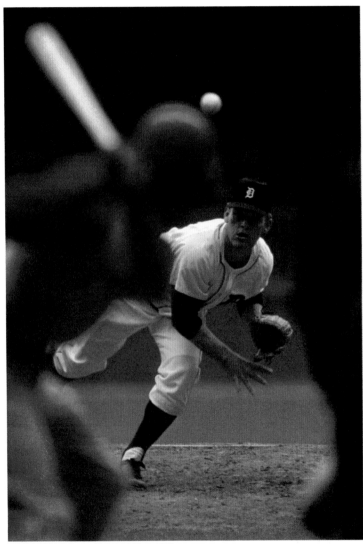

JAMES DRAKE: *Denny McLain at Work, 1968*

Denny McLain's ball is stopped in mid-air in this Detroit Tigers-Cleveland Indians game. A long 600mm lens projected the viewer from far behind the batter and plate umpire (at right) directly into the action. The blurred figures frame McLain and direct the eye to the ball.

After sunrise, George Silk took up a 3 a.m. dare and had himself hoisted in a boatswain's chair to the top of the aluminum mast of the 12-meter Nefertiti to capture this bird's-eye view. He used a wide-angle lens on his 35mm rangefinder camera, pointing it down at arm's length to get the ballooning spinnaker into the picture.

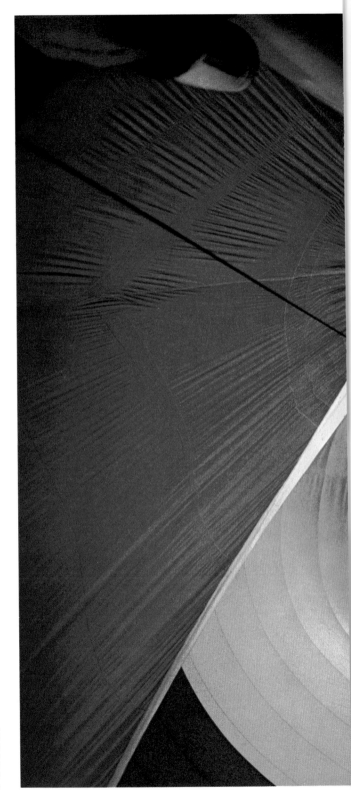

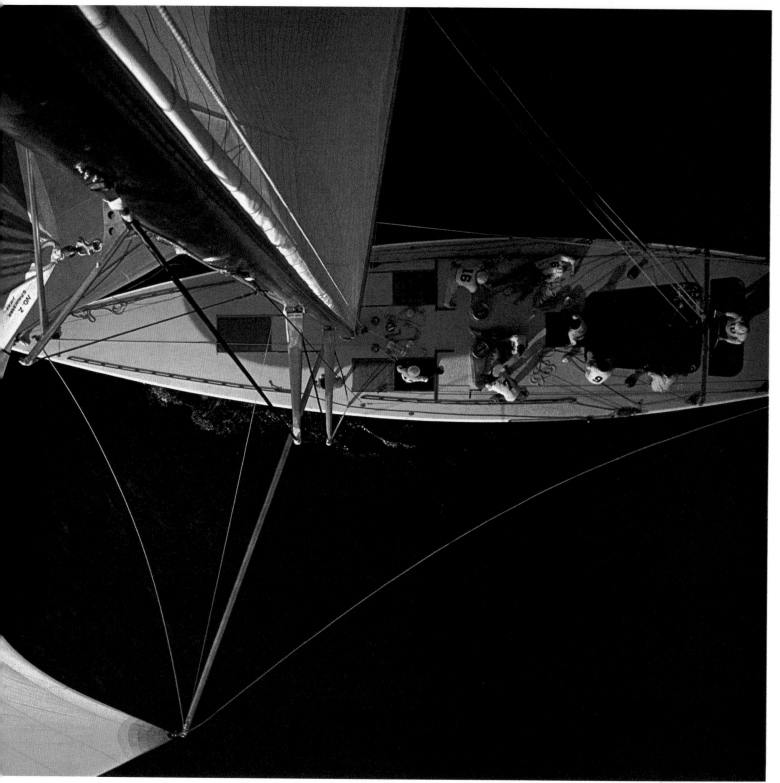

GEORGE SILK: *Nefertiti,* 1962

Daredevil Feats

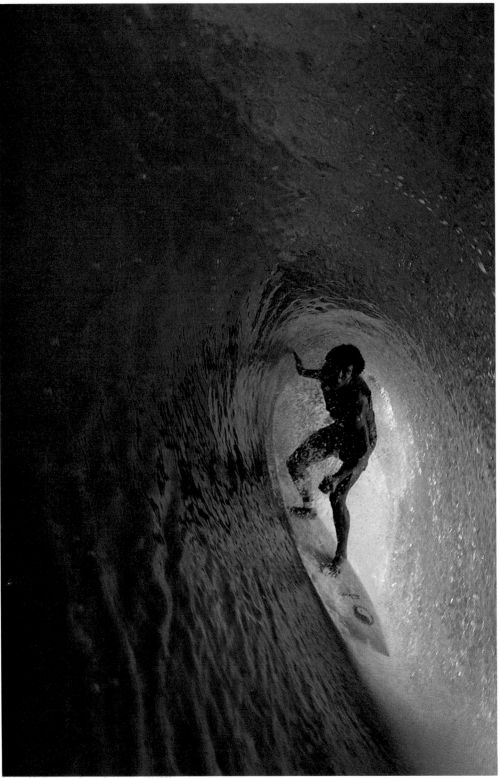

A professional surfer rides into the tunnel formed by a breaking wave —the "tube" in surfers' jargon— in this shot taken by a photographer who swims or floats on an air mattress among the waves to achieve his dramatic results. For this picture, taken with a 35mm SLR equipped with a motor drive and stored in the same hard plastic housing underwater photographers use to protect their gear, he bobbed for several hours in treacherous shallow surf off a beach in Hawaii. As this wave approached, he found himself inside the same breaker as the surfer and fired four shots during the few seconds before the wave crashed over the camera and the board sped by.

DAN MERKEL: *In the Tube, Oahu, Hawaii,* 1980

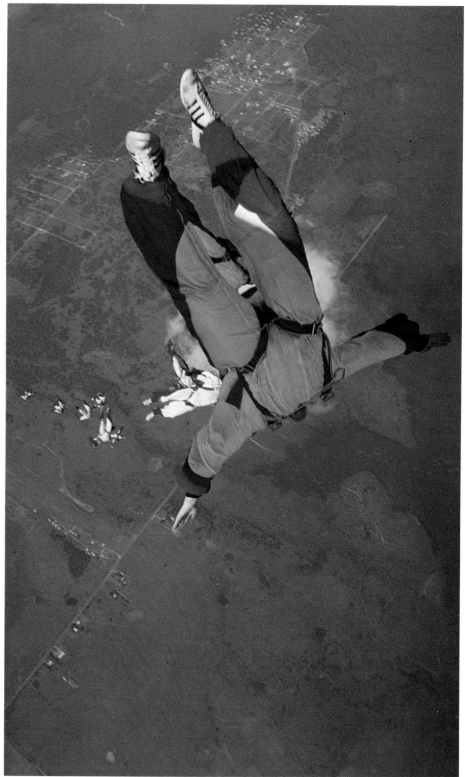

This flock of skydivers over Oklahoma, falling freely before releasing their chutes, was recorded by a photographer who was plummeting downward with them. A former paratrooper who had made more than 1,800 previous jumps, he used some military gadgetry to help get the picture. To the front of his helmet he bolted a motorized 35mm SLR that was triggered by a long control wire, then attached the sight from a World War II artillery gun to act as a substitute viewfinder. This setup enabled him to frame and shoot an entire 36-exposure roll of film during the 90-second free fall.

JERRY IRWIN: *Skydivers over Wagoner, Oklahoma, 1974*

Fresh Perspectives with Remote Control

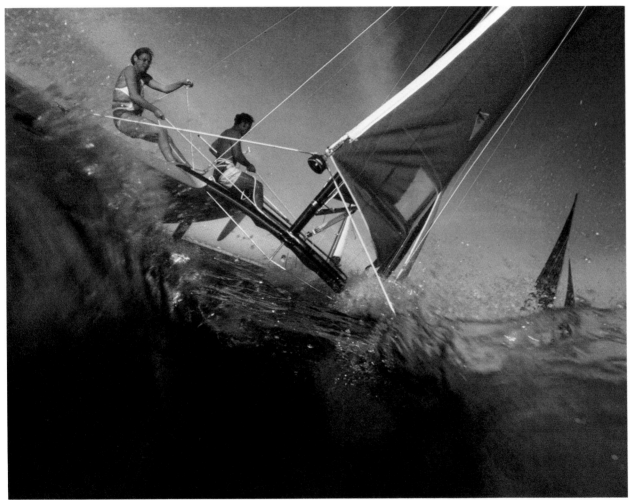

CO RENTMEESTER: *National Catamaran Championships, San Diego,* 1978

While her partner manipulates the sail of this twin-hulled catamaran, a young woman leans out over the water to balance the fast-moving craft during a race. No photographer was on board but a remotely controlled motorized camera was. It and a radio receiver in a waterproof housing were suspended between the twin hulls of the boat. The photographer triggered the camera by sending a radio signal from an observation boat a couple of hundred yards away.

For this unusual picture of a water jump in a ▶ steeplechase race, the photographer did not crouch alongside the other photographers at the side of the track (lower left); instead he rigged a remote-controlled camera fitted with a 17mm extra-wide-angle lens under the jump barrier. He shot into the sun, triggering the device from inside the track just after some runners had completed the jump. The circular pattern around the runners was caused by reflections from lens elements of the sun image.

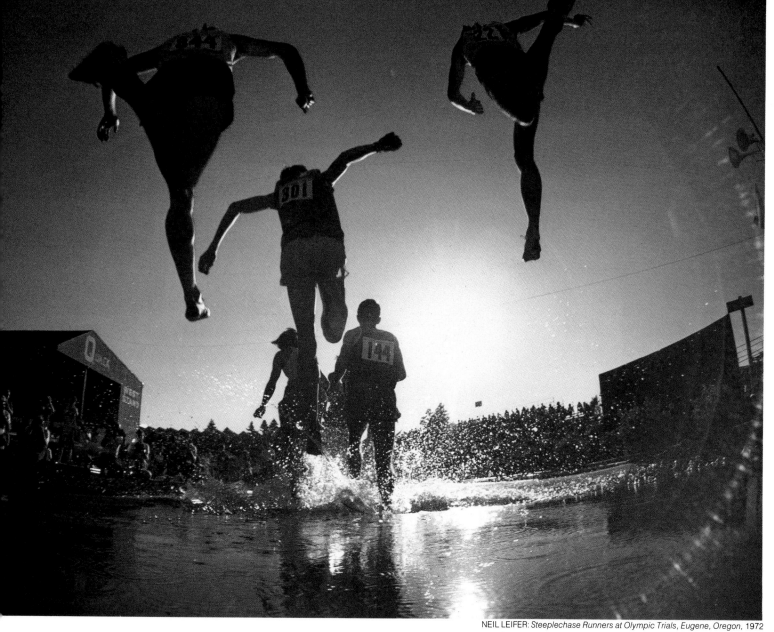

NEIL LEIFER: *Steeplechase Runners at Olympic Trials, Eugene, Oregon,* 1972

The Revealing Aftermath

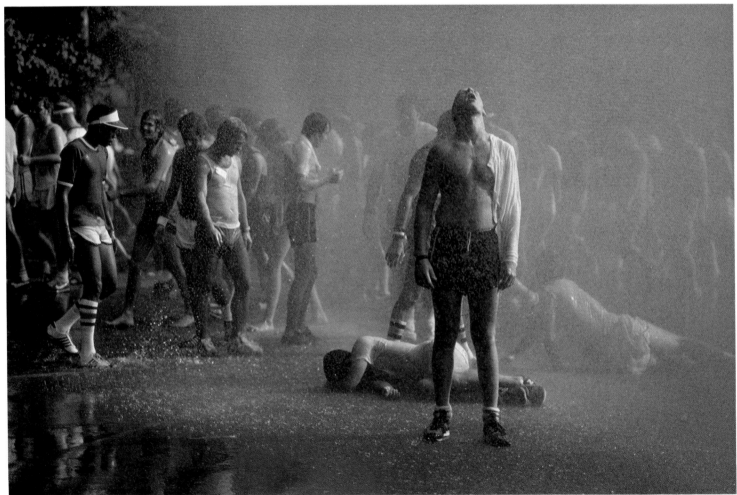

CHUCK ROGERS: *Marathon Man, Atlanta,* 1978

Of the more than 100 shots that he took of
The Peachtree Road Race in Atlanta in 1978, the one
that seemed to the photographer to capture the
essence of the grueling 10,000-meter run was this
one snapped after the finish. A fire hose had
been turned on to help cool the exhausted
runners; its cascading mist helped create this
impressionistic vignette.

The Assigned Problem 6

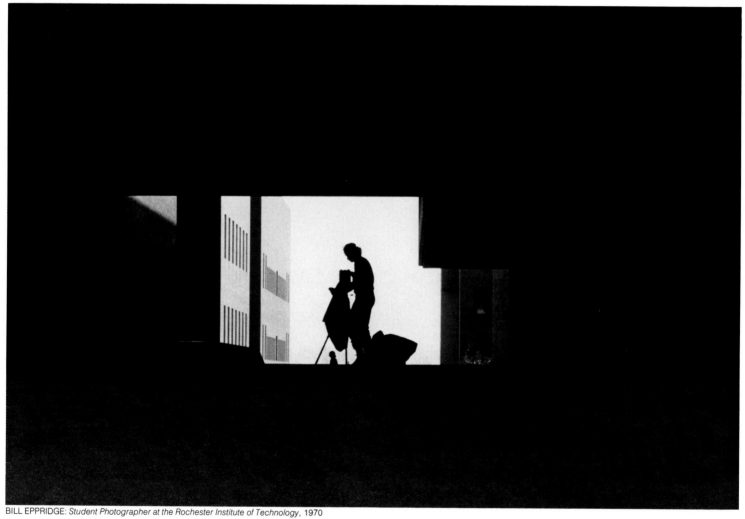

BILL EPPRIDGE: *Student Photographer at the Rochester Institute of Technology*, 1970

Photography in the Classroom

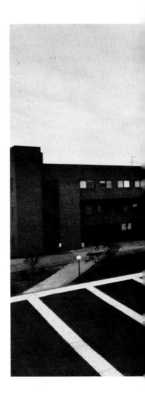

Today more and more people are finding out how to solve the problems of photography not by the haphazard process of trial and error but by going to school. In the past most young photographers necessarily learned by doing, for only a few American colleges and technical institutions considered photography an appropriate subject for study. "There was no place I could go . . . for photographic education," wrote Ansel Adams of his efforts in the 1920s to master the art of landscape photography. "Excepting the few kind individuals who provided assistance, and some nuts-and-bolts training in photofinishing shops, I trained myself—very inefficient!" To help aspiring young photographers avoid the frustrations he himself experienced, Adams started a photographic workshop in Yosemite, California. In doing so, he contributed to a growing national phenomenon.

According to a survey conducted in 1980 by a member of the Department of Cinema and Photography at Southern Illinois University, the number of American and Canadian colleges and universities that offer some instruction in photography had almost doubled in the previous 10 years, and the number of students had increased from 80,000 to 135,000. By the 1979-1980 school year, photography could be studied as a course in nearly 1,000 schools, and 846 of them offered degrees in photography. The range of subject matter that is taught in formal classes is very broad, covering courses in elementary introductions to picture taking and processing, advanced seminars in the history of photography, and such specialties as photography for television, medicine and law.

Photography is the major concern of a number of specialized private institutes and nondegree schools, where intensive training in photographic art and techniques is offered without the liberal arts courses that accompany most college programs. The institutions offering bachelor's degrees generally place photographic classes either in the journalism or art departments.

One school with an independent photography department is The School of Photographic Arts and Sciences, part of the Rochester Institute of Technology, which is located in upstate New York. The Institute, founded in 1829 when Rochester was a frontier farming community, is an enormous complex of science, business and arts colleges housed on a 1,300-acre campus of modern brick buildings on the outskirts of Rochester. The School of Photographic Arts and Sciences is one of the Institute's major entities and offers a greater variety of photography courses—more than 100—than any other institution in the country; it confers Bachelor and Master of Fine Arts as well as Bachelor and Master of Science degrees.

Like other students at the Institute, those in the School of Photographic Arts and Sciences tend to concentrate on the practical—understandably. Rochester is an industrial town, and one of the best places in the world to earn a living

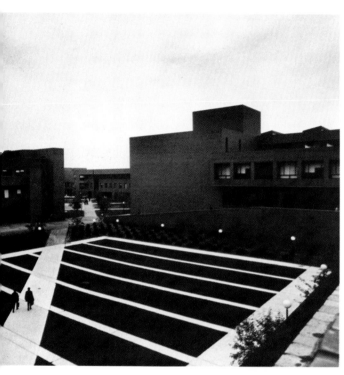

The campus of Rochester Institute of Technology, completed in 1968, includes 10 different colleges, as well as libraries, athletic facilities and a student housing complex. This view from the top of the College of Graphic Arts and Photography shows the College of General Studies (left) and the James E. Booth Memorial Building of Fine and Applied Arts.

in photography. Photography is in the air. It was here that George Eastman in 1888 began manufacturing the simple box camera that expanded picture taking from the hobby of a dedicated few into a national craze. It is here that the Eastman Kodak Company, now the world's largest manufacturer of cameras and film, maintains its headquarters.

Kodak lends close support to the photography school. It provides guest lecturers, sometimes offers advice on the curriculum, opens its libraries and gives technical advice to students working on special projects. It also hires many of them when they complete their education.

Partly because of this industrial backing, R.I.T. has the most elaborate facilities in the country. It is the only school to educate students for degrees in a technological specialty called Photographic Science and Instrumentation, turning out graduates who design new cameras, concoct new kinds of film and develop the complex photographic equipment used in many branches of scientific research. The even more specialized Department of Bio Medical Photography is one of very few in the country to offer a collegiate program in the techniques of photographing living organisms for scientific research.

Most of R.I.T.'s 1,000 photography students are concentrating on becoming well-rounded professional photographers. "We are preparing young people for meaningful careers," explained the school's director. In addition to basic classes in picture taking and laboratory techniques, the students can choose from a selection of elective courses such as portraiture, advertising photography, photojournalism and motion-picture photography. One major program in professional photography, leading to a Bachelor of Science, includes training in business management and accounting for students who plan to enter industry or to open their own studios. Another program concentrates on esthetics, and leads to the fine arts degree. In both, the emphasis is on learning by doing. From virtually the first day of class, students are assigned challenging photographic problems, and are sent out of the classroom to solve them. The aim of this guided do-it-yourself approach is to produce students with the ability to think and communicate in photographic images.

A Wealth of Facilities for Learning

R.I.T.'s School of Photographic Arts and Sciences is one place where a student can learn how to develop film in an automatic Versamat Film Processor—or how to use a video color-negative analyzer to gauge the proper color values for making a good print *(opposite, top right)*. Such highly specialized machines are part of a four-million-dollar inventory of photographic equipment.

Housed in a massive red brick building that it shares with the Institute's School of Printing, the photography school provides fully equipped motion-picture and television studios and a sound stage, still-photography studios, and processing laboratories for both black-and-white and color work. All together, the school has 178 darkrooms. Chemicals for processing film are mixed in waist-high, 200-gallon vats in a special room; 198 gallons of fixer alone must be prepared every week to fill the school's needs.

Aside from the equipment available in the still- and motion-picture studios, the students can execute assignments by choosing from among 206 cameras, including 55 motion-picture cameras and 101 view cameras, as well as a variety of lenses, electronic flash units, tripods and filters. As many as 1,000 items may be issued to students on a busy day. □

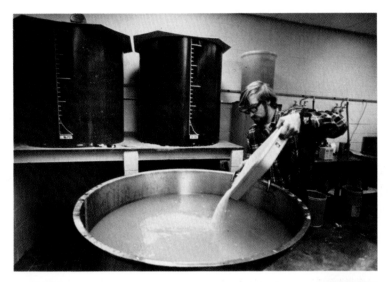

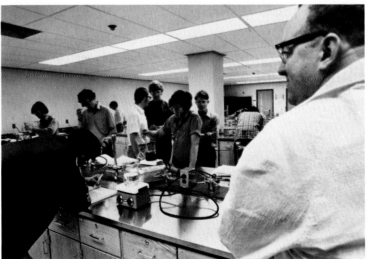

Preparing a supply of paper developer (top), extension student Gary Morse pours commercially blended chemicals into a vat in the chemical mixing room. Freshman students in the chemistry lab (bottom) learn to blend their own developers. In this experiment, they are required to eliminate one of the ingredients to discover the effect on processed negatives.

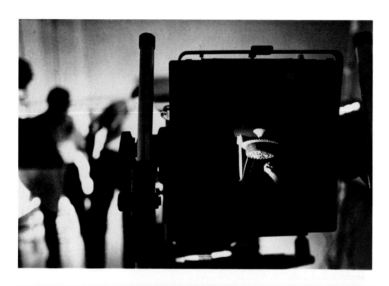

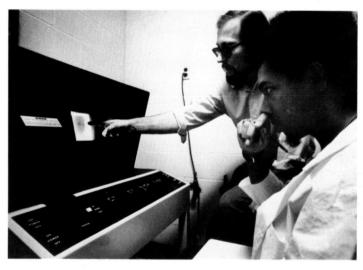

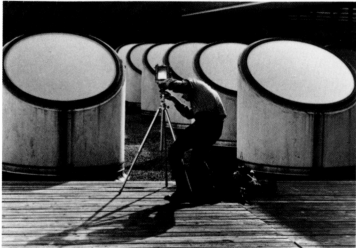

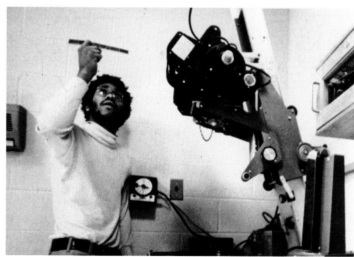

The inverted image of a chocolate cake on the screen of a studio view camera (top left) shows a student's effort to compose a still life. At top right, a teacher uses a color-negative analyzer to point out color values in a transparency to junior Denny Harrod. Freshman

Cary Keshen (bottom left) adjusts his view camera to photograph the futuristic skylights atop a campus building. In a color-printing darkroom (bottom right), sophomore Irving Baker inspects a strip of 35mm negatives before putting it into the enlarger at his left.

A Curriculum of Challenges

Ralph Hattersley, a former member of the R.I.T. faculty, once compared the teaching of photography with the classic tale of the blind men trying to describe an elephant: One man, who had taken hold of the elephant's tail, maintained the animal was long and slithery, like a snake; another who ran his fingers over the animal's leg insisted that an elephant is a huge, wrinkled cylinder, like the trunk of an enormous tree; still others, feeling other parts of the beast, described it in totally different terms.

Such is the case with photography, Hattersley said. The field is now so vast and complex that no one can grasp it all, and photography teachers must grope their way. "We have lost our main means for determining what goals our students should pursue," Hattersley wrote. "How can we know what to teach them?"

The faculty at R.I.T. decided to solve this predicament by teaching students to deal creatively with challenge. Photographic assignments would be treated as problems for the students to solve once they were provided with the necessary technical background.

Some of the problems might be purely technical: How to arrange the lighting for a strong, effective portrait; what kind of camera to choose, what film, what developing and printing methods. R.I.T. students are bombarded with technical data on strobe lights, umbrella reflectors, developing compounds and printing tricks.

But in most problems that students are asked to solve, technique merges into interpretation and the methods and tools used to solve them change as the styles and technology of photography evolve. For example, student photographs in the 1971 edition of this volume in the LIFE Library of Photography were all black-and-white; the present edition includes two pages of students' color photographs, reflecting the great increase in the use of color in photography.

Regardless of changes in the medium, however, students are required to master some basic skills. The photograph of a halved cabbage shown opposite result-ed from an assignment to produce a high-quality print using one of various lab techniques taught in the freshman introductory course. By emphasizing contrast, the student transformed the image of a humble vegetable into a design of singular beauty and originality.

The problems are even more challenging in the upper-class courses. One instructor assigned his second-year students to photograph any commonplace object—a water glass, a lamppost, a piece of Swiss cheese—and, by means of lighting and composition, to give it an aspect of monumentality. Another told his advanced students to create an image to represent the idea of communication for the cover of an annual report of an imaginary communications company *(pages 176-177)*. And still another teacher, who began his course by having the students shoot pictures of sugar cubes, ended it by asking them to indicate photographically their attitudes toward such sweeping concepts as death, sex and man's inhumanity toward man.

Assigned to produce "a print of outstanding merit," the young photographer picked a seemingly commonplace subject, a red cabbage sliced in half, which he photographed on Plus-X film with a 4 x 5 view camera. He printed on high-contrast paper to convert the image of the folded leaves to a powerful, convoluted design.

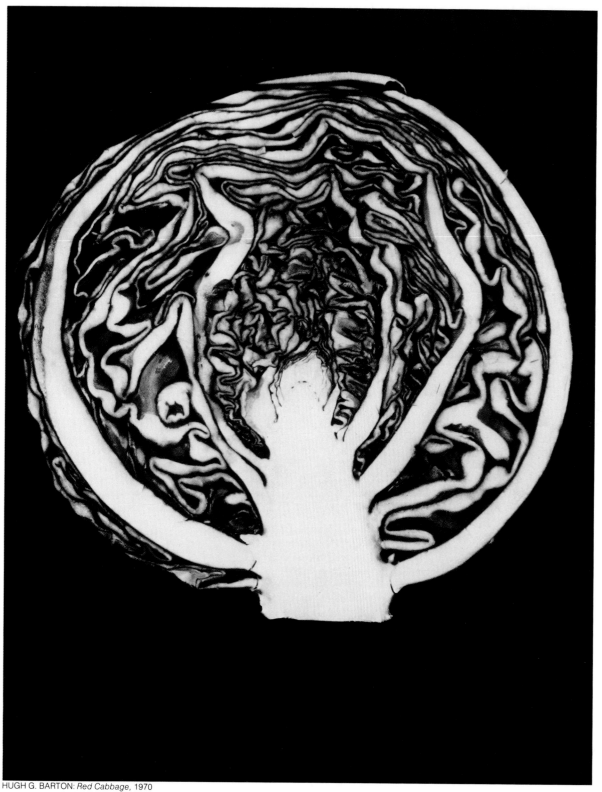

HUGH G. BARTON: *Red Cabbage*, 1970

New Light on the Common Egg

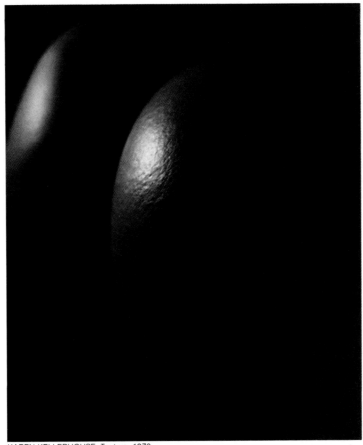

KAREN KELLERHOUSE: *Texture,* 1970

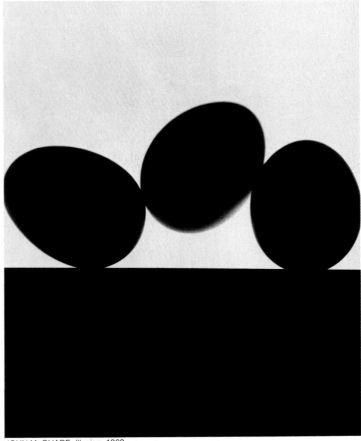

JOHN McQUADE: *Illusion,* 1969

No object seems more ordinary than a hen's egg. That is precisely why several classes of R.I.T. students were assigned to take pictures of eggs—to test their ability to show a mundane subject in an unusual way. The students, using different lighting and darkroom techniques, plus a liberal amount of imagination, made some extraordinarily varied statements about the properties of eggs. One focused a pencil-thin spotlight on a small part of the shell *(above, left),* creating a sense of texture that seems as warm and palpable as human skin. Another demonstrated the basic geometry of eggs *(opposite, top left),* photographing them from above in natural light and printing for maximum contrast to eliminate every quality besides shape. Still others *(opposite, bottom row)* seem to comment on the properties of light itself.

The precarious balance in the picture above is actually an illusion. The eggs were placed next to a piece of black cardboard on a glass pane, lighted from below and photographed from above. At left above, a spotlight reveals surprising texture in a supposedly smooth egg.

High-contrast printing turned eggs into circles ▶ of white space (opposite, 1). A tiny light beam aimed at each end of the hollowed-out shell in the foreground made it glow with a light of its own (2). A pattern of light streaks was thrown onto these eggs from a spotlight with a special lens (3). Two eggs are silhouetted against the large spherical disk of a floodlight reflector (4).

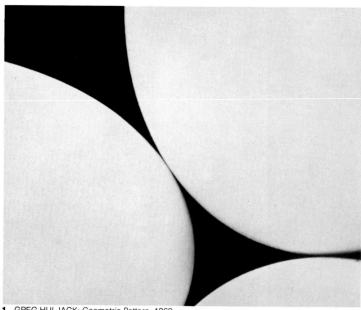

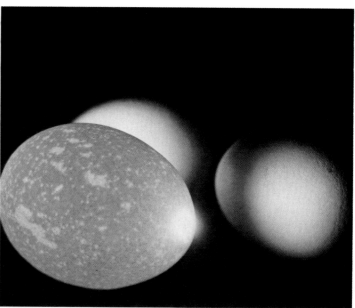

1 GREG HULJACK: *Geometric Pattern*, 1969

2 KEITH HUNT: *Inner Glow*, 1970

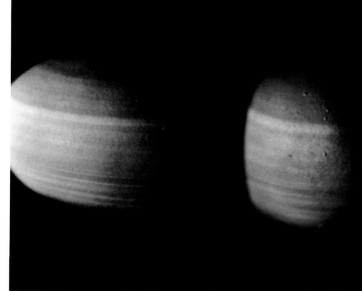

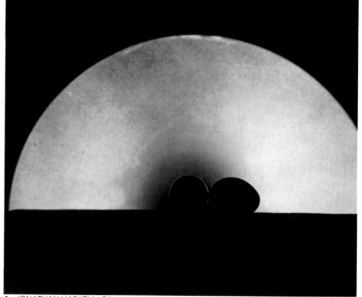

3 JONATHAN HASKELL: *Lightstruck*, 1969

4 JONATHAN HASKELL: *Silhouettes*, 1969

Private Views of a New Environment

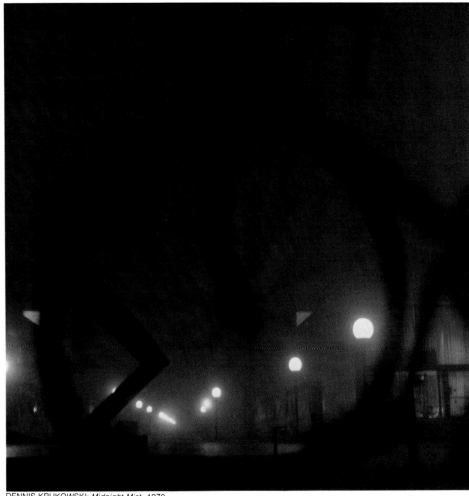

DENNIS KRUKOWSKI: *Midnight Mist*, 1970

A somber disquiet pervades this time exposure, made at night in a heavy fog, of lights and pathways receding into nowhere. The off-focus silhouette of the bicycle looms menacingly above the eye of the camera, which was placed on the ground; yet the bicycle also adds an odd human element to the seemingly vacant campus.

One of the first tasks that many teachers set for their freshman classes is to photograph the campus—not just as a collection of buildings, but as an environment. "R.I.T. offers you a new realm of experiences," said one instructor. "How you perceive, interpret and record these experiences is the essence of this project."

The instructor suggested three different approaches. The students could look for a way to express the clean, functional style of campus architecture. Or they could treat the assignment as a problem in photojournalism and show how other students were adapting to the campus. Finally, they might try to extend their vision into the realm of surrealism and convey a personal image of the campus in any form their imagination conceived—the approach adopted by two students whose photographs are shown here.

Stark black shapes silhouetted against the ▶ failing light of an evening sky give a strange emphasis to the modernistic lines of the R.I.T. campus. "I was purposely looking for a high-contrast effect, as this was my impression of the campus," said Jim Barstow, the student. "By overexposing and underdeveloping, I was able to catch the scene as I saw it."

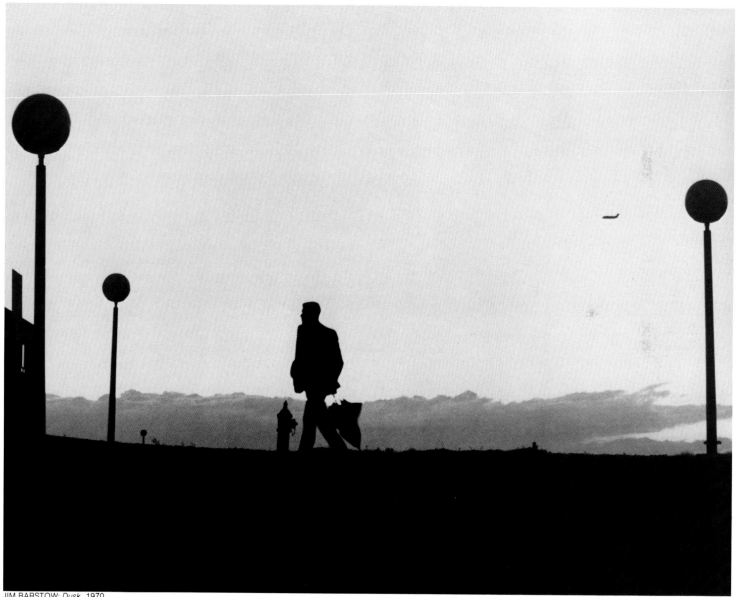

JIM BARSTOW: *Dusk*, 1970

Facing the Difficulties of Portraiture

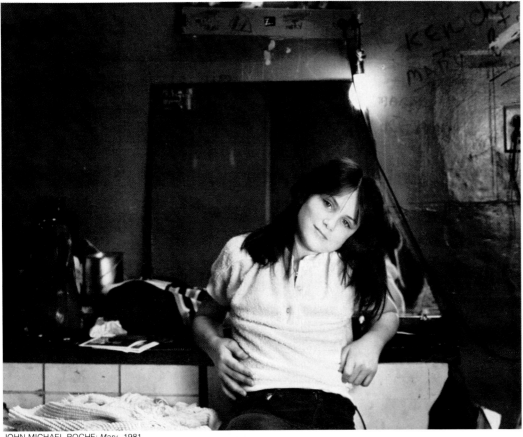

JOHN MICHAEL ROCHE: *Mary*, 1981

In this portrait of a 10-year-old girl, the photographer's main problem was getting the family to accept his presence, but he also had the technical challenge of creating suitable portrait lighting in the girl's starkly lit bedroom. He eventually set up three photoflood lamps, and left the room's single bare bulb burning as well.

What makes the difference between an ordinary likeness and a striking portrait is often the insight and imagination the photographer brings to it. As part of a course in photographing people, using mainly studio view cameras, R.I.T. students were asked to make two kinds of portraits: one in the sitter's home or place of work, and one in a studio. In both, the aim was not merely to produce a technically proficient result, but to express aspects of the sitter's personality that especially interested the photographer.

Both types of portrait present difficulties. When shooting in the sitter's own environment, careful advance work is often needed to accustom the sitter and anyone else on the scene to the camera and to make sure the necessary equipment is at hand. But the photographer can add an extra dimension to a portrait by a thoughtful use of the setting. In the location portrait of a Rochester youngster reproduced at left, the student photographer used the girl's untidy bedroom as a contrast to her beauty. But it took him three visits to her house to win her family's confidence and to work out all the technical details.

The problem of taking a portrait in the studio is just the opposite. The sitter is usually psychologically prepared to be photographed, there are no extraneous distractions and the photographer has all his cameras, lights and other equipment available. However, he must try to capture a spontaneous, natural quality in his subject in decidedly structured, unnatural surroundings. This often requires the combined talents of a psychiatrist and a film director—as well as a measure of luck—as one R.I.T. student found when taking an informal portrait of a lively fellow student *(right)*.

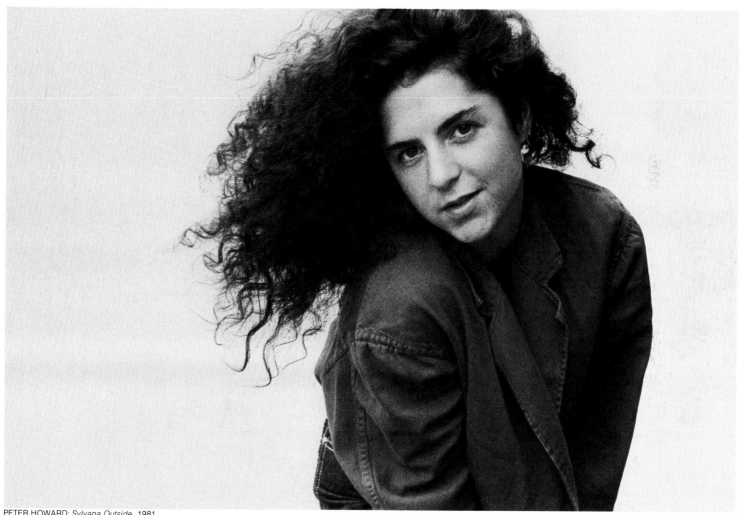

PETER HOWARD: *Sylvana Outside*, 1981

In an effort to capture the personality of his outgoing subject, the photographer took her out of the formal environment of the studio onto a shady balcony. There he chatted and joked with her and urged her to watch him, not the camera. When a breeze suddenly caught her hair and blew it across her shoulder, he made his exposure.

Illustrating an Idea

Professional photographers are frequently faced with the problem of expressing abstract concepts like "strength," "wetness" or "the future" with visual images. To give students experience in this type of work, teachers at R.I.T. developed a course called conceptual photography, in which the student is required to make an abstraction concrete—to reduce it to a simple visual symbol that will convey the idea in a picture. Although the students taking the course are often headed for advertising and commercial photography, the principles are fundamental to other types of photography as well.

The two photographs on these pages were made in response to an assignment to produce a cover picture for the annual report of an imaginary communications company. Rather than search for already existing visual equivalents for the ideas of communication, both students chose to create images in the studio—with arresting results.

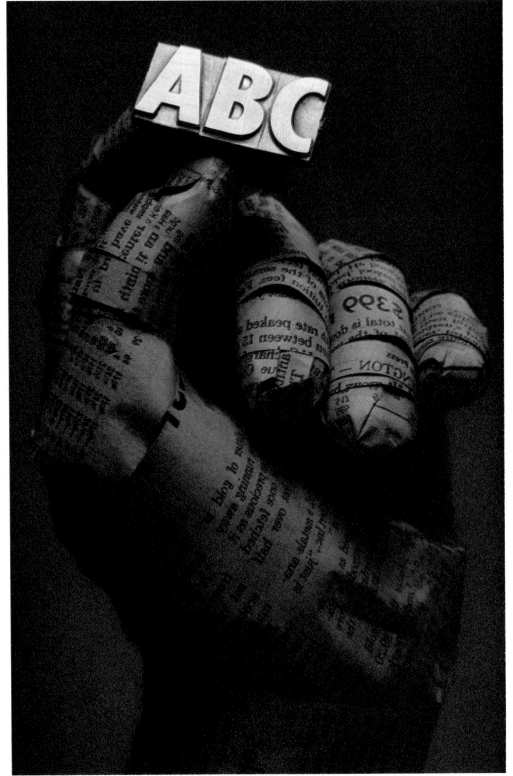

A hand wrapped in newsprint holding a block of type is one student's visual representation of the concept "communication." He took the simplest symbol he could think of for communication—the letters of the alphabet—and combined it with a human hand, symbol of the most sophisticated communicator, man.

DANIEL J. ROMENESKO: *ABC*, 1981

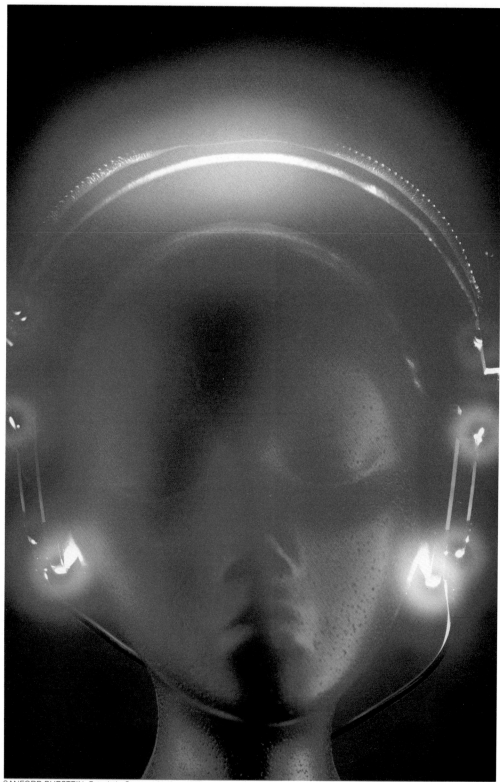

To convey the idea of communication in the space age, this student photographed a futuristic mannequin wearing earphones. He placed a violet filter over a floodlight to give the silver-painted foam plastic head its unearthly color, and he breathed on the lens to create the foglike flare that surrounds the highlights.

SANFORD BURSTEIN: *Futuristic Communication*, 1981

From Three Dimensions, a Flat Design

The distinguishing talent of Edward Weston, one of the masters of photography, was his ability to picture ordinary objects in such a way that their qualities of form and shape were emphasized, but the object itself remained recognizable. One of Weston's most famous pictures is a close-up of a ceramic toilet bowl he photographed from below to give it an odd sense of monumentality. The same utilitarian item, treated in a somewhat different way, was picked by R.I.T. freshman Judie Gleason for her own study in transforming normal appearances.

Miss Gleason's assignment was to photograph any three-dimensional object in such a way "as to reduce the illusion of three-dimensionality as much as possible," thus creating a flat pattern of light and dark shapes. At the same time, the object itself would have to retain its identity.

There is no mistaking the object Miss Gleason chose. Yet by a wise selection of visual design elements—a squarely overhead camera angle, careful framing and strong contrast of black and white—she has in effect created an optical illusion in which the solid toilet bowl seems almost as flat as the tile floor it rests on. □

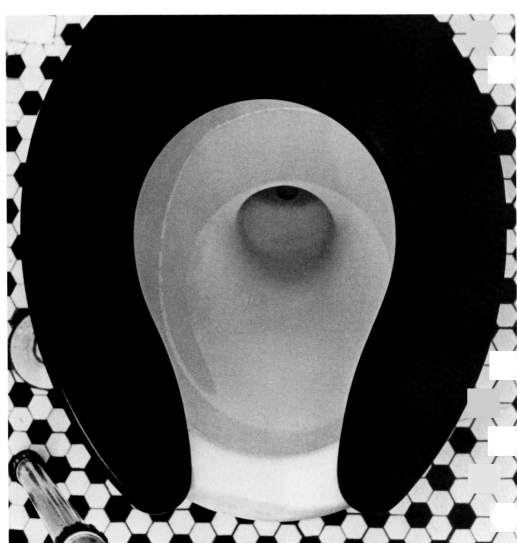

JUDIE GLEASON: *Toilet Bowl,* 1967

The main visual clue that lets the eye recognize three dimensions is gradation in shading between light and dark. By including a minimum of gray tones in this view of a toilet bowl, Miss Gleason produced a strongly two-dimensional pattern of black and white.

How to Succeed by Breaking the Rules 182

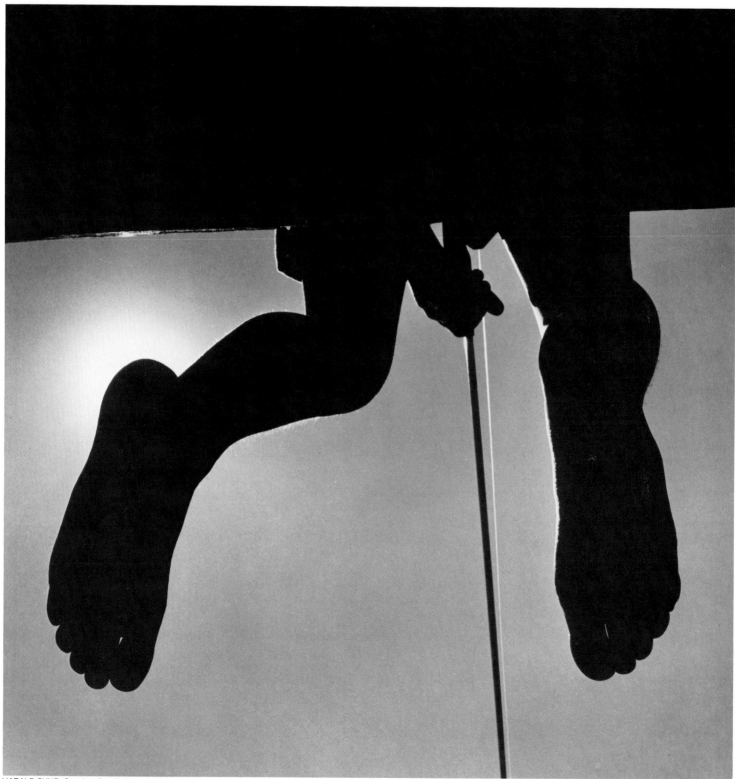

HARALD SUND: *Barefoot Boy Fishing,* 1967

How to Succeed by Breaking the Rules

It gets harder and harder to break the rules of picture taking accidentally, because so much photographic equipment is being designed to prevent mistakes that might mar the final image. For instance, it is impossible to make accidental double exposures with most of today's cameras: The mechanism that cocks the shutter is constructed to advance the film simultaneously, inextricably tying the two functions together and ensuring a fresh frame for every exposure. With cameras that set aperture or shutter automatically, even such common errors as overexposure and underexposure have become rarities.

If a photographer deliberately seeks effects that ordinarily are avoided, he might seem frustrated by the improvements engineers have labored to produce. Their success imposes limitations on the mistakes he can make. To thwart him further, few manuals include instructions on how to achieve other than the correct results in photography. But ingenious photographers continue to dream up unusual practices to create striking pictures. The great proliferation of new equipment actually makes it easier to experiment with unorthodox techniques. Occasionally an unusual method is discovered by sheer accident (as Lilo Raymond did when she produced the picture at right), but most are employed on purpose by photographers seeking to give their work graphic originality or to underscore its emotional content. For example, in the picture of a boy fishing on the preceding page, the photographer deliberately underexposed the subject to produce a striking silhouette.

If a photographer wants to make multiple images, there are several ways he can double-expose his film. On some cameras, the linkage that prevents double exposures can be disconnected. And even cameras lacking such an override can be manipulated to keep the film from moving as the shutter is cocked. With most 35mm single-lens reflex cameras, the following procedure will work. After making the first exposure, hold the rewind crank with the left hand to keep the film from advancing; then press in on the rewind button with the little finger of the right hand, and use the right thumb to operate the film-advance lever. This will cock the shutter, making possible a second exposure on the stationary film. A more elaborate technique involves rewinding the film into its cassette (being careful to leave the end protruding), then putting the film through the camera a second or third time; it is necessary to take pains to align the sprocket holes in the same relative position to get exposures in good register.

When using any of these multiple-exposure methods, be sure to allow for the extra light that will reach the film; underexpose each of the overlapped pictures by one or two f-stops, depending on how many shots are combined. Multiple images may also be made in the darkroom either by combining two or more negatives into a "sandwich" before enlarging them or by projecting them one after the other onto the same piece of printing paper. Two transparencies can also be placed in the same slide holder and projected together.

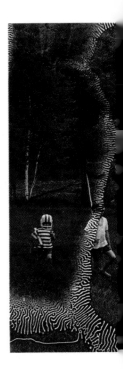

To shoot some pictures of children staging a make-believe parade, Lilo Raymond used orthodox equipment—a 35mm camera with a 50mm lens—and technique; she exposed at f/8 for 1/125 second. The rule she broke belongs more to the housewife's code than the photographer's: Always empty the pockets of any garment headed for the washing machine. When she put her jeans into the laundry, she forgot to take the finished roll of film out of one pocket. And a washed, rinsed and dried roll came out with the washed, rinsed and dried jeans. Miss Raymond "was heartbroken—I knew the roll would have been good—but I decided to process it anyway." This proved difficult, what with layers of film sticking to each other and the emulsion cracking and peeling in spots, but in the end it was all worthwhile: A zebra-stripe pattern formed a delicate tracery across each picture and served to frame the children like figures in a fantasy landscape.

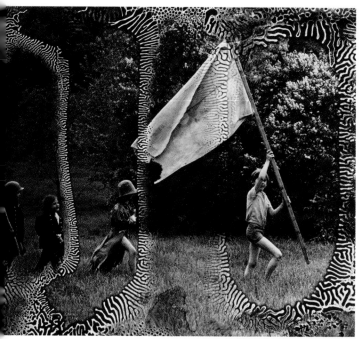

LILO RAYMOND: *Children Playing,* 1968

Special efforts are needed even to create the image distortions that inadequate lenses caused in the camera's early years. Various methods will serve. Shooting through raindrops on a window is a favorite way of achieving distortion and since any highly polished curved surface reflects a distorted image, it too can be used to get the effect. Often it is possible to photograph a reflection of the subject in the chrome trim of a car—a bumper, a wheel cover, even the bright strip around a headlight. In order to get equally clear images of both reflection and reflector, the lens must usually be stopped down to increase depth of field and keep all planes in sharp focus *(pages 58-59).*

Unlike distorted images and double exposures, a few other kinds of deliberate mistakes are now easier to make because they depend on equipment not generally available in the old days. Perspective, for instance, can be altered by using a long-focal-length or a wide-angle lens since both lenses change the size relationships that normally assist the eye in determining distance. A long lens, which makes foreground and background objects appear to be about the same size, makes background objects seem closer than they are, while a wide-angle makes far objects appear smaller than—and farther away from—near ones. A good example is Philippe Halsman's wide-angle portrait of Louis Armstrong *(page 187),* a carefully calculated distortion that shows a huge trumpet being held by the musician whose body tapers off into tiny feet.

The photographer who puts his mind to it will find many ways to do things wrong in order to get the right picture. Deliberate underexposure, for example, can be used to produce harsh contrasts, silhouettes, or intensely rich colors—in general, to eliminate detail so that a picture suggests more than it shows. Unorthodox use of an electronic flash unit can turn a car into a phantom *(pages 96-97)* or give a subject gleaming red eyes. Ignoring the recommendations for color film use can turn hues topsy-turvy or render a colorful scene in monochrome. But whatever the technique adopted, rules are broken at the breaker's peril. They exist because, in most cases, they are necessary. Successful violations generally depend on knowing in advance the effect that is wanted, rather than on random, trusting-to-luck trials.

Making a Point by Chopping Off Heads

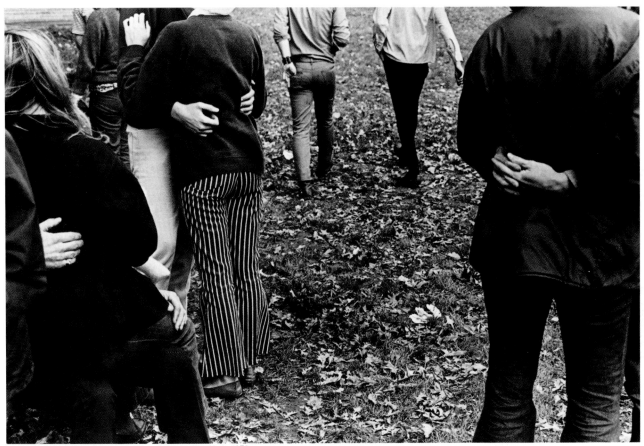

ANTHONY SZCZYGIELSKI: *Varsity Club, Palmyra, New York, 1970*

One of the first things a photographer learns is not to take pictures that chop off people's heads. Decapitation is easy to do in close-ups made with some cameras that have a viewfinder lens separate from the taking lens. Unless the two lenses are interconnected, the photographer sees a slightly different view of the subject from the view that will go through the lens to the film. And even with cameras that display on their viewing screens exactly what the film will record, part of a head may inadvertently be left out if a photographer is shooting on the run and fails to frame his composition on the screen. The loss, particularly of the eyes, may rob the picture of its most expressive elements—but, by directing attention to other elements, a partial image of the subject may say a great deal more than a complete view possibly could.

This group shot was taken with a 24mm wide-angle lens to get everybody in the frame—but without their heads. The picture was meant to emphasize the social nature of students, and eliminating heads concentrates the essence of the idea, revealing the young people's emotional interrelationship through the linkage of their hands and the closeness of their bodies.

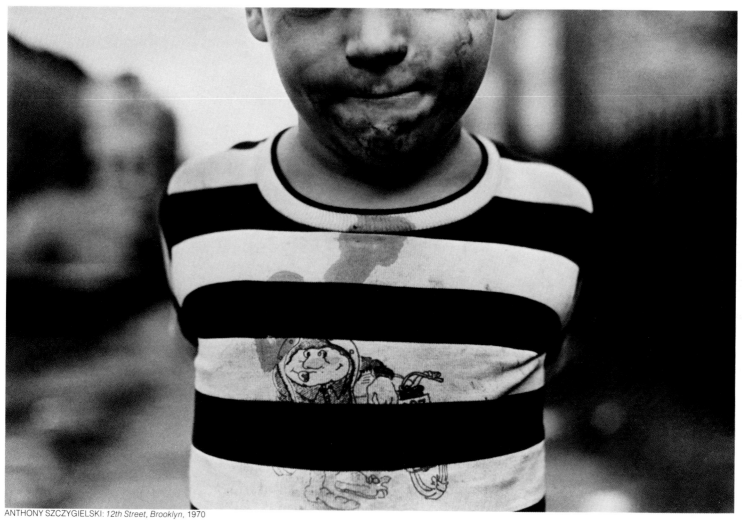

ANTHONY SZCZYGIELSKI: *12th Street, Brooklyn,* 1970

This picture is part of a study the photographer made of neighborhood youngsters, of whom he says, "Dirt and ice cream are a quality of childhood, or at least of this group of kids —they're rambunctious and proud of being dirty." He composed the picture deliberately to crop off the top of the boy's head, thus underlining the cocky bravado of the facial expression and the pulled-back shoulders beneath the ice-cream-streaked T-shirt.

The Impact of Distorted Perspective

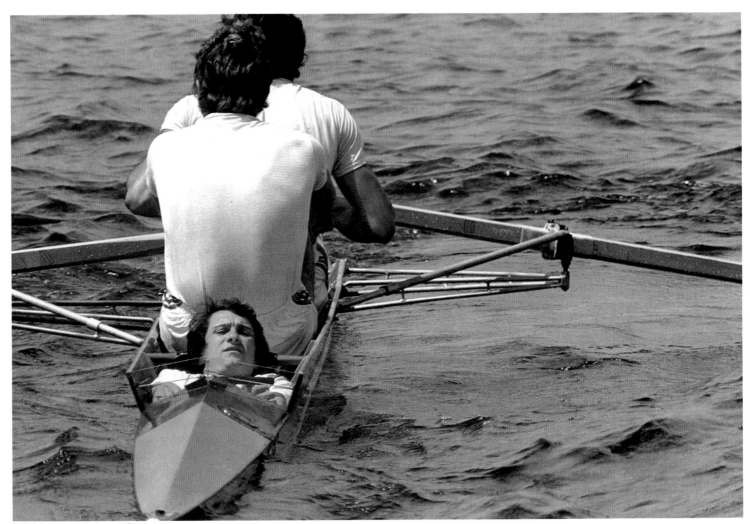

CHRIS SMITH: *Heady Race,* 1976

Photographers who rely on wide-angle or long-focal-length lenses learn to guard against the apparent distortions in perspective that they can produce. Long lenses draw nearby objects and distant ones dramatically closer together; wide-angle lenses make them seem to be farther apart. However, such compression or extension can produce arresting and artful results, as seen in the images here.

The coxswain of an Italian Olympic crew lies feet forward at the bow of his shell. The 400mm lens that was used for the picture so foreshortened distances that there appears to be no room in the shell for the crewman, and he looks like a disembodied head.

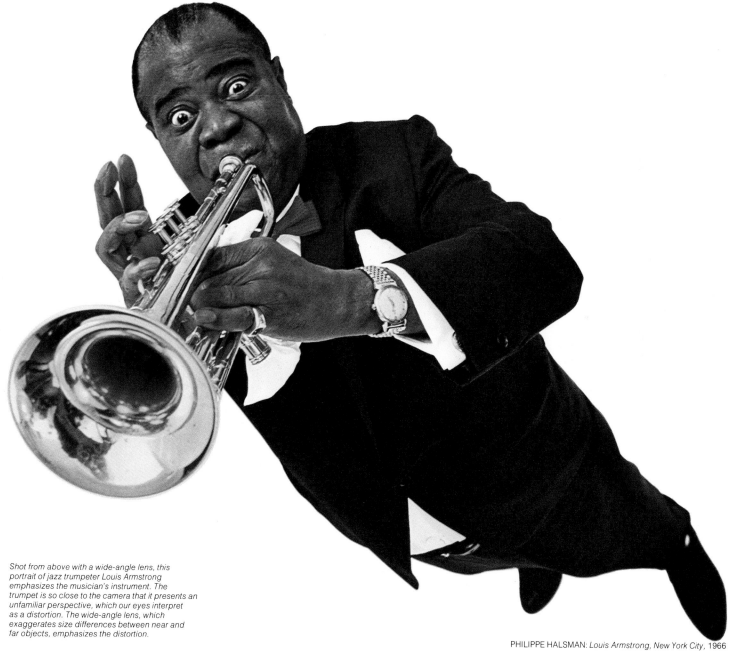

Shot from above with a wide-angle lens, this portrait of jazz trumpeter Louis Armstrong emphasizes the musician's instrument. The trumpet is so close to the camera that it presents an unfamiliar perspective, which our eyes interpret as a distortion. The wide-angle lens, which exaggerates size differences between near and far objects, emphasizes the distortion.

PHILIPPE HALSMAN: *Louis Armstrong, New York City,* 1966

Shifting Focus for an Air of Mystery

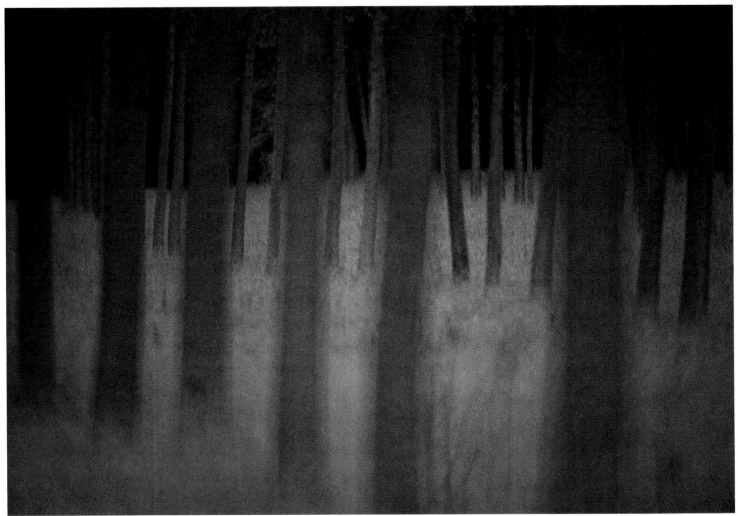

ANDRÉ MARTIN: *Poplar Wood, France,* 1975

To produce a clear image of the main element in his picture, a photographer is taught to adjust his camera's depth of field to get that element in focus. Yet he may violate this rule with profit if his purpose is ambiguity; one way to endow a subject with mystery is to make it prominent but somehow secondary.

To create mystery in the forest picture above, the photographer reversed the normal expectations of the viewer: The trees in the foreground have been deliberately blurred, while those in the background are sharp. The car is the principal element in the photograph at right, but its lines have been half-submerged in the texture of the curtain through which the camera was aimed.

A long lens was used to give the woodland scene at left a slightly ominous feeling. Capitalizing on the lens's shallow depth of field, the photographer focused on a spot that would bring distant trees into focus; this caused those nearest the camera to blur.

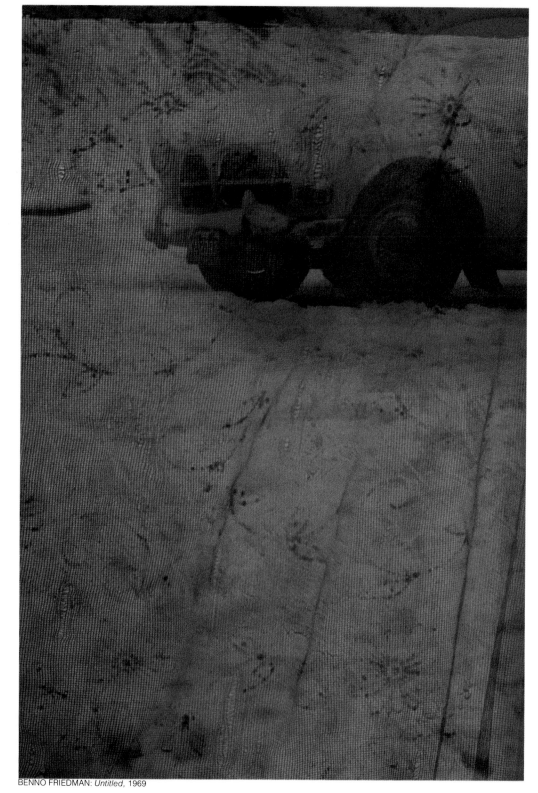

The great depth of field of a wide-angle 28mm lens solved the problem of balancing the objects in this composition. The lens got sharp detail in the window curtain in the foreground, making this subordinate element seem almost as important as the car outside, which stands out because it too is in focus.

BENNO FRIEDMAN: *Untitled,* 1969

Suggestive Blurs

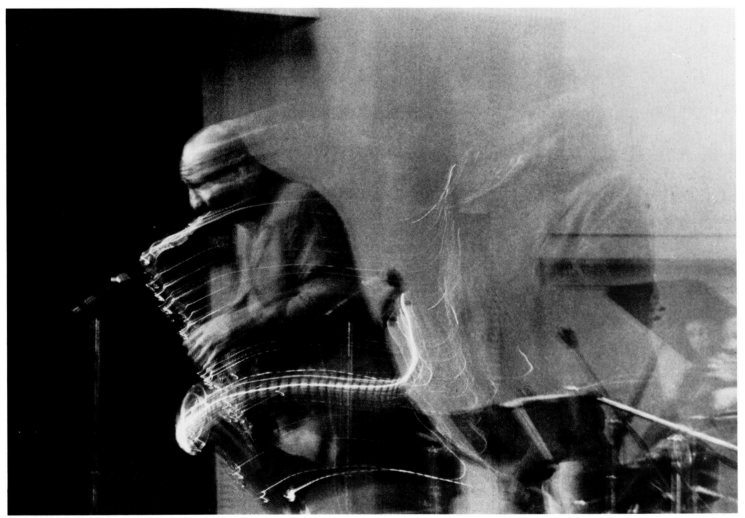

CLARENCE E. EASTMOND: *Sound in Motion, New York City,* 1968

A rock-steady camera and a motionless subject are the conventional requisites for getting a sharply focused picture with a slow shutter speed. They are especially important with long-focal-length lenses that magnify the subject—and subject movement as well. But to convey a feel-ing of action, subject motion or camera blur may be more desirable than sharp-ness. The picture above used a slow shutter speed to trace the rhythmic per-formance of a jazz musician, while the photograph at right used controlled blur to convey the frenzy of birds taking off.

Tenor saxophonist Sonny Rollins appears to vibrate across the stage of New York City's Town Hall during a jazz concert. Hand-holding a 35mm SLR with a 135mm lens, the photographer took a 1-second exposure of the dimly lit musician, relying on a combination of camera and subject movement to produce sweeping, graceful trails of light that match the mood of the performance.

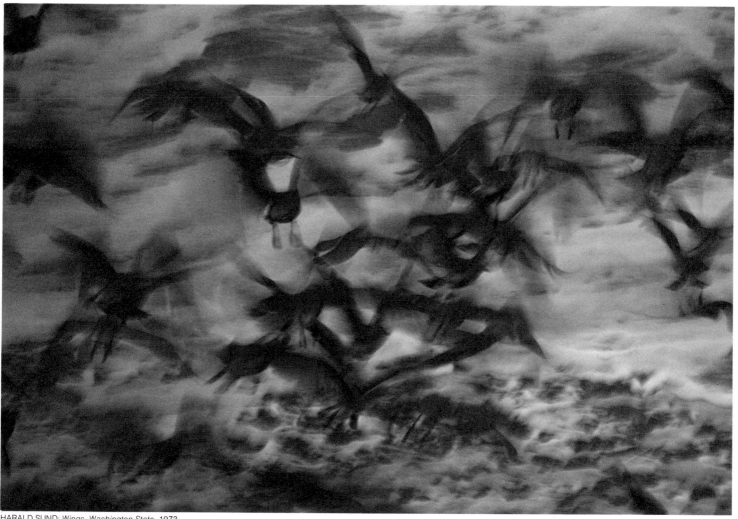

HARALD SUND: *Wings, Washington State,* 1973

A chance encounter with a flock of resting seagulls in the faint light of a foggy morning resulted in this impressionistic view of shorebirds in motion against a background of surf and rocks. Photographer Harald Sund had no tripod to steady his 300mm telephoto lens when he came upon the birds, but he decided to "let the light dictate" his technique. He set his camera for the ½-second exposure the low light required, walked toward the birds, and opened his shutter as the startled flock flew up in front of him.

Shadows to Startle the Eye

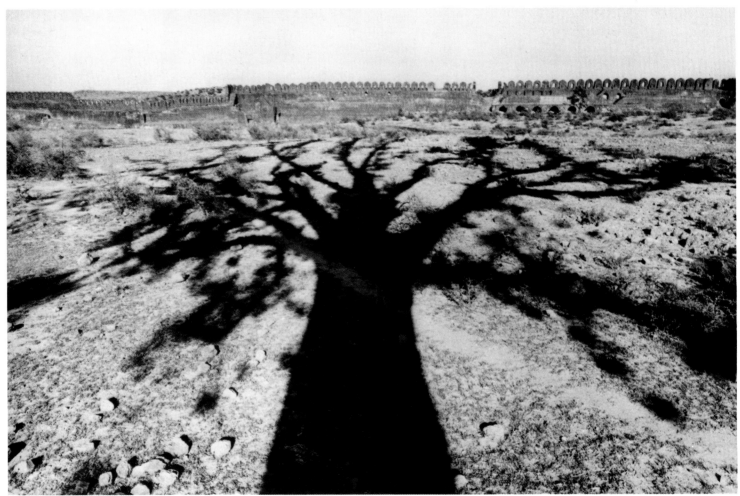

RENÉ BURRI: *Shadow of a Tree*, 1963

*Like a thick black-velvet carpet that divides into
narrow strips radiating out to cover the desert,
the shadow of a tree links foreground to
background in this picture, which was shot near
the city of Rawalpindi in Pakistan. Rohtas
Fort, a 40-foot-thick, three-mile-long wall
that was built in the 16th Century, stretches
across the far horizon in a geometric frieze.*

Every photographer who has ever read a manual knows that he must watch out for shadows; they obtrude into pictures, obscure subjects, distract viewers from the point of the picture. But far from being awkward mistakes that stamp the pictures as the work of amateurs, the shadows in the photographs on these pages command attention—and make the pictures successful.

René Burri's tree shadow *(opposite),* with its sparse branches spreading out over a backdrop of dry, rocky terrain, produces a pattern that seems to have a palpable texture of its own. Ken Josephson's shadow image of himself photographing his infant son makes the baby appear to be floating in a state of suspension against a vertical wall. Josephson decided to present himself, the photographer, as a presence visible along with his subject. He liked the result so well that he used it on his holiday greeting cards for the year.

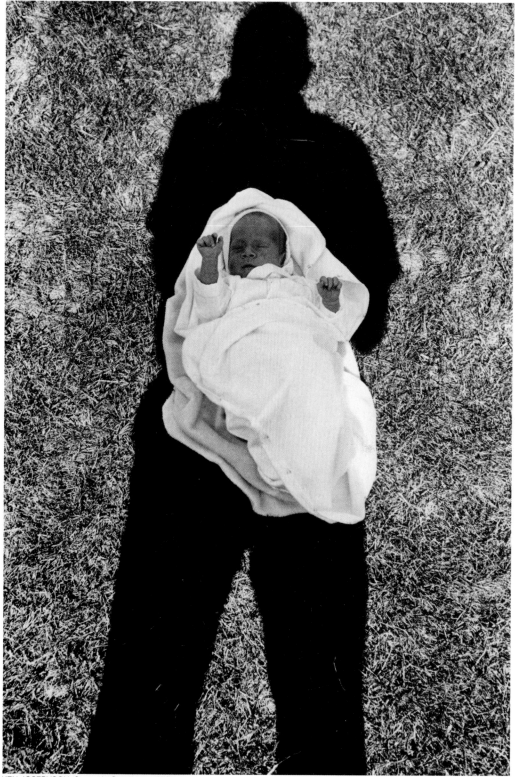

His father's shadow looms above and below two-month-old Matthew Josephson, lying asleep on the grass. The picture was shot on a bright, sunshiny day and overexposed slightly to make sure that the image of the baby would emerge clearly from its dark surroundings.

KEN JOSEPHSON: *Season's Greetings,* 1963

Shooting into the Light for Drama

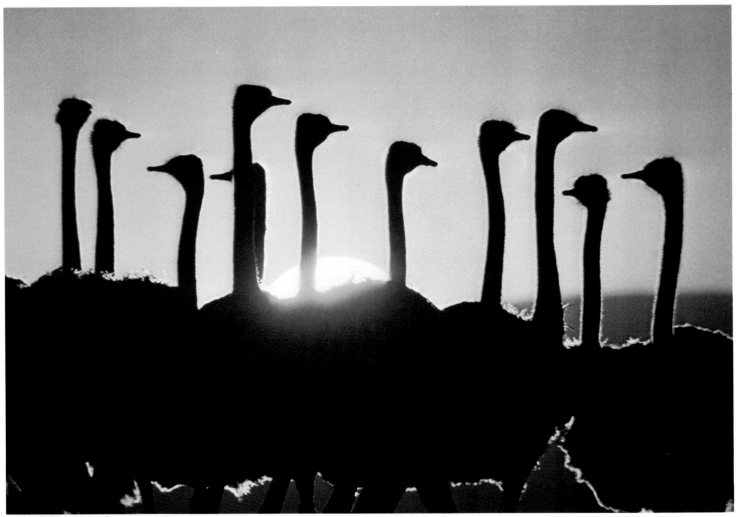

PETE TURNER: *Ostriches, South Africa,* 1970

The injunction against pointing the camera at a strong light source is a sound one. Not only can the light cause flare as it is reflected by lens elements, but it can also confound light meters, which are designed to read more evenly illuminated scenes. However, highly dramatic pictures, such as those reproduced here, can be achieved by photographers who flout this rule when conditions are right.

The setting sun silhouettes a flock of ostriches on a South African veld. The photographer used a 400mm lens to keep his distance from the birds and to enlarge the sun. He based his exposure on a light reading of the sky away from the sun. The setting—f/11 at 1/125 second—produced a richly colored sky with the sun slightly overexposed and the ostriches dramatically underexposed.

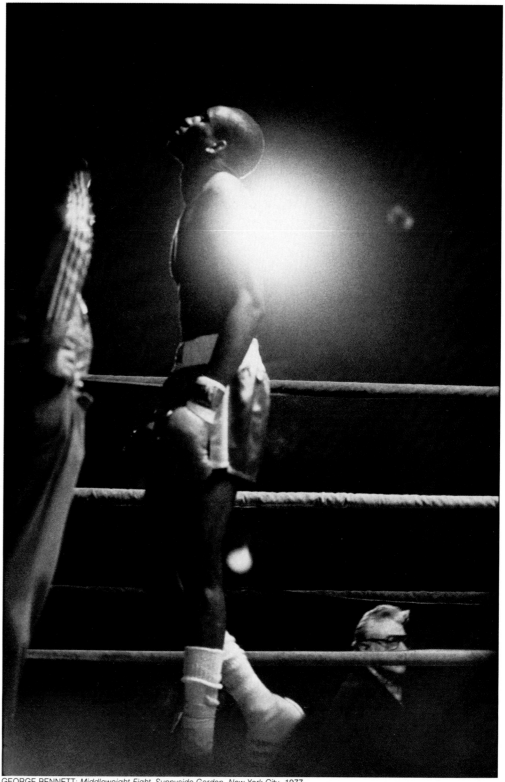

To give his shots of a boxing match the striking graphic effects of strong backlighting, the photographer selected a vantage point opposite an exceptionally bright floodlight. Using a hand-held incident-light meter, he measured the light falling on the boxer from other lights above and around the ring. When the photographer included the floodlight in his frame, it penetrated the picture—otherwise properly exposed—like a ball of fire.

GEORGE BENNETT: *Middleweight Fight, Sunnyside Garden, New York City, 1977*

An Unearthly Effect from Flash

An annoying problem when taking color portraits with flash is the spot of red that often appears in a subject's eyes. This phenomenon, known as red-eye, occurs when the flash unit and camera lens are placed close together and the subject looks straight into the camera. The redness is a result of light from the flash hitting the eyes' blood-rich retinas and reflecting back to the lens.

In this picture of a pond full of alligators, red-eye was just what photographer George Shelley was hoping for. He knew that alligators' eyes reflect so brightly that poachers usually find their prey by shining a flashlight in their eyes. Shelley planned to get the same effect using an electronic flash shortly after sunset, when he calculated that it was dark enough for the eyes to glow yet still light enough to reveal the alligators' distinctive shapes.

Pairs of alligator eyes reflecting light from a flash unit peer through the darkness settling over a farm in south Florida where the creatures are raised. The photographer's assistant dropped some marshmallows into the pond to attract the alligators; as they looked up expectantly for a second course, the photographer took a ½-second exposure. He supplemented available light with a burst from a wide-angle flash that was powerful enough to light up their eyes but not so strong as to overpower the natural illumination.

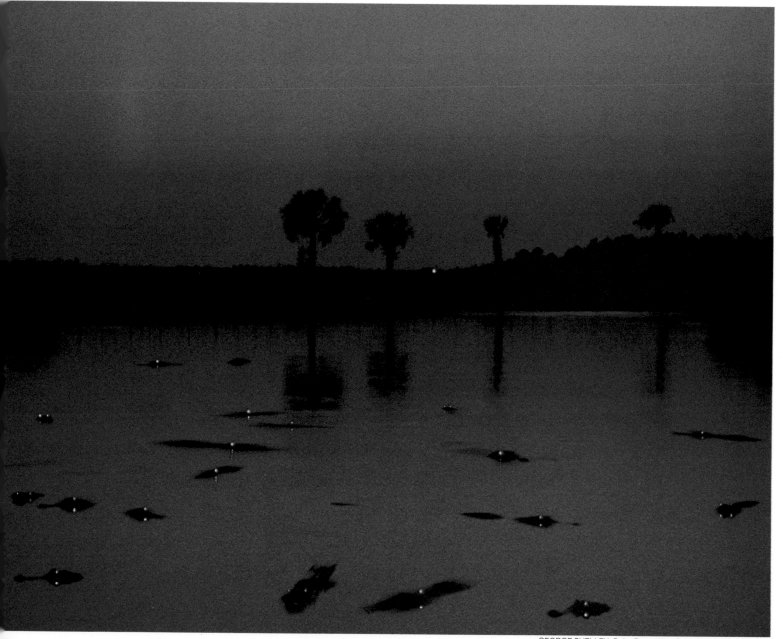

GEORGE SHELLEY: *Ruby Eyes, West Palm Beach, Florida,* 1979

Sacrificing Detail for Bold Shapes or Delicate Moods

JAY MAISEL: *Figure in Red, Ghana,* 1966

If the photographer had taken his exposure reading from the shadowed face of this dark-skinned subject, an enormous amount of light would have reached the film, draining the color from the T-shirt and washing out the surrounding scene. Instead, he took a reading from the bright sky behind the man, which considerably reduced his exposure. The resulting setting — f/8 at 1/250 second — dramatically underexposed the man's face but created rich colors overall and a strong poster-like design.

In both of the pictures shown here, the photographers have used exceptionally strong lighting—and unconventional exposure techniques—to turn the figures in them into shadowy forms, almost devoid of detail. But each photograph achieves its special effect with a different method.

By ignoring conventional procedures and exposing for the brightest areas of a scene instead of the dimmest, as in the picture at left, the photographer can reduce dark elements to silhouettes and greatly simplify the ideas they represent.

Quite a different effect is obtained if the picture is not only silhouetted but also thrown out of focus and overexposed *(right)*. Detail is again eliminated, but now outlines are also distorted, partially because overexposure tends to spread the effect of bright light on the emulsion. This spilling over of light may wash out narrow dark areas such as the arms of this dancer, which are so thinned that the figure becomes an exuberant, unearthly wraith.

To catch the gaiety of a young woman frolicking on a Cape Cod beach on a summer day, the photographer "played around with the focus until I got a blurry, elongated silhouette," then shot at 1/125 and f/4. This overexposure further softened the image and made the figure seem as ephemeral as a water sprite come to life.

WHITNEY L. LANE: *Sea Nymph,* 1970

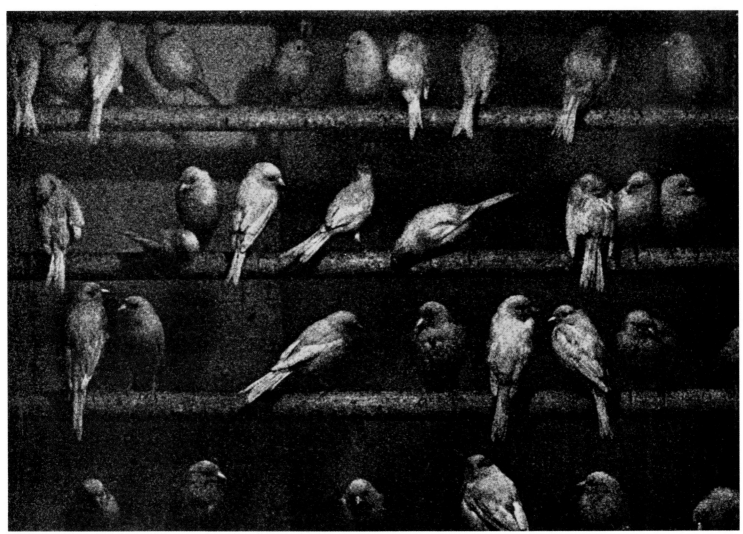

GEORGE KRAUSE: *The Birds, Mexico,*1964

The grainy texture of this shot of canaries in a pet shop was achieved with a chemical bath called an intensifier, in which the photographer soaked the developed negative. Particles of mercury in the intensifier bonded to the silver in the negative, producing the clusters of metal that form grain.

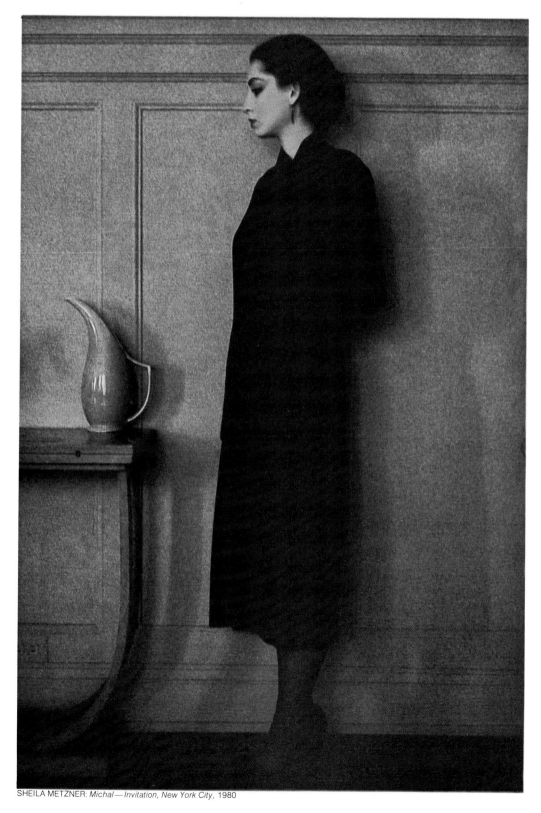

Softening with Grain

Graininess—the mottled appearance in a print caused by uneven clumping of silver particles—was long a concern of users of small-format, fast films. Such films contained large silver particles, and even a slight clumping became obvious in an enlargement. Grain was emphasized by underexposure and overdevelopment, a technique common when shooting in low light, where fast film is most often used.

But graininess is not always something to be avoided. In photojournalism, it contributes documentary excitement. And in other kinds of pictures, it adds texture and masks detail so the scene is simplified and the basic elements gain power.

Making grainy pictures today, however, requires more than fast film, underexposure or overdevelopment. Even fast films now have a relatively fine grain, requiring an enlargement of more than 16 times for graininess to become apparent. Photographers must take more extreme measures to obtain the effect.

The study of birds by George Krause shown on the opposite page illustrates one method: He bathed the negative in a special chemical normally used to add contrast. Sheila Metzner used a different method for the portrait at left. After taking the picture on ordinary slide film, she had the image printed by an old-fashioned process that exaggerated graininess.

This portrait, taken on conventional color slide film, gained a mottled softness when the slide was enlarged and printed by the Fresson Quadrichromie process. This process, an adaptation of a 19th Century printing technique perfected in France by the Fresson family, uses particles of carbon and color pigments that are suspended in a light-sensitive emulsion of potassium dichromate and gum arabic. Graininess results because the image-forming particles are much larger and less evenly distributed than the silver and dyes in standard photographic paper.

SHEILA METZNER: *Michal—Invitation, New York City, 1980*

Stark Black and White for Emotional Power

One of the marks of the great photograph has always been a great range of tone—the maximum number of subtle shades of gray, delineating detail in exquisite precision. And yet some subjects are best rendered in solid blacks and whites with few gray shades between. In these harshly unequivocal tones almost all detail is lost, but the very lack supplies raw force to a grotesque natural form such as a weirdly gnarled tree, or to a tense street scene such as the one at right.

The stark black-and-white effects are achieved by deliberately heightening the contrast of negative or print or both together. Some materials are specifically designed to increase contrast. Copy film, for example, is a high-contrast film. (A low-contrast print may be copied on it to increase contrastiness.) There are also high-contrast developers, such as Kodak D-11. And printing papers are available in many grades of contrast.

A good technique for getting high contrast is to underexpose the film and then overdevelop it. With underexposure, relatively few crystals in the emulsion are affected by light; these are completely converted to silver by overdevelopment to provide the print's blank whites, while the unaffected areas of the emulsion remain empty to provide the print's solid blacks.

Raising the temperature of the developer solution above the level that is recommended by its manufacturer makes its action more rapid and produces overdevelopment in a conveniently short period of time. This is the method Peter deFrancis used to get the high contrast shown in the picture at right.

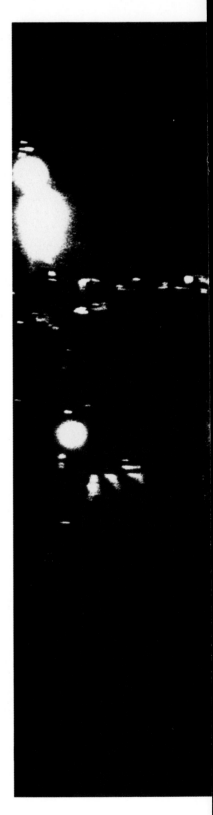

A nighttime demonstration in Washington, D.C., held in 1970 after a fatal confrontation between students and National Guard at Ohio's Kent State University, was a subject whose drama seemed best rendered in the bold blacks and whites of high contrast. To achieve maximum contrastiness, photographer Peter deFrancis, who uses only his last name professionally, employed a very high-speed film but exposed for only 1/60 second at f/2.8—about a fourth as much as the meter reading called for. He then exaggerated the effects of underexposure by overdeveloping the film. According to the guide provided by the manufacturer, developing at 68° F. for eight minutes would give normal contrast. But deFrancis went beyond that, advancing the temperature of the developer to 90° F. Finally he printed on extra-contrasty paper.

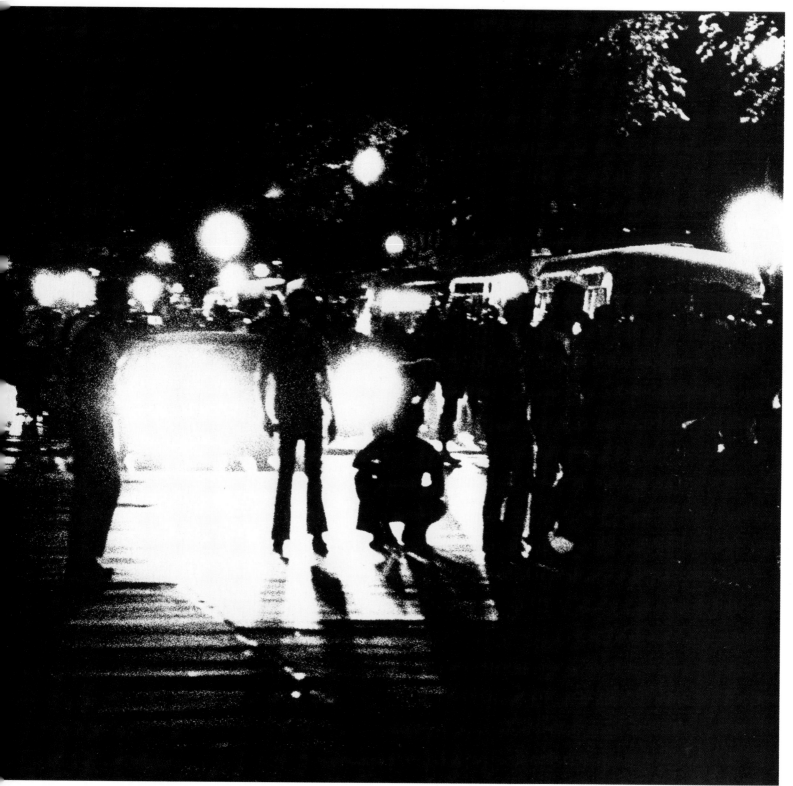

deFRANCIS: *Counterpoint,* 1970

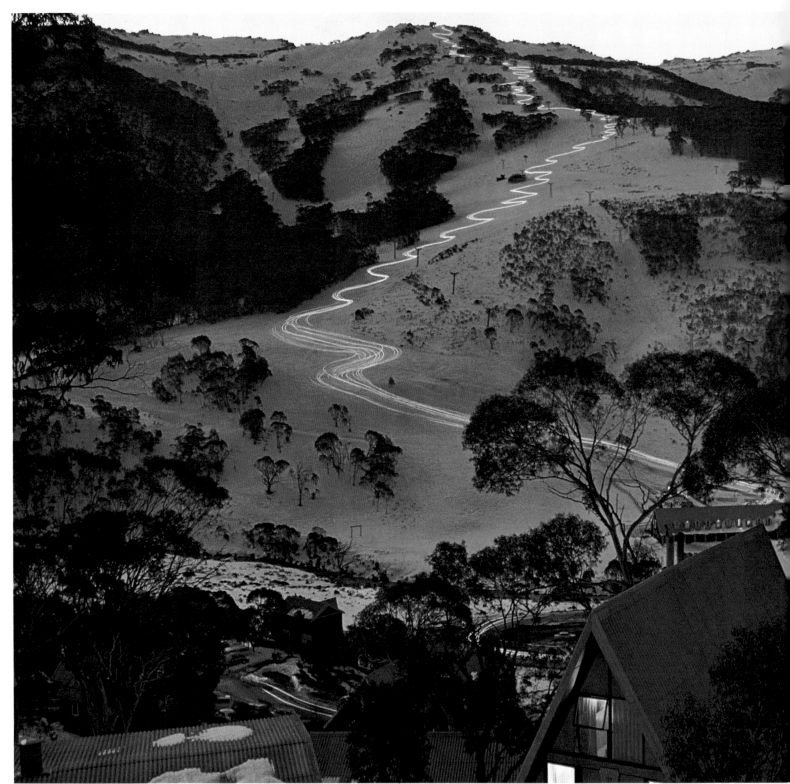

DAVID MOORE: *Torchlight Procession of Skiers, Australia*, 1966

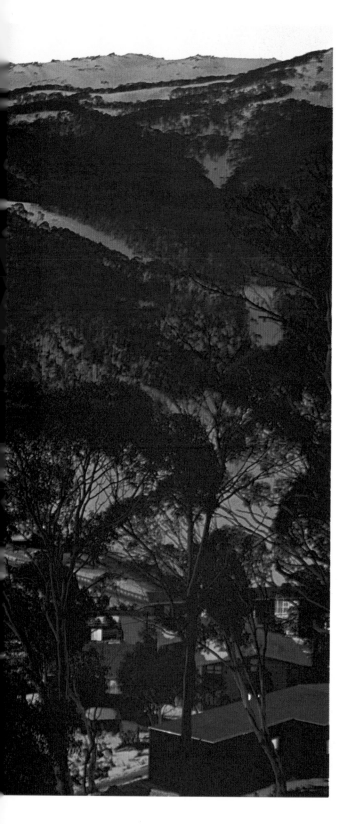

Mellow Tints from Reciprocity Failure

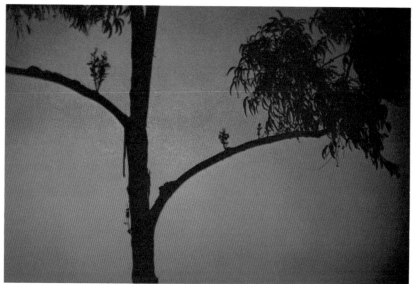

PETER DeLORY: *Summer,* 1970

The warm purple tint over the snow (left) and the two-toned sky in the picture above were produced by reciprocity failure. Both pictures were shot in the dim light of dusk and given lengthy exposures; David Moore exposed for

the full 5 minutes it took the skiers to run the trail (the zigzag thread of light that bisects his picture). To avoid overexposure, he set his aperture at its smallest opening, f/22, thus reducing the amount of light admitted.

The "law of reciprocity" states that a long exposure in very dim light should give exactly the same result as a short exposure in very bright light. (In technical terms, the effects of light intensity and exposure time are reciprocal; an increase in one factor precisely counterbalances a decrease in the other.) That is the law. Film emulsions obey it—most of the time. The law breaks down, however, if film is exposed for more than 1 second in an extremely dim light, or for less than 1/1000 of a second in a very strong light; then the phenomenon known as reciprocity failure occurs.

Its cause is not entirely understood; most experts think it results when light is insufficiently intense to trigger the silver bromide crystals in film into forming a latent image. Reciprocity failure slows the speed of the film, which gives an underexposed, darkened black-and-white image. Something more happens with color films. Because color film contains three separate emulsion layers, each of which may be affected differently, the varied speed losses change the color balance. The result is color shifts, like those that give a pleasing cast to the two pictures shown on these pages.

An Inferior Lens for Superior Effects

One reason for the high price of a good camera lens is the need for several separate elements, each shaped to work with the others in creating a sharp image. But a sharp image, every line and color in its proper place, would have dissipated the charm of the picture at right, which was made with a simple lens similar to a magnifying glass and prone to the defects so expensively removed from a fine camera lens.

A simple lens made of a single piece of convex glass causes blur in a number of ways. For one thing, it cannot get the edges of the image into sharp focus (unless the aperture used is extremely small); to correct that error, at least one other, differently shaped lens element must be added. For another, the single lens makes overlapping images of each of the colors in the spectrum. It bends each color to a different degree, thus splitting a ray of light into its component colors and bringing each of these separate components to a focus at a different point on the film. Correcting this "chromatic aberration" requires another lens element to cancel the color effects of the first; it must be made of a different kind of glass and shaped to bend light in a compensating direction. Because it lacks such corrections, the simple lens seldom produces a faithful reproduction of a subject—but it can transcend direct reproduction to create scenes of unusual beauty.

"This was a different approach to shooting fall —an attempt to capture pattern, line and design in an abstract view of fall foliage," says Henry A. Shull of his close-up of a sprig of maple, which he found beginning to turn color on an overcast October day in Vermont. He photographed it from a distance of two or three feet, using a Nikon set at f/2 and 1/500—but with the standard lens replaced by a piece of convex optical glass. This simple lens blends colors together to create surprising shades in the developed print.

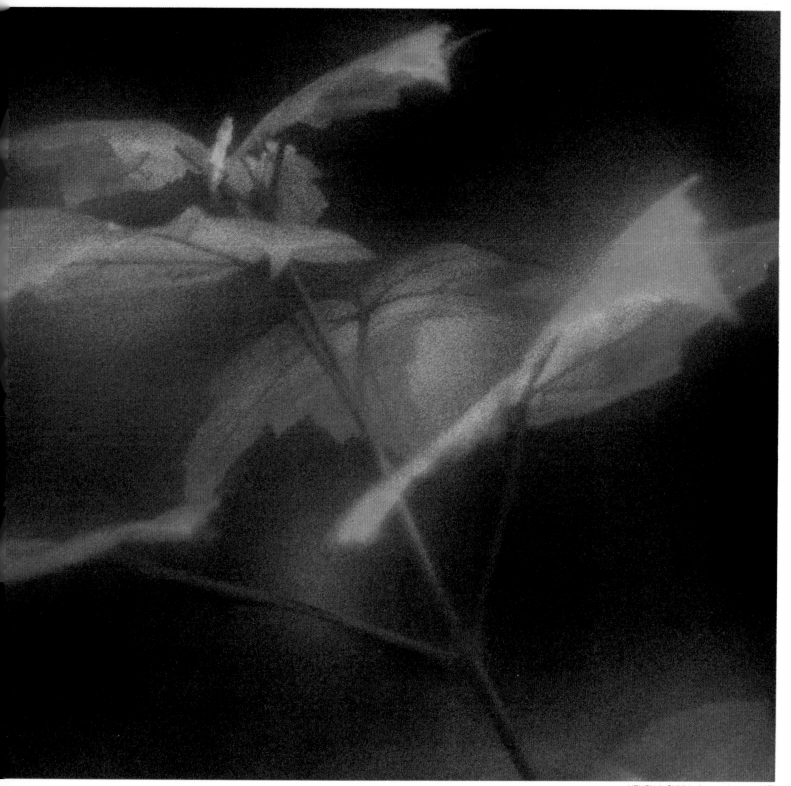

HENRY A. SHULL: *Autumn Leaves*, 1970

207

Indoor Film to Create an Altered View of the Outdoors

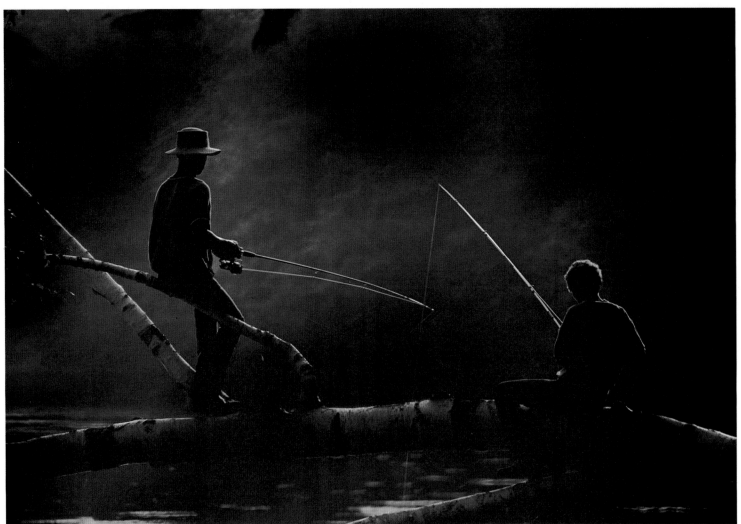

STEPHEN GREEN-ARMYTAGE: *Two Boys Fishing,* 1970

If a photographer wants to emphasize a blue tone in his outdoor scenes he can use indoor color film, which is very sensitive to blue light. When the film is used indoors this weighting counterbalances artificial light's lack of blue and over- abundance of red, making the result look natural. Outdoors, where light colors often tend toward the blue tones, it can give a pleasantly monochromatic effect. (Conversely, outdoor film that is used indoors produces yellowish-red results.) □

When indoor film is used to take a picture in daylight, the result is the blue cast that gives this picture its distinctive quality. The photographer could have "corrected" his color to achieve naturalistic lighting by using a yellow filter, but he preferred the monochromatic tints because he felt they would simplify the content of his picture.

Bibliography

Adams, Ansel, *Natural-Light Photography*. Morgan & Morgan, 1952.

*Birnbaum, Hugh, and Don Sutherland, *Photo Guide for Travelers*. Rivoli Press, 1970.

Croy, O. R., *Creative Photography*. Focal Press, 1965.

*Department of the Navy "Photographic Bulletin —Tips for Cold Weather Photography." COMNAVSUPPFOR.

Eastman Kodak:
Adventures in Existing-Light Photography, AC-44. Eastman Kodak, 1980.
Color As Seen and Photographed, E-74H. Eastman Kodak, 1972.
Kodak Color Films, Color Data Book E-77. Eastman Kodak, 1980.
Kodak Guide to 35mm Photography, AC-95. Eastman Kodak, 1980.

Kodak Professional Photoguide, R-28. Eastman Kodak, 1979.

Notes on Tropical Photography, C-24. Eastman Kodak, 1980.

Photography under Arctic Conditions, C-9. Eastman Kodak, 1977.

Prevention and Removal of Fungus on Prints and Films, Service Pamphlet AE-22. Eastman Kodak, 1980.

Evans, Ralph M., *Eye, Film and Camera in Color Photography*. Wiley, 1969.

Focal Press Ltd., *Focal Encyclopedia of Photography*. McGraw-Hill, 1969.

Fritsche, Kurt, *Faults in Photography: Causes and Correctives*. Focal Press, 1968.

*Hertzberg, Robert E., *Photo Darkroom Guide*. Amphoto, 1967.

*Jonas, Paul, *Manual of Darkroom Procedures and Techniques*. Amphoto, 1967.

Karsten, Kenneth S., *Science of Electronic Flash Photography*. Amphoto, 1968.

Mees, C. E. Kenneth, *From Dry Plates to Ektachrome Film*. Ziff-Davis, 1961.

Mueller, Conrad G., and Mae Rudolph and the Editors of TIME-LIFE Books, *Light and Vision*. TIME-LIFE Books, 1969.

Pittaro, Ernest M., *Photo-Lab-Index*. Morgan & Morgan, 1970.

Smith, Edwin, *All the Photo Tricks*. Focal Press, 1959.

Spencer, D. A., *Color Photography in Practice*. Focal Press, 1966.

Stroebel, Leslie, *View Camera Technique*. Hastings House, 1972.

Acknowledgments

The index for this book was prepared by Karla J. Knight. For the assistance given in the preparation of this volume, the editors would like to express their gratitude to the following individuals and institutions: Barbro Dal, Bonnier Fakta, Stockholm, Sweden; Berkey Marketing Company, Woodside, New York; Canon, Lake Success, New York; Walter Clark, Rochester, New York; George A. Doumani, Science Policy Research Division, Library of Congress, Washington, D.C.; Empire Exposure Meter Service, New York City; Werner A. Fallet, Assistant Sales Manager, Zeiss-Ikon-Voigtlander of America, Inc., New York City; Martin Forscher, Professional Camera Repair Service Inc., New York City; Alfred Geller, Royaltone Inc., New York City; Professor L. Fritz Gruber, Cologne, Germany; William Harmon,

Nikon Inc., Garden City, New York; Thomas Iten, School of Photographic Arts and Sciences, Rochester Institute of Technology, Rochester, New York; Rudolf Kingslake, Retired Director of Optical Design, Eastman Kodak Co., Rochester, New York; Phillip Leonian, New York City; Wayne Lennebacker, Altamont, New York; John Loengard, Picture Editor, *Life;* Robert E. Mayer, Manager, Photographic Services, Bell & Howell Photo Sales Co., Chicago; Scott Mlyn, New York City; Nikon Inc., Garden City, New York; Minolta Corp., Ramsey, New Jersey; Pentax Corp., Englewood, Colorado; Pioneer & Co., Inc., Westmont, New Jersey; from the Rochester Institute of Technology, Rochester, New York: Lothar K. Engleman, Dean of College of Graphic Arts and Photography, William S. Shoemaker, Director of

School of Photographic Arts and Sciences, John F. Carson, Staff Chairman, Photographic Science and Instrumentation, Edwin M. Wilson, Staff Chairman, Professional Photography, Tom Muir Wilson, Staff Chairman, Photographic Illustration, and the faculty and staff of the School of Photographic Arts and Sciences; Joe Scherschel, Assistant Director of Photography, National Geographic Society, Washington, D.C.; Melvin L. Scott, Assistant Picture Editor, *Life;* A. S. Smith & Son, Philadelphia; Cleveland C. Soper, Research Associate, Eastman Kodak Co., Rochester, New York; Mike Sutkowski, Office of Public Relations, Singer Diversified Worldwide, New York City; Union Carbide Corp., Battery Products Division, New York City; Vivitar Corp., Santa Monica, California.

Picture Credits

Credits from left to right are separated by semicolons, from top to bottom by dashes.

COVER: Emil Schulthess from Black Star; Robert B. Goodman

Chapter 1: 11: Bradford Washburn, courtesy Museum of Science and Hayden Planetarium, Boston. 13: Ralph Crane for *Life*. 16: Stan Wayman for *Life*. 18: Co Rentmeester for *Life*. 22: Hank Walker for *Life*. 24, 25: Fil Hunter. 27: Charles Moore from Black Star. 28, 29: Loren McIntyre. 30, 31: Robert B. Goodman from Black Star. 32: Michael Rougier. 33: John Dominis for *Life*. 34, 35: John Dominis for *Life*; Co Rentmeester for *Life*. 36, 37: Leonard McCombe for *Life*. 38, 39: John Olson for *Life*. 40, 41: George A. Doumani. 42, 43: Robert R. Nunley, courtesy Naval Photographic Center, Washington, D.C. 44: Emil Schulthess from Black Star.

Chapter 2: 47: Evelyn Hofer. 50, 51: Enrico Ferorelli. 52, 53: George Haling. 54, 55: Enrico Ferorelli. 56, 57: Bob Walch. 58, 59: Wolf von dem Bussche. 60, 61: Fil Hunter. 62, 63: Enrico Ferorelli. 64, 65: Henry Groskinsky. 66, 67: George Haling (2)—Bob Walch (2). 68, 69: John Neubauer, except cameras, Fil Hunter. 70, 71: John Neubauer (2); Fil Hunter. 72: Fil Hunter (2); John Neubauer (2).

Chapter 3: 75: Yale Joel for *Life*. 77: Bob Walch—drawing by Otto van Eersel; Tony Triolo for *Sports Illustrated*. 79: Yale Joel for *Life*; drawing by Otto van Eersel. 80: Tony Ruta for *Time*—drawing by Frederic F. Bigio from B-C Graphics. 81: Ralph Morse for *Time* (2); Tony Ruta for *Time*. 82: Bruce Dale, © National Geographic Society. 84, 85: Drawings by Frederic F. Bigio from B-C Graphics; Bruce Dale, © National Geographic Society. 87: Michael Nichols from Woodfin Camp and Associates. 88, 89: © 1980 Harald Sund. 90, 91: Douglas Kirkland from Contact Press. 92, 93: © 1980 Harald Sund. 94, 95: Steven C. Wilson from Entheos. 96, 97: Gregory Heisler for *Life*. 98, 99: Co Rentmeester for *Life*. 100: © Lennart Nilsson.

Chapter 4: 103: Henry Groskinsky. 107: Courtesy *Modern Photography*. 108: Drawing by Herbert H. Quarmby. 109-111: Sebastian Milito. 112: Drawing by Frederic F. Bigio from B-C Graphics. 113: Fil Hunter. 114, 115: Sebastian Milito. 117: George Constable. 118: Sebastian Milito. 119: Robert G. Mason. 120, 121: Patricia Maye—Don Hinkle. 122, 123: Gerald Jacobsen. 124: Don Hinkle. 125: Sebastian Milito. 126, 127: Fil Hunter. 128: Walter Iooss Jr. for *Sports Illustrated*.

Chapter 5: 131: © Phillip Leonian. 138, 139: Co Rentmeester for *Life*. 140, 141: George Silk for *Life*. 142: Neil Leifer for *Sports Illustrated*. 143: All Sport/Tony Duffy. 144, 145: Walter Iooss Jr. for *Sports Illustrated*; Andy Hayt for *Sports Illustrated*. 146, 147: John Zimmerman for *Sports Illustrated*.

148, 149: George Silk for *Life*. 150: Neil Leifer for *Sports Illustrated*. 151: Al Freni. 152, 153: Horst Baumann. 154, 155: James Drake for *Sports Illustrated*; George Silk for *Life*. 156: Dan Merkel. 157: Jerry Irwin for *Life*. 158, 159: Co Rentmeester for *Life*; Neil Leifer for *Sports Illustrated*. 160: © 1978 Charles B. (Chuck) Rogers.

Chapter 6: 163-167: Bill Eppridge. 169: Hugh G. Barton. 170: Karen Kellerhouse; John McQuade. 171: Greg Huljack; Keith Hunt—Jonathan Haskell (2). 172: Dennis Krukowski. 173: Jim Barstow. 174: John Michael Roche. 175: Peter Howard. 176: Daniel Romenesko. 177: © Sanford Burstein. 178: Judie Gleason.

Chapter 7: 181: Harald Sund. 182, 183: Lilo Raymond. 184, 185: Anthony Szczygielski. 186: Chris Smith. 187: © Philippe Halsman. 188: André Martin, Paris. 189: Benno Friedman. 190: Clarence E. Eastmond. 191: © Harald Sund. 192: René Burri from Magnum. 193: Ken Josephson. 194: © Pete Turner. 195: George Bennett. 196, 197: George Shelley. 198: © 1981 Jay Maisel. 199: Whitney L. Lane. 200: George Krause. 201: Sheila Metzner, courtesy Daniel Wolf Gallery. 202, 203: deFrancis from Soundandfury film ltd. 204, 205: David Moore from Black Star; Peter DeLory. 206, 207: Henry A. Shull. 208: Stephen Green-Armytage.